DARK
PSYCHOLOGY *and*
MANIPULATION

Discover **40** Covert Emotional Manipulation Techniques,
Mind Control & Brainwashing. Learn How to Analyze People,
NLP Secret & Science of Persuasion to Influence Anyone

William Cooper

Download the Audio Book Version of This Book for FREE

If you love listening to audio books on-the-go, I have great news for you. You can download the audio book version of this book for FREE just by signing up for a FREE 30-day audible trial! See below for more details!

Audible Trial Benefits

As an audible customer, you will receive the below benefits with your 30-day free trial:

- FREE audible book copy of this book

- After the trial, you will get 1 credit each month to use on any audiobook

- Your credits automatically roll over to the next month if you don't use them

- Choose from Audible's 200,000 + titles

- Listen anywhere with the Audible app across multiple devices

- Make easy, no-hassle exchanges of any audiobook you don't love

- Keep your audiobooks forever, even if you cancel your membership

- And much more

Click the links below to get started!

For Audible US

For Audible UK

For Audible FR

For Audible DE

Table of Contents

Chapter 4: The 10 Best Techniques of Dark Psychology 49

Chapter 5: 8 Advanced Techniques of Mental Manipulation 63

Introduction

While Psychology can be defined, in general, as the study of human behavior and the functioning of the mind, Dark Psychology studies the human condition concerning man's natural unconscious and emotional predisposition to prey and subjugate others.

Dark Psychology, persuasion, and manipulation are everywhere: in friendship, in love relationships, in advertising, in the workplace, in the news, etc. It doesn't matter where you look or who you're talking to. The situation is, either you are going to persuade someone, or someone will persuade you. Think about it for a moment, if you don't convince your boss you deserve a raise, he will convince you that you are not ready for it. So, you will walk out of his office thinking you need to work another year, or even longer, before you deserve it.

This penchant for Dark Psychology is innate within each of us. As people get smarter and smarter and want to prey on us, we also must adapt our responses to these deviant behaviors. That's why I decided to write this book.

Dark Psychology and Manipulation is the result of 7 years of studying the art of influencing human behavior and research in the psychological and social fields. This book will reveal all the mechanisms psychologists have discovered in recent years to manipulate and persuade people's minds to do what you want them to do, as well as the most effective strategies to defend ourselves against mental control.

In the next chapters, you will find a collection of the most powerful persuasive and manipulative techniques used by advertisers, emotional predators, vendors, politicians and all those who are able to change the thoughts of an individual or a group of people. You can use these techniques both to protect yourself from manipulation by narcissists, or social predators, and make a person do something they would not do. Knowing these techniques will allow you to succeed in relationships in general and especially at your work. Whatever your motivation is, in the following pages, you will find the tools you need.

Whether you are conversing with your friends, your partner, writing a work email, telling a story, or selling a product, you need to know the methods that the masters of persuasion use to change people's thoughts and make them act.

This book is not designed for academic purposes. My goal is to present persuasive language and behavioral patterns with many practical examples and begin to apply them immediately after reading them. These tools can be so effective and powerful; so please use them ethically because it can be good or do a lot harm to those around you.

Be careful! This book may hurt some people's feelings. Please read it only if you really feel prepared to improve your communication with an ambitious goal. If you are a sensitive person, this book is not for you. Everything you will learn here is simple, easy to put into practice and it also works. You will learn to take advantage of our natural decision-making process. It has been shown that decision-making is primarily based on emotions and assumptions rather than logic—in the following pages you will learn how to take advantage of this "glimmer."

If you want to move mountains, you have to be able to move people first. Most people try to motivate others by praying them until death. When that doesn't work, they despair and start reprimanding, imposing, or deceiving to get the results they want. If you try to motivate people directly, you will fail. If you have already tried to change someone's behavior, you will know that this is painfully true. As an old saying goes, "You can take a horse to water, but you can't force it to drink." However, you can make him thirsty. Consequently, the secret of motivation, influence, and persuasion, lies in learning to create the conditions for the mind to become "thirsty" so that the body follows it. The good news is that most minds are already thirsty in some way. We all live our lives driven by a series of necessities and desires, and you just need to go a little deeper to find those needs and take advantage of them. How? Through the use of language patterns and cognitive shortcuts that I will reveal to you.

Our brains love shortcuts. The world is a complex place, and your brain is constantly being attacked by an enormous amount of sensory information, for which it has a series of pre-programmed responses to help you resist this deluge. That's why when you hear a sudden loud noise, your body jumps. When you see good food, your mouth produces saliva. When the room is dark and warm, you get sleepy. It all happens automatically. You don't have to think about it, it just happens. These "conditioned responses" are activated because your brain has learned to anticipate what comes next. So, is it possible that there are such "cause and effect" answers when we listen to certain words? Or is it possible that certain parts of human communication universally command a specific "shortcut" reaction?

The short answer is YES!

The interesting thing is that every time you talk to someone, consciously or unconsciously, you are influencing that person's mind. Even if you choose not to talk, your own silence can affect them. Your verbal and non-verbal communication changes the neurochemistry of those around you. People normally do not want to accept this truth because they are afraid of being considered manipulative. Some people don't like the idea of influencing other people's thoughts for obvious ethical reasons, and some simply don't want to accept this responsibility. However, to communicate effectively, you must accept this fact. Whether you try it or not, you are manipulating the thoughts, feelings, and actions of others.

When we think in manipulation, we think of some manipulators in history, such as Adolf Hitler, Frank Abagnale Jr., Bernie Madoff, or any other people who use the same skills to sell our used cars in bad condition, get guilty people acquitted or cheat millions of poor people. But let's not forget the other great manipulators of history, such as Mother Teresa, Martin Luther King Jr., Winston Churchill, Gandhi and many others who have used the power of words to move people to fight for human rights, to abolish slavery, to give more power to the weak or to initiate political reform.

Both groups have influenced the thoughts, emotions, and actions of hundreds of thousands or millions of people, but the difference lies in the intention. No one doubts that communication is a powerful tool. Like any other tool you have at home, communication can be used to build or destroy. In the hands of a chef, a knife is a useful tool, while in the hands of a murderer, it is a deadly weapon; what matters is not the knife itself, it's the intentions of the person who uses it. In the rest of this book, I will provide you with powerful tools that will allow you to get what you want.

Surely you've already imagined what you can achieve when you've enhanced your powers of persuasion and manipulation, so now I'll tell you what will happen if you don't, that is to say, without these abilities:

- If you're an employee, you won't get a raise from your boss;

- If you're a parent, you won't be able to get your kids to make their bed;

- If you're a victim of a manipulator, you won't realize it, and you won't be able to react to get rid of his negative influence;

- If you're a salesman, you won't be able to sell your products easily;

- If you're a team leader, you won't be able to motivate your team members to work harder or more efficiently;

- If you're completing a negotiation, you won't get any concessions from the other party;

- If you're an entrepreneur, you won't get your employees to accept your vision;

And the list goes on.

As a result, without the capacity for manipulation and persuasion, you simply will not be able to influence people's behavior. Therefore, improve these skills by reading this book, and you'll get pretty much anything you want.

Are you ready? Now it's time to begin this fantastic "journey" into the human mind to discover its secrets.

Happy reading!

Chapter 1

The Fundamentals of Dark Psychology

What is Dark Psychology?

To understand what Dark Psychology is, first of all we must start from the basics and understand what Psychology is. It can be defined as the science that deals with the study of human behavior: how people perceive, think, and react to various situations based on emotional, cognitive, and social elements.

Dark Psychology, instead, can be defined as the study of the human condition about a man's natural unconscious predisposition to prey on and subjugate others for personal gain.

The use of Dark Psychology can be found everywhere—in love relationships, at work, in relationships with friends, on TV, in advertising, in politics, etc. (1).

---

(1) Vance Packard (2007) – *The Hidden Persuaders*. Ig Publishing.

This dark aspect of psychology is inherent within each of us, no one excluded, and is part of the most unconscious part of our mind.

How is it possible to use psychology to take advantage on others? Simply, by using devious techniques of influence and mental manipulation to induce others to do something they would not normally do. Many psychological experiments show how this is possible. I will give you a proof of this in the remaining of the book!

The secrets of Dark Psychology reside in the knowledge of hidden psychological principles. Some of these powerful techniques and tactics are used by influencers to manipulate people's minds and their choices.

Dark Psychology, as well as the principles and techniques that surround it, can be used in romantic relationships and help in your career path. Of course, this is not to encourage you to become an emotional or social predator; however, knowing these techniques will give you a great advantage from others.

Why do we need to understand Dark Psychology? This is present every day around us and, therefore, it cannot be ignored.

You have the power to choose whether to continue ignoring the secrets of Dark Psychology with the consequence of becoming a victim, or decide to know about it and exploit it to your own advantage, either to protect yourself from mental manipulators, or to influence others to do actions they would not generally do.

Perception

This is a set of cognitive abilities that allows us to acquire information coming from the outside and is re-elaborated in our mind. Perception is therefore that process by which everything we see, hear, and notice with all our senses is then modified by our brain and given some meaning.

Man, by natural predisposition, tends to save cognitive energies through what are called "cognitive or reasoning shortcuts", to conclude with a minimum of effort in the decision-making process as fast as possible. The effort is a cost and our brain tends to limit it as much as possible. Laziness is deeply rooted in human nature.

During human evolution, we have developed a capacity for reasoning. This decision-making skill allows us to be extremely effective and fast. Since prehistoric times, when in the presence of danger, for example in front of a starving beast, humans did not think about all the possible options. Still, he chose from a few available alternatives:

1) or either run away from the animal *(escape)*;

2) or attack the beast *(attack)*;

3) or he would freeze to avoid detection *(freezing)*.

This speed of decision-making, on the one hand, has obviously allowed us to evolve but, at the same time, it has generated what is called COGNITIVE BIAS, which is the cause of many errors of logical, and above all, decisional type (2).

In other words, this reasoning capacity exposes us quickly to the possibility of being conditioned and influenced by others in our choices.

All the most common techniques of mental influence to impact a person's decision-making process will be revealed to you in this book. *Anchoring Bias, Ingroup Bias, Halo Effect Bias, Bandwagon Bias, Confirmation Bias,* are some Cognitive Bias that will be explained in the next chapters.

Persuasion

"Persuade" and "manipulate" are two verbs that are often used as synonyms, but, on the contrary, have very different meanings.

(2) Kahneman, D. (2011) – *Thinking, fast and slow.* New York: Farrar, Straus and Giroux. A. Tversky, D. Kahneman (1974) – *Judgment under Uncertainty: Heuristics and Biases.* Cambridge University Press.

Galperin, A., & Haselton, M. G. (2013) – *Error management and the evolution of cognitive bias,* in J. P. Forgas, K. Fiedler, & C. Sedikides (Eds.), Sydney symposium of social psychology. Social thinking and interpersonal behavior (p. 45–63). Psychology Press.

Do you want to see more on cognitive biases? In this link 188 of them in one infographic. https://www.visualcapitalist.com/every-single-cognitive-bias

As we will see shortly, the difference between Persuasion and Manipulation lies fundamentally in the "techniques" and "methods" used to convince another person.

Persuasion is the art of changing someone else's attitude or behavior through a mutual exchange of ideas. Unlike manipulation, it uses only words and logical arguments to put the interlocutor into a specific state of mind to which the persuader points. It can be said that persuasion aims at obtaining approval and trust through a gradual and systematic work of conviction.

Richard M. Perloff (3) defines the persuasion as "a symbolic process in which communication seeks to convince other people to change their attitudes or behaviors about a problem through the transmission of a message in an atmosphere of free will." In persuasion, the person makes his choice of his own will, even when the persuader uses motivating tactics to guide the subject in a certain way. The person will still be able to choose the direction he wants to take.

The art of Persuasion can be compared to a knife. It can be used either to cut a cake or food or to kill a person. Objectively the knife is not made to be a weapon, but could be used as a weapon. In the same way, also persuasion techniques can be used for both "good" and ethical purposes (e.g. to defend yourself against those who want to use them against you), or they can be used for "evil" purposes.

So consider this book as a real knife and learn to use it in the right way. Everything will depend on you!

Manipulation

Unlike persuasion, Manipulation is a type of social influence aimed at changing the perception or behavior of others using linguistic tricks, devious schemes, subliminal, and deceptive methods that can also lead to both psychological and physical abuse.

---

(3) Richard M. Perloff (1993) – *The Dynamics of Persuasion: Communication and Attitudes in the 21st Century*, Hillsdale, New Jersey: Lawrence Erlbaum.

Manipulation can be said to be aimed at the coarse reworking of elements, mostly for tendentious or fraudulent purposes.

Etymologically, manipulation means "forcing someone to do something."

The Manipulator tries to lead the other towards his own ideas for personal gain and very specific interest and can do this either, by using sneaky manipulation techniques or by using extreme persuasion techniques. In any case, most of the tactics he will use will be deceptive and exploitative.

But how do you manipulate a person? Manipulation often occurs through the use of deception or illusion, i.e., by altering or distorting the vision of the person's reality you want to manipulate, to the point of using coercion and punitive practices.

But how exactly do manipulators create this illusion of reality? The first tool most used by manipulators is the use of lie to deceive others.

Lying, deception, generating guilt, fear, or even more serious anger, are all tools used to manipulate people.

In addition, manipulators in action will resort a series of underhand manipulation techniques such as intimidation, emotional blackmail, or methods of mind control or brainwashing.

Dark Psychology vs. Covert Emotional Manipulation

What is the difference between Dark Psychology and Occult Emotional Manipulation?

Dark Psychology can be defined as the process of mental influence that consists of making people do things against their self-interest. This lacks morality, precisely because its function is immoral.

Secret Emotional Manipulation is the process in which a person tries to influence another's decisions and feelings in a hidden way, not necessarily for immoral purposes. Basically, Secret Emotional Manipulation involves masking the real intentions of the manipulator. This type of person focuses on the emotional side of the individual because he knows that a person's emotions are the key of their personality.

While secret manipulation focuses on an individual to achieve the ultimate goal, Dark Psychology can be used on a person, but it can also be used in larger groups to influence an entire group or, sometimes, a society to influence their thinking. This shows how frightening and dangerous dark persuasion can be: it can be used to change the minds of groups of people altogether.

The History of Persuasion

Throughout time, persuasion has evolved and changed from its early days. For many years, this has existed; it has indeed been present since ancient Greece. That doesn't mean the art and persuasion process is exactly the same as before. Nevertheless, the art of persuasion and how it is used in today's times have changed considerably.

Richard M. Perloff spent quite a while researching traditional ideologies, how they are used, and how they can affect culture as a whole. He has written a book entitled *The Dynamics of Persuasion: Communication and Attitudes in the 21st Century (4)*. The book discusses different ways in which current values were used in past times. He explains that the number of messages considered as persuasion has risen in precarious numbers. In ancient Greece, this was used only in writing and in debates between the elites. There wasn't much influence, and you wouldn't see it very often.

Without some persuasion message accompanying you in modern times, it is difficult to get anywhere. Consider the different types and sources of ads that exist today; up to 3000 of these are found every day in the United States. Besides that, people knock at your door (or you might find them on the street) often trying to make you buy something, convincing you to believe in what they are selling, or inducing you to try something new. This is, more than ever in history, a part of the modern world.

---

(4) Richard M. Perloff – *The Dynamics of Persuasion: Communication and Attitudes in the 21st Century,* Hillsdale, New Jersey: Lawrence Erlbaum, 1993.

We can say that Persuasion travels very fast. It could take weeks or longer to get a persuasive message from one point to another in ancient Greece.

The power of persuasion was, therefore, limited as most people could not get the message. In the sense of face-to-face contact, many acts of persuasion had to be undertaken this way. In modern times, the use of the Internet, radio, and television is a reasonable source of persuading messages in hardly any time over a long distance.

In just seconds, political candidates can be able to appeal to their constituents all at once, and each message can be quickly transmitted. This plays a significantly greater role if it can be distributed too quickly.

Persuasion can also mean a lot of money—businesses have learned the power of persuasion, and they do all they can to make it work for them. The more successful they are to persuade consumers to buy their goods, the more money they get.

Many organizations are only interested in the persuasion process, including public service firms, marketing companies, or advertising agencies.

Other companies will be able to use the persuasive strategies provided by these organizations to meet and surpass their marketing targets.

Persuasion has become subtler than it was in the past: at the start, the persuader will make his points of views clearly to the whole group, to make everyone change their minds. The past is gone; nowadays the persuasion process is far more discreet, and hidden.

Chapter 2

The 6+1 Weapons of Influence by Dr. Robert Cialdini

Dr. Robert Cialdini is an international expert in the field of persuasion, conditioning, and negotiation. He is a professor of psychology at the Arizona State University and his most important book, written in 1984, is *Influence: The Psychology of Persuasion* (5). The book is an exhaustive collection of studies, tests, experiments, and theories of many researchers who want to explain how and why you end up saying YES.

People are surrounded by stimuli that increase more and more every day; that's why our brain reduces the fatigue of the active decision-making to simplification mechanisms. Without the instinct, we'll succumb to information overload, so we use mental shortcuts *(cognitive bias)* (6).

---

(5) Robert B. Cialdini, (1984) – *Influence: The Psychology of Persuasion*. HarperCollins.

(6) Galperin, A., & Haselton, M. G. (2013) - Error management and the evolution of cognitive bias, in J. P. Forgas, K. Fiedler, & C. Sedikides (Eds.), Sydney symposium of social psychology. Social thinking and interpersonal behavior (p. 45–63). Psychology Press.

Today, the evolution of technology is very fast. Our natural ability to process information looks increasingly insufficient to handle the overload of changes, choices, and novelties of modern life.

We have created our own inadequacy by building a world of radically greater complexity.

But why talk about these topics? Because our choices are 95% based in an unconscious level of decision making.

Let's see in detail the 6+1 universal rules of persuasion discovered by Robert Cialdini and the respective psychological mechanisms of mental influence that underlie them.

1. Reciprocity

According to the "reciprocity rule", if a person receives a gift, a concession, or a favor, which he perceives as spontaneous or disinterested, he feels obliged to give something back.

This psycho-technique is based on the fact we feel instinctively inclined to reciprocate what a person has given us or the favor we have received, just as we have been educated from an early age by our society.

A strategy of persuasion that exploits this principle is the "tasting technique." At the supermarket, they invite you to taste a product so that when you feel you have received a gift you feel almost obliged to return it, and the purchase of the package is almost guaranteed.

Or think of the street stalkers, those who ask for alms with various excuses and pretend to give you a small item and even put it in your hands, as a flower; if you notice, as soon as you take it, they start asking you for money.

Remember that you often return the gifts you receive unfairly; that is, by exceeding their value, because psychologically you want to repay them in a dignified way. This mental trap is often exploited by those who want to manipulate us.

How to Avoid Falling into the Trap of the Reciprocity Rule

If a person makes a favor, don't feel obliged to return it. If he does it with his heart, he should not want anything in return; but if he wants something back, avoid falling into it.

In fact, it is good to avoid accepting those gifts or those offers that give you the suspicion they are oriented towards a profit. So if you have the impression that whoever is giving you a gift is not a benefactor but a taker, you can easily refuse the gift with good assertive communication.

Also, when someone gives you a positive identity, they sometimes will make it to manipulate you. If, for example, a person says to you, *"You, who are a smart person will surely approve..."* don't fall for the trap! He might do it to push you to act in line with the image he's given you. And you, who are a smart person, certainly won't fall for it.

2. Scarcity

The rule of scarcity is that mental concept whereby we tend to attach greater value to objects we think might run out; that includes items we believe are rare and uncommon.

According to this principle, the more something is scarce, the more it is desired. It is the assumption that underlies collecting.

Marketing experts know that a product becomes more attractive when its availability is limited.

There are two strategies to create scarcity in a sale:

1) Create a "time restriction" of the special offer, for example: *"offer valid until tomorrow night"* or *"offer valid only for a few days"*;

2) Use the "product limitation," e.g., limit the special offer *"only to a certain number of items"* or *"only to the first 20 calls."*

This is what happens on travel sites like Booking when we're trying to book a room in a hotel and a pop-up says *"only 3 rooms left available."*

Also, this is what happens on airline websites when we are trying to buy a ticket and a pop-up appears with the words: *"Last 5 seats available."*

The rule of scarcity acts deep in the consumer's psyche because it leverages on his fear of losing the product, or the opportunity to save money if it does not act quickly.

How to Defend Yourself against the Scarcity Rule

When an opportunity is limited in time, this does not mean that it has to be precious and to be seized at once. Evaluate if you really need that product or that information and don't let your instinct advice you.

3. Social Proof

On average, when people are confused or in a situation with a lack of information, they tend to consider the behavior and choices made by a large number of people to be more valid. This rule exploits the cognitive *"Bandwagon Bias"*.

It's a bit like what happens when we get out of the subway, not knowing in which direction we have to go to find the exit; we instinctively follow the flow of people, believing that they know the right path.

If I have to buy a product on the internet, I will not only choose the one with the best reviews, but I'll go for the one with the most ratings.

This is what happens on Tripadvisor with the reviews and opinions that customers give about the restaurants or hotels they have gone to (7).

The same occurs for the number of "Likes" on a Facebook page because their high number gives the idea that people like it; or try to think about the high number of views of a video on Youtube.

In practice, the mechanism works like this. If interest or behavior is very widespread among people, automatically it will appear more interesting and attractive for us too. If you think about it, "fashions" work exactly like this.

This stratagem is used in political elections with polling data. If those say that a certain political party is very successful among the people, I will have the feeling that it is worth voting for it too.

---

(7) Cialdini, R. B. (2001) – *The science of persuasion*. Scientific American, 290, 31-54.

This technique is also often used in marketing: when you see a line of people outside a store, you feel more like going in, because you ask yourself: "What on earth will be in there? I'm going in there too!" Usually, in a disco, they keep people outside to create the "queue effect," even if there's nobody in the club. On the contrary, when you walk into a restaurant and realize there was no other customer, you will leave; I have done it before. It happens because, in cases like this, we are led to think that there is something wrong; and when we are in doubt, we go away.

How to Avoid Falling into the Trap of the Rule of Social Proof

Try not to fall into the trap of "If many people think so, then it's right." If, for example, they recommend a restaurant, a movie or a book, the one preferred by more people is not always the best.

4. Liking

As a rule, we tend to like people attractive people in general and those similar to us (in clothing, interests in opinions, hobbies, etc.). For this reason, we are more inclined to follow them and accept their offers. This rule exploits the cognitive *"Halo Effect Bias"*.

By working on building a bond of "sympathy" and "similarity" between persuader and victim, it is easier to achieve results than a change of attitude.

This pleasantness can involve many other features: it can be physical attractiveness, sympathy, familiarity, a form of kindness, and all characteristics that make a person-pleasant.

How can it be created? By identifying the points in common with the interlocutor, deepening on them, bringing them to the foreground, and then leveraging them: it is a confirmation technique; in practice, one does nothing but reflect the other.

To build a "bond of sympathy," we can make appreciations. It is quite natural that I have more sympathy for those who compliment me, who esteem me, or who love me in general.

To build a "bond of similarity," we can bring out one or more features in common. Similarity is mutual in persuaders; if you tell him for example "I'm from New York," and if he can't tell you he's from New York, he'll say: "I visited it last year it's a beautiful city and I'd like to live there." In this way, he'll immediately appear more sympathetic and you'll tend to follow him.

The rule of sympathy and pleasantness is the "identification mechanism" that lies at the base of what is called "Influencer" or "Testimonial;" who is a known person who recommends openly or indirectly a certain product praising its qualities. Typically he uses the various social media, publishing photos with a certain item to influence his followers to buy it, creating a process of identification (8).

How to Defend Yourself from the Liking Rule and Pleasantness

If someone you've just met sells you a product or service and you realize you like it too much compared to others, it turns on a "wake-up call". To do this, try to separate the "product or service" from the "person proposing it;" objectively assess what he or she is proposing. Take some time to evaluate the purchase calmly, without the presence of the person who might influence you.

5. Authority

In general, we have a sense of deference to authority, so we tend to obey orders given by a person in uniform or follow advice given by an authoritative person in a particular field.

This is why in marketing we use dentists in toothpaste or toothbrush commercials, chefs to recommend a kitchen brand or sportsmen and women to advertise products for those who practice certain sports.

A recent example of a company that has turned its fortunes around through an important figure is Herbalife, with Cristiano Ronaldo.

In order to appear authoritative, a persuader could adopt a decisive attitude, and a posture that imposes itself. He could display his diplomas or academic titles on the wall of his office, conveying an

---

(8) Jonah Berger, (2016) – *Invisible Influence: The Hidden Forces that Shape Behavior*. Simon & Schuster.

idea of authoritativeness all the more so if, for example, he wears a uniform.

I have always been struck by the fact that two different lawyers, separately from each other, told me that they could not wear a shirt worth less than $100 because otherwise, they would lose clients. They believe that, indirectly, wearing that shirt testifies to their professional success.

How to Defend Yourself from the Rule of Authority

When an idea or behavior is suggested to you by someone of authority, it does not mean either that it has to be the right one, nor has to be the wrong one. Let me give you this advice as an expert on the subject.

6. Commitment and Consistency

The "rule of Commitment and Consistency" is based on the fact that people tend to be consistent with what has been said or done before.

We are all instinctively inclined to take positions, in general, because we give a vague opinion about something. But once we have committed ourselves, especially if we have done it in front of more than one person, we automatically tend to maintain it. It's as if something inside our mind makes us do it. This happens because psychologically, we need to feel and appear consistent with the choices we made previously.

The "rule of commitment and coherence" is much more effective if the commitment is made, and, besides being said, is also WRITTEN. At the same time, if what has been said and written is also made PUBLIC, then the technique becomes extremely powerful (9).

---

(9) Cialdini, R.B., Wosinska, W., Barrett, D.W., Butner, J. & Gornik-Durose, M. (1999) – *Compliance with a request in two cultures: The differential influence of social proof and commitment/consistency on collectivists and individualists.* Personality and Social Psychology Bulletin, 25, 1242-1253.

The mechanism of this persuasive technique consists in making a person express a general judgment on anything and then immediately attach a request to it.

A strategy used on the street by those who want money, is to ask the first passer-by questions like: *"Excuse me; do you have something against drug addicts?"* The average person will answer no; then they will be invited to sign in favor of, for example, a popular petition to promote the social reintegration for drug addicts. Next, they will be asked for a small donation in support of the initiative he signed a few seconds earlier.

The secret lies in using an argument the interlocutor will certainly agree. For example: *"Are you in favor of saving poor children who are dying of hunger?"* Or, *"are you in favor of protecting the environment and avoiding pollution of the planet?"* The answers to these questions will, on average, always be in favor. So the trap of commitment and consistency with the demand for money to support the initiative will be set. The passer-by is, therefore, likely to agree to give the offer to be consistent with what was said just now.

This technique works even better if the person you want to persuade responds publicly in front of several people or in the presence of a friend. In order not to make a bad impression, they will try to be consistent with what they have said until the end.

Another way to exploit this rule consists of a manipulative technique called "Foot in the door", which aims to create a contact with the interlocutor, a small glimmer, and then gradually make him accept something more challenging (10).

A typical example of "Foot in the door" is the pitfall technique or asterisk: it is an offer at a very low price with an asterisk (*) next to it. For example, imagine you see a sign in the window of a travel agency with a sign saying, "Flight to and from Miami at $97.00 (*)." Attracted by the offer, we decide to enter and ask to buy a ticket. But when we read what the asterisk indicates in small letter, we discover that the offer is valid only under certain conditions and does not include taxes, etc. So, the total cost of the ticket is $ 197.00. In these cases, it is very likely that, ever since we entered the office and

---

(10) Cialdini, R. B. (2001) – *Influence: Science and practice* (4th ed.). Allyn & Bacon.

expressed our interest in buying a ticket, we finally decide to pay the much higher amount; all just because of consistency.

How to Defend Ourselves from the Rule of Commitment and Consistency

Countering the "rule of Commitment and Consistency," is very difficult, and to say NO, you have to be very aware of what is happening. Consistency is the element that makes us decide automatically, allowing us, in most cases, to make the right decision quickly.

To avoid being a victim of this kind of manipulation, therefore, it is necessary to be aware of the processes behind this principle to understand that you can get out of this trap at any time you want.

If, for example, a decision is no longer optimal for us, no matter how much energy we have spent to achieve that goal, it will probably be more advantageous to let it go. If, on the other hand, you realize you are a victim of this kind of manipulation, you can use appropriate assertive communication to tell the person you are interacting with that you are not willing to fall into that kind of trap and be manipulated.

After the fear of scarcity, the praise for sympathy, the deference for authority, and the power of reciprocity and consistency, I will deal with the last rule of persuasion stated by Robert Cialdini: Units.

7. Units (The Community Effect)

The seventh rule is a rule developed by Robert Cialdini later, precisely in 2016 in his last book *Pre-Suasion: A Revolutionary Way to Influence and Persuade* (11), i.e., the idea that by sharing an identity with someone else, one is then more inclined to accept his requests. This rule exploits the cognitive *"Ingroup Bias"*.

Communicators who can identify "Units" will be able to get positive responses to their proposals and recommendations. A tool used to study (and exploit) the units are certainly the Facebook groups,

(11) Cialdini, R. B., (2017) – *Pre-Suasion: A Revolutionary Way to Influence and Persuade*. HarperCollins.

capable of triggering a sense of belonging such that commercial proposals are not only accepted but desired.

Among many, one of the most striking examples is certainly the Apple that gathers a group of people who identify with the values of the product, makes them similar to each other, and has even managed to make the same group of individuals also have a "common enemy," embodied in Android devices.

"Groupthink" or "group thinking" has been the subject of many experiments that have shown how individuals are strongly influenced by group opinions, perceptions, and behavior *(Bias Ingroup)*.

Solomon Asch, a Polish social psychologist, demonstrated its validity in 1956 through one of his experiments (12). This consisted of including some subjects in small groups. They were shown three lines of very different lengths, and were asked to indicate which of the three corresponded to, for example, one meter.

The other members of the group, accomplices of the experimenter, unanimously gave an obviously wrong answer. Well, 33% of the

(12) Asch, S. E. (1956) – *Studies of independence and conformity: A minority of one against a unanimous majority. Psychological Monographs,* 70 (Whole no. 416).

Asch, S. E. (1951) – *Effects of group pressure upon the modification and distortion of judgment.* In H. Guetzkow (ed.)

subjects let themselves be conditioned by this answer and indicated the clearly wrong length.

If the attitude socially accepted by the group, even if wrong, is that it is normal to wait for months to collect the salary, a great number of subjects will let themselves be conditioned by such an answer.

How to Defend Yourself from the Unity Rule

Contrasting the rule of "unity," is very difficult because belonging to a "community" in which we reflect and identify ourselves, conditions us both in ideas and especially in purchasing choices.

Therefore, to avoid being a victim of this type of manipulation, it is necessary to be aware of the processes underlying this rule in order to understand that it is possible to get out of this trap at any desired time. If, for example, a product or service is not suitable for us, either because of its quality or cost, it will be more advantageous not to buy it.

Chapter 3

8 Common Methods of Dark Psychology

In this chapter, we will center on some of the most common but effective methods out there. You will find this discussion is rather detailed and aimed at providing deep insight into how these strategies are effective.

You will notice some of the methods we will get into a very common and rather overt, while others are rather subtle and go unnoticed. In fact, some of these tactics are so subtle that you don't even know they are there; but they are.

Deception through Lying

Regardless of the manipulator's ultimate objective, lying is almost always their favorite go-to maneuver. In a manner of speaking, it is the foundation of their playbook. Manipulators will often resort to lies to gain any kind of advantage. Pathological liars are those who compulsively lie all the time, even if there is no need to. When the manipulator is deceptive, it's because they realize that the lies go much better than the facts (13).

There are several deceptions the manipulator can use to help them achieve their ultimate goals. Firstly, there are flat-out lies. If the victim doesn't know any better, they will fall for the ruse. The deception takes place as the target is simply misled by the false information. This is a pretty straightforward issue.

Things change when the manipulator seeks to cleverly disguise lies by wrapping them up in a context in which they may seem accurate but are truly false. The phenomenon known as "fake news" comes to mind. In fake news, the manipulator will present fraudulent information, which is not known to be true, but also not known to be untrue. So, the target cannot distinguish fact from fiction. The manipulator does everything to persuade others that they are sincere, while the information presented seems to be credible. In the end, the victim has no choice but to go along unless they are willing to do their own research to determine if the manipulator is truly lying or being truthful.

What makes fake news even more powerful is when the source of information is credible. While there is always the possibility they could simply be wrong about the information they are presenting, manipulators always seek to build up as much credibility as they can. That way, victims will take them at face value. When this occurs, manipulators can become quite dangerous.

Manipulators who lie to their targets are usually good at it. Targets may also find it hard to tell when they are lied to. Generally, it is too late to do anything about the obvious fib by the time the subject figures it out. The only way to ensure the target eliminates their risk of being manipulated is to look after the different types of characters that are specialists at trickery and deception. The manipulator lies about anything to get through, and most of the time his targets won't know until it is too late to do anything about it.

---

(13) Carson, Thomas L. (2012) – *Lying and deception: theory and practice.* Oxford University Press.

Lying by Omission

This approach is similar to the previous one, with a few slight differences to the above-described method. The lie is a bit subtler because the manipulator will tell a few things about the truth but will reject some key issues. This may be called "faking out" in some instances. The manipulator may argue that they must borrow money to get gas or food, but they really need the money to buy drugs or alcohol. In this example, they are telling the truth about needing the money. What they are leaving out is the real reason why they need the money.

This is why you need to think things through. If you just blurt out lies without actually thinking about them, then you are liable to make a mistake. If you do, then you'll get caught and your cover will be blown.

In order for this technique to be effective, you need to mix lies in such a way that they make sense with scrutinized and contrasted with the truth. They need to be credible and presented in a manner that makes sense to those who will hear them. Often, manipulators add or omit details that are convenient to them. So, the information is true, on the whole, but the details of the truth are twisted to suit your benefit. As the saying goes, "the devil is in the details."

A good means of implementing half-truths is through rumors. Nowadays, social media is a great way of spreading rumors. In fact, it is so effective that you don't really need to get people to believe it; all you need is to sow a seed of doubt. As long as you can get people to doubt the accuracy of the information, or partially accept its validity, then you have done your job. By the time the affected parties seek to restore their reputations or set the record straight, it will have been too late. That is why you need to strike first and often. That way, the victim will have no choice but to go into crisis mode.

If you fear such an attack on yourself, then you need to hit the manipulator back where it will hurt them. You need to discredit them at all costs. That will sow the seed of doubt on the source of the information and give you a fighting chance to defend yourself.

Denial

Denial is a form of lying as it entails pretending that something happened when it didn't or trying to hide the fact that something didn't happen when it did. A simple form of denial is trying to avoid responsibility for an action. This is common when a person does something inappropriate but wishes to avoid the punishment associated with their actions.

When the manipulator appears to be truly sincere in their defense, the confusion created in those around them can ultimately lead to the planting of the seed of doubt. This is how skillful trial attorneys are able to convince jurors that their client is not guilty. Please note that we're not saying that the accused is innocent. What we are saying is that the accused is not guilty as the other party was unable to prove the suspect's culpability beyond a reasonable doubt.

Avoidance

This occurs when manipulators don't give straight answers or move the discussion into a different topic utilizing diversion tactics. In a dialog, avoidance occurs by rambling, or otherwise talking endlessly in a meandering fashion. Their ultimate game is to confuse the target, which makes them question the true version.

When a manipulator changes the topic, it can be gradual and not entirely obvious.

The manipulator takes advantage of the frustration of the other party. The best manipulators have a way of transitioning attention away from their deeds and on to what they really want to achieve. So, don't be surprised if you are dealing with a manipulator if they are constantly trying to dodge your questions or conversation.

Over time, the target can find it difficult to determine what is genuine or not since the manipulator can cause them to question every fact they know or think is valid (14).

---

(14) Carson, Thomas L. (2012) – *Lying and deception: theory and practice*. Oxford University Press.

Generalizations

These types of statements are very dangerous insofar as they are intended to be direct attacks on one particular person or group of people. Generalizations can be very unfair, especially when they are intended to characterize a group of people in a certain manner. For instance, when you say things such as "all men are..." or "all women are..." you are misrepresenting people in a truly unfair manner. Yet, when attempting to confuse and deceive people, these statements can be quite effective at creating a negative atmosphere. Manipulators love nothing more than to create animosity among people. After all, one of the fundamental tenets of manipulators is "divide and conquer." Blanket statements are great at achieving that.

Playing the Victim

When we act like victims, we manipulate others. We've learned that since we were kids, if you wanted your parents to do something for you, you would lock yourself in your room crying, and this behavior certainly attracted their attention; even today a little victimhood will help you achieve this result. Through victimhood, you can make a person do something for you.

This is one of the reasons why many people go into depression and stay in it. The "feeling special in their problem" allows these individuals to attract the attention of others to feel important in their eyes. This is a sneaky way of manipulating others but equally present in many people.

Generate Fear

The news bulletins are a champion in this. The news tends to terrify us because the more scared we are, the more vulnerable we will be and, therefore, more susceptible to manipulation. Through the use of fear, rulers have the opportunity to manage us better and keep us under control. One remedy we all have at our disposal to defend ourselves against this devious technique is not to watch the news every day. By watching the news we satisfy what is called the need for "security."

The classic example we can say to understand this technique is when a mother educates her child. If she doesn't want her kid to do something, she tells him something on purpose that frightens him; for example: *"if you touch the stove you will burn your hand and then we have to take you to the hospital."* In this way, the child will never go near the kitchen!

It is not necessary to shout or make direct threats to intimidate. Manipulators are experts at sowing fear, many times imperceptibly. It is a matter of announcing dangers in the face of certain behavior.

They manipulate you, for example, when they tell you that you "must" act in a certain way. Otherwise, you run the risk of a certain undesirable situation occurring. Apparently, they are appealing to reason, after all, they are just trying to condition you through fear.

Create Insecurity

One of the most powerful techniques of mind control is to continuously question everything our interlocutor is telling us. For example, if you say to me: *"you know that I was able to achieve this result,"* I could reply saying *"but are you sure that the result you have achieved is thanks to you?"* That way, if we question what others are saying to us, and we do it repeatedly, eventually, others will tend to question it!

There are situations where our weaknesses and convictions or self-love are highlighted and we take advantage of them.

Negative criticism of what we do or say is manipulative mechanisms based on insecurity. It also happens when they try to confuse us by making our mistakes look more complicated than they are or by making us believe that they know us better than we do.

Chapter 4

The 10 Best Techniques of Dark Psychology

Thus far, we have talked about methods used in dark psychology. Indeed, we have only skimmed the surface as there is quite a bit to discuss when it comes to manipulation tactics.

Now, the reason why dark psychology techniques are effective lies in the way they interact with your psyche. The human psyche is structured in such a way that it is capable of filtering out stimuli that somehow don't conform to the patterns, beliefs, and values that permeate the psyche. For instance, if you believe in peace, your mind will reject any notion of violence. By the same token, if your mind is centered on greed and avarice, you may place minimal restrictions on schemes aimed at getting money.

However, the subconscious mind, the layer that exists beneath the conscious mind, is unfiltered but equally able to process the stimuli that enter it. This is why the manipulator's true goal is to access your subconscious and implant ideas at that level. When that happens, the chances of ideas and beliefs sticking are very high.

This is why advertising is so repetitive. Think about it. If you only hear an advert once, the chance of you recalling it would be very slim. However, if you hear adverts over and over, there will come a point where your conscious mind will stop putting up a fight. When that occurs, the message can seep through into your subconscious. This is the secret of brand positioning. So, if you think advertising, at least good advertising anyway, is about selling stuff, guess again. Good advertising is all about getting you to constantly think about a brand or a product.

The Door in the Face!

Directly from the experience of door-to-door salesmen, I present the technique of the door... in the face! (15). When we want to obtain a certain result from our interlocutor, we should make a request we consider too high and unreasonable: this request will undoubtedly be followed by a metaphorical door in the face, a refusal. At this point, we should immediately follow the real request that we had in mind: compared with the first, in fact, the new request will appear more modest and reasonable.

This technique bases its effectiveness on the natural tendency of our mind to make comparisons. If we provide the right term of comparison, no request will appear excessive.

This technique works because it arouses in the person a sense of guilt and an idea of concession. In other words, your renunciation will be perceived as a concession and then, it is a sneaky application of the "reciprocity rule", which has been widely discussed in the second chapter.

Foot in the Door

This tactic is implemented in increments. This begins with the manipulator asking for small favors. Every time the victim complies, the manipulator will ask for increasingly bigger favors until they get what they ultimately want, or they exhaust their victim. At that point, the manipulator needs to move on to a fresh victim.

(15) Burg, B. (2011) – *The Art of Persuasion: Winning Without Intimidation*. Tremendous Life Books.

Consider this example:

A manipulator wants a large sum of money. Yet, they know they won't get it if they just ask for it. So, they ask for a tiny sum. Then, they pay it back. Next, they ask for a bigger sum and then pay it back. They do this as they build up trust capital until one day; they get what they want, never to be heard from again.

This example clarifies why this technique is called put your "foot in the door"... and make room with your whole body...

A more rudimentary approach consists in asking multiple people for money with no intention of paying it back. Eventually, they exhaust the people around them. So, they need to move on and find new victims.

In the **"foot in the door"** technique, smaller requests are asked to gain compliance with larger requests, while the technique **"door in the face"** works in the opposite direction, where larger requests are asked with the expectation that it will be rejected, to gain compliance for smaller requests (16).

"Yes-set" Technique

The technique of the "yes-set" consists of asking several questions to the interlocutor, for which he can only agree and answer "yes." This will create a light conditioning that will also make him answer yes to your real request. It is a short-term freezing effect that causes the person to enter into a certain response perspective.

4 or 5 harmless questions in the preamble are enough (17).

For example, you want to watch a specific program on TV, knowing that the choice of your partner will probably be very different:

YOU: *It was nice today, huh? It feels good to get some sun!*

HIM/HER: *Yes, it was.*

---

(16) Morin, C. (2019) – *The Persuasion Code: How Neuromarketing Can Help You Persuade Anyone, Anywhere, Anytime.* Wiley.

(17) Dilts, R., (2017) – *Sleight of Mouth: The Magic of Conversational Belief Change.* Dilts Strategy Group.

YOU: *Are you watching TV tonight?*

HIM/HER: *Well yes, I think so.*

YOU: *Remember the movie we saw the day before yesterday?*

HIM/HER: *Yes.*

YOU: *I liked it. He was practically the main actor, right?*

HIM/HER: *Yes, he was.*

YOU: *Do you agree to watch the 1:00 movie tonight? I think it'll be okay.*

HIM/HER: *Yes, if you want, what is it?*

A funny little demonstration of this principle that I'm sure you already know. Ask someone to repeat the word "white" 10 times, and then ask the question "What is the cow drinking?" The wrong answer will have been conditioned by the previous repetition.

The mechanism behind this technique is based on the use of "rhetorical questions" or statements that are true, taken for granted, or otherwise verifiable in the direct experience of the person.

In these cases, the person "leading" the report prepares the ground with a series of questions to which the interlocutor will surely answer yes; that is why it is called "Yes-Set."

In all three cases, some truisms or true and/or verifiable statements are followed by an "unverifiable statement" which is an induction (or command) or a demand taken for granted.

Linguistic Presupposition

Some very insidious communicative maneuvers consist of asking the interlocutor questions to which it is not possible to answer simply with a "YES" or a "NO", but that trigger in the subject of the actions as an answer to a command. For example, if I ask a person if he *"can turn off the light, there on his right?"* apparently I am asking if he can do it, but in practice, I will get the switch off, which is actually what I wanted.

In other words, through the linguistic form of "embedded commands," you can skillfully camouflage a command into a question, as in the following example: *"Do you want to tell me now what's bothering you or would you rather wait a while?"*

With this sentence, I create in practice an alternative through the construction of more proposals, where I take for granted that in any case, the subject will reveal to me what worries him.

The Linguistic-Presupposition is one of the most powerful and easy to use tools to give someone "apparently" a choice and at the same time "trap" them inside your idea, almost without any way out.

Bind is a hypnotic technique used to force a choice with words. It is also called the "illusion of alternative."

Let's see some examples:

- *"After you go to buy bread, could you come by the newsstand and buy me the paper?"*

- *"When are you going to take me to the movies?"*

- *"Have you decided which foreign country to take me to for our anniversary?"*

Each of these questions already provides a choice, and the trick is to take for granted a fact that is slightly hidden.

Reverse Psychology

This technique consists of assuming a behavior opposite to the desired one, with the expectation that this "prohibition" will arouse curiosity and therefore induce the person to do what is really desired. For instance, when you tell a child not to do something, that is the first action they do. This type of response persists throughout a person's life.

It's a way of getting things done, giving the opposite of the command you want to give. If I say things like, "don't be offended," "don't worry," I get the opposite effect; I will make my interlocutor stiffen.

Some people are known to be like boomerangs because they refuse to go in the direction they are sent but take the opposite route. This type of behavior can be used by a dark persuader because it is a weakness that the victim has. Take an example of a friend who loves to eat junk food at any opportunity they get. The dark persuader knows this and therefore will suggest that they should eat healthy because it will be good for them, knowing that the friend will choose fast food anyway.

When individuals are told that they should not believe one thing or the other, they will pay closer attention to it (18).

Consider this situation:

You are looking to force your employees to work overtime without questioning it. However, getting them to log the hours can be challenging as no one is keen on staying beyond their usual shift. So, you really can't do much to convince them to work overtime.

Then, you get an idea: Why not ban overtime? That is, anyone who wants to work overtime cannot do so. The justification behind it is that since no one wants to stay longer hours, then there will be no overtime. In fact, you could take it a step further and hire temp workers to fill in the extra hours. Now, your regular staff is concerned that others are encroaching upon their jobs. In the end, you may get resistance from your usual staff, who is now demanding to work overtime in order to get rid of the temp workers.

In the end, you have successfully manipulated your staff to work overtime. You were able to play with their sense of security by banning overtime and then bringing other workers to cover the hours they wouldn't.

A convention playbook would have sought to incentivize workers so they would be more willing to stay longer hours. But this would have meant paying more or offering greater benefits. In the end, your manipulation attempts were successful without conceding any additional benefits.

---

(18) Tali Sharot. (2018) – *The Influential Mind: What the Brain Reveals About Our Power to Change Others*. Picador USA.

Negative Hidden Commands

A negative hidden command is a specific linguistic model of reverse psychology in which instruction is formulated negatively so that it is perceived by the unconscious mind, bypassing the "critical guardian" of our interlocutor.

An interesting aspect of the unconscious mind is that, compared to the conscious one, it does not understand negation. This happens because our mind works by images and because there is no mental representation of the word "NOT." Therefore, the unconscious does not perceive it. In other words, our brain cannot deny experiences related to the senses without first visualizing them.

Generally, in the books of Guerrilla Marketing, NLP, the psychology of communication, and neuro-marketing, two examples are given below to explain this concept.

- Read the following sentence and do what it says: "Don't think of a pink elephant."
  What were you thinking? Almost certainly a pink elephant, <u>even though you were asked not to.</u>
- Now I ask you not to think of a yellow lemon. Think about what you want, but don't think of a yellow lemon. Don't think of a big, juicy yellow lemon, its intense aroma, its sour taste. Don't think about cutting the yellow lemon in two, squeezing half of it in your mouth, and drinking its sour juice (19).
  Did you do it? Most likely not, in fact maybe you even felt your salivation increase, swallowed, and felt some chills.

How did that happen? Simple: Our brain can't deny sensory experiences without trying them first.

The second case is even stronger than the first because it contains many more details and ideosensory contents that activate with more energy the mental representation it intends to suggest.

This mechanism is very useful to us because we can use negative hidden commands while stimulating a positive response in the recipient of the message.

---

(19) Kevin Hogan and James Speakman (2006) – *Covert Persuasion: Psychological Tactics and Tricks to Win the Game.* Wiley.

In order to use negative hidden commands, it is sufficient to say what we want to happen and to precede it with negation.

Some examples:

- *"I'm not asking you to go on vacation with me."*

- *"I'm not asking you to trust me."*

- *"I'm not here to list all the advantages of our proposal."*

- *"You don't have to decide right away, take all the time you need."*

With negative hidden commands, we can prevent the conscious mind from blocking our messages—filtering them to check whether or not to accept them—because rationally it is not receiving them, unlike the unconscious mind.

Anchoring

Anchoring or "conditioning" is a psychological tool that is used to associate sounds, visuals, or other stimuli to certain feelings and sensations. It should be noted that these feelings and sensations can be both positive and negative.

Ivan Pavlov, a Nobel Prize-winning Russian scientist, has managed to demonstrate this mechanism by conducting experiments on dogs. He first began by feeding some dogs, always preceding the "lunch" by the sound of a bell, observing how the animals reacted to the sight of food with intense salivation, a symbol of a natural reflex of the dog, functional to digestion and associated with hunger.

After a certain period of training, Pavlov subjected the dogs to the sound of the bell without giving them any food; the animals reacted with the same salivation, which was a sign of an emotional expectation.

With conditioning, it is possible to connect certain emotional states and cognitive responses to external stimuli through forms of association. This type of stimulus-response behavior is at the basis of manipulation and is the tool used by manipulators.

Remember always the rule that decision-making is primarily based on emotions rather than logic.

Let's consider a classic example of positive anchoring: what sound does the ice cream truck make? Can you recall the music? What thoughts come to mind when you hear that sound?

The same goes for songs, slogans, logos, scents, and so on. These stimuli are developed with the intent of associating a specific feeling in your mind. Skilled marketers are masters at exploiting these feelings in their audiences.

The easiest way to understand this is to focus on price anchoring, which is generally done with the whole $9.99 deal. Another way to get you to think you're getting a great deal is to create a sense of belonging or an anchor of ownership. An example of this would be Starbucks. They have overpriced and not so great coffee, but the barista writes your name of the cup, and automatically, the product value increases in your mind. They have included you in the making of this product, and now the product itself seems like it is yours (20).

Dark persuaders use anchoring as an easy fix for most of the monetary sale they want to encourage.

By "anchor effect" (which is based on *Anchoring Bias*) we mean the tendency, when a decision has to be taken, to rely excessively on the first information offered to us (the anchor, precisely). In the moment in which this point of reference comes fixed, the judgment will consider it the best.

As an example, in the process of purchase of a good, the initial price gives the basic setting to all the negotiation, for which prices inferior to that one of anchor can seem reasonable even if they remain superior to the effective value of the good. Or, on the contrary, the price devaluation applied by competitors creates an anchor in the customer, which they consider unjustifiably higher prices for a product they consider similar (21). In this regard, Daniel Kahneman, Nobel Prize winner for his studies on cognitive psychology, said that it is completely wrong the very common theory that, in a negotiation, the second counterpart is in advantage;

---

(20) Starch, D., (1996) – *Measuring Advertising Readership and Results.* Effects of the Advertising Message, McGraw-Hill

(21) Jonah Berger, (2016) – *Invisible Influence: The Hidden Forces that Shape Behavior.* Simon & Schuster.

according to him, thanks to the anchoring effect, in negotiations there is an important advantage "of the first move" that allows to set the point of reference for the discussions, proposals and counterproposals that will serve to reach agreement (22).

Blackmail

Blackmail is commonly known as having some type of information or knowledge that, if revealed, can be very damaging to the victim. Therefore, the victim doesn't have much choice but to comply with the manipulator. The end result is a negative feedback loop in which the victim has no choice but to go along until they have a chance to escape the trap.

Blackmail is one of the first tools a manipulator would use. It is commonly seen on TV and in the movies. Manipulators use personal or sensitive information about a person to extort them. The result of extortion is the gain of some kind of benefit from that person. In the movies, you commonly see manipulators threatening to reveal damaging personal information about a person unless they comply with their wishes. This is a form of coercion and doesn't necessarily need to be accompanied by threats of physical violence. If the victim is weak enough, they will cave and comply with the manipulator's requests. However, if the victim decides to confront the manipulator, they may face the consequences of the information being revealed about them.

It should be noted that extortion is generally a threat of physical harm unless victims comply with the demands of the aggressor. Typical extortion does not involve any kind of personal information. Rather, it seeks to use physical violence to compel others to act in accordance with the manipulator's desires. This generally includes some kind of payment in exchange for "protection." The victims usually have one of two options, either face the extortionist and fight them or run away. Generally, the latter is the best course of action.

---

(22) Kahneman D., Jack Knetsch J., Richard Thaler R. (2008) – *The Endowment Effect: Evidence of Losses Valued More Than Gains*, in Handbook of Experimental Economics Results, vol. 1, pp 939-948

In the workplace, blackmail can be an incredibly damaging tool. However, it is not to be used often as blackmail uncovers the identity of the manipulator. While there may be anonymous blackmail threats, generally speaking, a manipulator will have to reveal their true identity in order for the victim to see them as a credible threat. Once the "cat is out of the bag," the manipulator will have to eventually move on to another victim because they have exhausted their current one.

Love Bombing

This statement is a simple strategy involving a brilliant, abrupt, and vigorous show of favorable feelings toward the victim. It is essential to remember that manipulators generally use this strategy at the beginning of their relationships. This strategy seems a little odd when you really dig deep into it. This is because an individual who intends to extract some type of gain from their victim initially says and does kind things for them. Yet, the manipulator may have very little regard for their victim. So, it's rather perplexing on the surface but makes perfect sense when viewed from the angle of their deception.

The concept behind love bombings is quite easy because its main aim is to generate a sense of love, confidence, and adherence for the manipulator within the intended target. The degree to which love bombing is used may depend on the target itself (23).

What does this imply?

Take a person who looks quite desperate, hopeless, and solitary, for example. The manipulator is more prone to choose this person as a target, as they are conscious of the fact that instead of more selective in their choice of partner, the target may essentially "take what they can get." As a result, the target, out of desperation, may become a sitting duck for love bombing. Initially, the target may not believe

---

(23) James, O. (2018) – *Love bombing: Reset your child's emotional thermostat*. Routledge.

they are the subject of such affection. However, they may come crashing back down to reality at some point.

It should be noted that the manipulators' modus operandi when it comes to love bombing is a combination of physical attraction and charming nature. The manipulator will go out of their way to seem physically attractive while also appearing to be a pleasant person to get along with. As such, they will seek out victims who are vulnerable. Vulnerability generally boils down to being the right place at the right time. For instance, a manipulator will seek out a victim who has been through a tough breakup, such as divorce, and is extremely vulnerable emotionally. Also, manipulators seek out people with low self-esteem. This makes them especially prone to affection and attention. In some cases, targets may be so starved for attention and affection that even when they are aware of the love-bombing, they will go along with it for as long as it lasts.

In the end, love bombing is an effective technique when done right. However, it is hardly the best way of building a long-term relationship. Therefore, the manipulator needs to move on at some point from their target and seek out a new relationship. This can leave the victim absolutely devastated in addition to what they lost to the manipulator in terms of possible material possessions.

Now, love bombing isn't always intended to lead to a relationship. It can be something quite benign, such as flirting to get something from someone in a very brief interaction. This is commonly seen in a number of ways. For instance, an individual may flirt with receptionists or security guards in order to gain access to a location. Other times, the manipulator may flirt with co-workers and colleagues so that they can "help" the manipulator. The best manipulators lead others on without the actual intention of allowing them to get close. In fact, when the time comes to move the relationship forward, they back away. This generally leaves the victim feeling deceived as they acted in good faith, believing the manipulator indeed had a genuine interest in them.

This type of behavior is predicated on the liberal use of flattery, which is intended to appeal to the target's self-esteem or lack thereof. While it's clear that some individuals are far more susceptible to flattery, it should be noted that it won't necessarily work in every circumstance. That is why you generally see manipulators going around trying to see who is more susceptible to flattery. When they find such individuals, they will exploit the proclivity as much as possible. In fact, flattery can open the door to love bombing at some point down the road.

One last point about love bombing: this maneuver isn't necessarily related to romantic relationships. As a matter of fact, love bombing can be a manifestation of "kissing up" to someone. For instance, you see workers in a company "kiss up" to their boss. The boss enjoys the adulation and will grant special attention and favor to those who praise them. This is especially useful when an individual shows signs of having a narcissistic personality. Since narcissists crave constant attention, they are especially susceptible to adulation, flattery and, of course, love-bombing.

However, there is a catch to adulating someone. If they are clearly incompetent or inadequate, the adulation may seem like an obvious lie. And while the victim may "drink the Kool-Aid" so to speak, others around the manipulator will catch on to the maneuver. As such, the manipulator may have no choice back to off or risk being criticized by those around them.

Positive Reinforcement

Positive reinforcement differs from love bombing as it is intended to "praise" or reward the type of behavior congruent with the manipulator's wishes and desires. Consequently, the manipulator will use affection, flattery and "love-bombing" to reinforce this behavior. Now, it should be noted that positive reinforcement is a commonly used technique and perfectly normal.

But then again, there's a moment when the manipulator may overdo it at some point. This is especially true when it's evident the victim's behavior isn't particularly special or noteworthy. A great example of this can be seen in a company in which executives surround themselves with "yes" men. A "yes" man is typically a low-level collaborator who always agrees and praises their boss in the hopes of keeping their job at the very least, or perhaps getting promoted in the best of cases.

In another sense, positive reinforcement can be utilized to get people to act in accordance with the desires of the manipulator. Positive reinforcement can be seen as the opposite of blackmail insofar as using positive outcomes as compared to coercion and fear. While it is true that fear is a much more powerful force, in the long run, positive reinforcement tends to go well within a longer lasting relationship.

On the flip side, manipulators need to be careful not to lay it on too thick. By this, we mean that manipulators should be careful to avoid making their praise too far-fetched lest they lose credibility. Unless the manipulator is dealing with a delusional tyrant, there is a limit to how far they can take positive reinforcement. That is why manipulators end up resorting to some sort of violence once the effect of positive reinforcement has run out. By then, the manipulator will be left with no choice but to find some other type of resource which can ensure that they maintain their control over the victim.

Now that we have explored these techniques, take the time to reflect on the relationships around you. You might find these tactics to be far more common than you could have ever imagined.

Chapter 5

8 Advanced Techniques of Mental Manipulation

So far, we have discussed a great deal of the dark psychology and manipulation techniques known to date. These techniques vary in their degree of sophistication and may be used across a wide range of situations or may be more suited for specific purposes.

In this chapter, we are going to be taking a look at some advanced dark psychology and manipulation techniques which are highly effective and are generally regarded as favorites for well-versed manipulators. If you happen to fall into one of these traps, you'll be surprised at the level of sophistication attached to them. Moreover, some manipulators may be so good that you will hardly notice you have fallen into such traps.

If you are entertaining the possibility of using these techniques for your own benefit, please be advised that employing dark psychology tactics such as these may get you what you want, but the cost to others may be quite high. You do need to be prepared to face the consequences should others be potentially harmed in this situation.

In addition, these techniques do take some time to perfect and develop as they require a good degree of skill and experience. That being said, your ability to make the most of the dark psychology tactics in the pursuit of your personal goals may lead you to gain deeper insights into the world of human psychology and how the human psyche works.

Gaslighting

This technique has a bit of an unusual name, but its overall effectiveness is remarkable. Its effect lies is getting people to question their own perception of reality. As such, gaslighting consists of manipulating the victim into believing what the manipulator wants them to believe, even when there is clear evidence against what the manipulator is saying.

It can be used, for example, in a discussion when one partner accuses the other of betraying it.

The "gaslighting" strategy is used to destabilize and make the other person doubt in order to make them believe they are living in an imaginary reality. In these cases, one of the most commonly used phrases is "It's all your imagination."

Another classic example of gaslighting can be seen in cases of abuse. The abuser repeatedly tells the victim that there is no such abuse happening, even when it's clear that the victim has been abused in some manner. This type of denial forces the victim to question their own perception of the events that have taken place. When effective, the victim may not necessarily accept what the manipulator has said, but rather, will question their own perception to the degree that they have no way of differentiating abuse from non-abuse situations (24).

Gaslighting is commonly used by politicians. This is why their first reaction is to deny everything when a scandal breaks. Nine times out of ten, politicians get away with initial denials. Unless the media decides to dig deeper and produce compelling evidence supporting claims, politicians will simply stonewall everything. This is intended to get voters to question the media's accuracy. The intent is not to convince the public, they have done no wrong; the intent is to generate enough confusion to where the public gives politicians the benefit of the doubt even when they are clearly guilty.

---

(24) Abramson, Kate (2014) – *"Turning up the Lights on Gaslighting"*. Philosophical Perspectives. p.28

Expert gaslighters are so charming and persuasive that they are generally given the benefit of the doubt. The fact of the matter is that this is all they need. So long as they are not indicated in the minds of others, they will feel content. To the degree in which the manipulator is able to sow the seed of doubt in the minds of others, they know they will always have the upper hand.

It should also be noted that there is a clear difference between simply denying facts and gaslighting. In order for gaslighting to be truly effective, it is necessary some credible explanation which can supplant the real events. This occurs when manipulators are able to come up with clever explanations for things that happen. That often entails playing the blame game or evading personal responsibility by concocting schemes. Then, there is always the possibility of creating a "boogeyman," which is a fictional character created as a means of having something to pin blame on. Now, the boogeyman does not need to be real. In fact, it doesn't even need to be a real person. The main function of the boogeyman is to have something which people can hate, fear or blame for the events that happen around them. Expert manipulators can milk a boogeyman for a long time, but will have to eventually move on to another one. In the end, it is nothing more than a fabrication.

The best antidote to gaslighting is to keep a close eye on details. Please don't forget that the devil is in the details. And so long as you can keep your eye on the details, you will be able to tell when you're being gaslit (25).

The Long Con

This is a slow method of persuasion. It is very useful when people resist giving into persuasion because they feel like they are pressured or there isn't any trust between the victim and the persuader. The dark persuader will invest their time in taking to understand their victim, befriending them, and ensuring the victim develops a sense of trust and affinity. To do this, the dark persuader builds an artificial rapport and uses other ways to make the victim

---

(25) Stern, Robin – *The Gaslight Effect: How to Spot and Survive the Hidden Manipulation Others Use to Control Your Life* (2008)

feel comfortable. After the victim has been prepared psychologically, the dark persuader begins their attempts. They can start by trying to lead their target into making choices that will be in the best interest of the manipulator. The purpose of beginning like this is firstly to accustom the prey to being persuaded. And second, to lead the person to consider the relationship between them and the dark persuader as a positive one; one they will benefit from. Once the victim trusts the manipulator, the target is vulnerable to the persuader's actions and does not stand a chance.

The long con is a long-term plan which generally entails a great benefit at the end. A good example of this is people who woo and eventually marry their target. The target falls head over heels for the dark persuader. The manipulator, in reality, is just interested in the victim's wealth, social status or influence. Once the manipulator has exhausted the resources of the victim, they will be prone to discarding the victim as they are no longer of use to them. This is the point in which divorces happen, leaving the victim devastated and emotionally shattered. Ultimately, the manipulator gets away with their machinations unless something is done in the meantime to stop them.

In the worst of cases, the long con can go on for decades. Think about financial crimes and fraud in which conmen deceive their investors. These schemes usually take years to hatch and even longer to unravel. By the time investors catch wind of the monkey business going on, they stand very little chance to get their money back. All that is left is a painful lesson on trusting others without doing their due diligence.

Covert Deception

Masking true intentions of the dark persuader is another tactic a manipulator will use to get what they want. A manipulator will disguise their true intentions from their victims and can use different approaches depending on their targets and the surrounding circumstances. One approach a dark persuader can use is using two requests consecutively because people find it hard to refuse two requests in a row. Take this example; a manipulator wants $500 from their victim. The dark persuader will begin by explaining why they are needed of $1000 while stating what will happen if they are not able to come up with that amount. The victim may feel some form of guilt or compassion, but will kindly explain to the manipulator that they cannot lend the amount because, quite frankly, it is more than they can manage to give. This is when the conman will lessen the amount to $500, which was what they wanted from the beginning. They will attach the amount with some emotional reason where the victim will be unable to refuse the second request. The deceiver walks away with the original sum, and the victim is left confused about what happened.

Creating an Illusion

Skilled manipulators can replace reality with an alternate version of it. These manipulators are able to take what they have seen to be real and replace it with an alternative version which is more convenient to them. For instance, manipulators may go as far as fabricating a whole new persona for themselves. This may include changing their name, faking an accent or even producing falsified documentation to accredit a different place of birth, nationality or family name. These elaborate hoaxes can lead to high-level deception. When you think about this type of scheme, some of the most elaborate fraudsters in history come to mind.

On a lesser scale, illusions can be created through flat-out lying, that is, providing false accounts of which never even took place. These false accounts may simply frame events in a different light that is more suitable for the manipulator's schemes. Moreover, manipulators can use embellishment to make events seem much larger than they really are (26).

Embellishment is often used to create grandiose accounts of a person's accomplishments. For instance, a job applicant may include that they were at the top of their class in college when, in reality, they were in the middle of the pack. Another type of embellishment is "name dropping." This is commonly used by manipulators to appear they are connected despite having very loose connections, at best, with the people they are mentioned.

The most skilled manipulators are able to mix lies with the truth. This enables them to paint a more credible illusion as the kernels of

---

(26) Dantalion, J. (2008) – *Mind Control Language Patterns*. Mind Control Publishing.

truth embedded in the illusion give those around them the impression that what they are saying is actually real. As a result, they may get away with their lies. However, please bear in mind that the devil is in the details. So, if you knit pick long enough, you may find out you are dealing with an impostor. That's why it's always a good idea to take everything you hear with a grain of salt. If you choose to take everything you hear at face value, you may become disappointed when you realize you believed someone who was deliberately trying to fool you.

The Big Buildup

Manipulators don't always act in haste. In fact, there are manipulators who take their sweet time. They are not concerned with immediate gains. Rather, they are interested in long-term sustainable results. But to achieve this, a gradual approach needs to be taken.

Think about advertisers.

Brand positioning is not something that happens overnight. As a matter of fact, positioning a brand is an endeavor that takes a long time, often years. But once the brand is positioned, they become entrenched in the minds of consumers. While there is nothing wrong with positioning a brand over time based on quality products and good service, the manipulative aspect of this type of advertising occurs when advertisers do their best to persuade consumers of their brand. As such, there is no substantial quality of product behind the brand but just clever advertising. So, it's up to consumers to discern if a product is really worth all the hype. Nevertheless, most consumers fall to the hype surrounding the brand.

Putting the Other Person Down

The manipulator has other options available to help them reach their ultimate goal. One tactic that can be quite effective consists in putting their target down on a regular basis. However, this isn't done through insults or threats. This covert technique is very useful because the manipulator uses it in a very subtle manner. This can be seen in the abundant use of sarcasm or perhaps passive-aggressive attacks. For example, the manipulator may say, "don't we look lovely today" when it is clear that the victim is not at their best. A passive-aggressive approach might be something like, "I'm just going to have to take you in for a good scrubbing and a haircut." It might say in a playful tone, but the subtext is far more sinister.

As for the target, they may not realize they are the subject of manipulation. They may feel terrible as a result of the interaction, but may not notice they are being deliberately acted upon by the manipulator. Consequently, the target is left to wonder what the motives might be for being treated in such a manner. Honestly, it doesn't really matter, at least not to the manipulator. What does matter is that the target is left feeling vulnerable and exposed. This is where the manipulator can make the most of their efforts. When a victim is left feeling defenseless, the manipulator is in a prime position to take advantage (27).

On the contrary, if a person feels safe and empowered, the likelihood of them being manipulated is quite low. That's why manipulators prey upon people with low self-esteem. If a person has high self-esteem, then they won't be easily manipulated. If anything, put-downs and insults will spark a defensive reaction. That would leave the manipulator with no choice but to move on to the next victim.

It should be noted that manipulators are always looking for easy targets. They avoid hard targets at all costs since manipulators have a proclivity for getting ahead as easily as possible. Hence, they will shy away from hard work in favor of embracing the easiest way out possible.

The same goes for cases in which you're dealing with a kind person and then you are suddenly confronted by an aggressive individual. When this occurs, the shock that goes in your mind may be enough to get you into a state of panic.

Depending on how mentally tough someone is, they may break down and hold out for a longer period of time. In some more extreme cases, interrogators may resort to torture tactics in order to

---

(27) John Marks (1979) – *The Search for the Manchurian Candidate: The CIA and Mind Control*, Times Books, p. 77

extract information from a suspect. While this is illegal in a criminal case, it is commonly used in the underworld of espionage.

To play this game with people, all you need to do is keep them off balance. While this doesn't mean that you should be moody, it means that you shouldn't be predictable. Otherwise, people around you will know what pushes your buttons and then choose to use that against you. That's why you need to measure your reactions and use them to suit your goals. If you feel that being nice will get you ahead, then be nice. But if you feel that you need to make an example out of someone, then you may have no other choice.

Leading Questions

This involves the dark persuader questions that trigger some response from the victim. A persuader may ask a question like, "do you really think so-and-so is that mean?" This question implies the person being referred to is bad in one way or another. An example of a non-leading question is, "what do you think about so-and-so?" When using leading questions, dark persuaders ensure they are carefully worded. Dark persuaders know that once the victim feels like they are being led in order to trigger a certain response from them, they will become more resistant to being deceived. When the manipulator gets a feeling that the victim appears to be catching on, they will immediately change tactics and return to asking the leading questions only when the victim has dropped their guard. This is a tactic commonly used in interviews or during interrogation, such as when police is questioning a suspect.

Financial Obligations

Often sects and cults create economic dependence in the followers or induce the donation of property, both real estate and money. Let's see what happens in some co-ops.

First phase: It is accepted by all employees to receive salaries late, 2 months become 3, 4, sometimes 5 and touch peaks of 6 months. Those who just can't make a living ask the leader for advance payments that are weighed as "personal favors" (economic dependence) for which you are in debt and must show gratitude.

Second phase: Employees no longer receive salaries and are told that there is no money, so they have to embrace a new ideology. The ideology of financial obligations provides that employees must give up wages that have not yet been collected in order to acquire the new status of working partner (28).

This status costs at least 6 months' salary and is sold as a business opportunity. The new ideology becomes the object of Group Thinking and those who do not adapt are isolated. Isolation weakens the victim and makes them more vulnerable to mental attacks.

(28) Cacioppo, John T., Petty, Richard E. (1984) – *The Elaboration Likelihood Model of Persuasion*, in *Advances in Consumer Research, Association for Consumer Research*

Chapter 6

7 Powerful Covert Emotional Manipulation Techniques

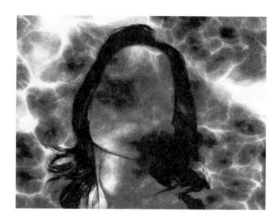

Emotional manipulation can happen at various levels. We have already discussed how fear is a very powerful emotion. But that's not the only one.

How about greed? That works just a good as fear. People who are driven by ambition can be easily had with statements such as "think of all the money you could make." Such a statement would drive a greedy person over the edge.

By the same token, if you're dealing with someone who is overly frugal, a statement such as "think of all the money you could save" would hit their sweet spot. The point here is that you need to know the person you're dealing with in order to make your manipulation attempts ring true.

So, let's take a look at some emotional manipulation tactics which you can use in a given situation.

Emotional Blackmail

While blackmail is very common as far as holding damning information on someone, emotional blackmail can be just as damaging. This occurs when the manipulator has some type of control over the victim and then uses it to extort the victim.

Consider this situation:

The manipulator knows that the target is very insecure about their past. The victim was once an addict and had a stint, or two, in rehab. The manipulator knows that the prey is very concerned about turning over a new leaf and put that past behind them. However, the manipulator threatens to bring up the victim's past every time they want to get something out of them.

Now, you might be thinking, "why doesn't the victim just get away from the manipulator?" That is a fair assessment in the vast majority of cases. However, the manipulator that is able to latch on to their target does so because the victim is in a vulnerable position.

That is the main takeaway here. When the manipulator is able to recognize the victim is in a vulnerable position, they will use that position against the prey. It's important to recognize if you happen to find yourself in such a situation. That way, you can guard against unwelcome attempts.

The manipulator may try to inspire empathy and remorse for themselves as a part of this strategy. Both of these feelings are the most effective people can feel and often enough to motivate the victim to behave in the manner the manipulator needs. The manipulator will use this to get what they want; they will make use of the empathy and remorse that they generate to others to go along with or support them. Using this form of manipulation is about relying more on the subject's emotions rather than their logic. The object constantly faces a risk, primarily in the form of emotional pain and suffering. The manipulator may resort to any maneuvers to trigger feelings powerful enough to compel their target to follow suit. Although the target may assume they support the manipulator out of their own free will, in reality, they are acting as a response to the manipulator's scheming (29).

(29) Forward, Susan (1997) – *Emotional Blackmail.* Tremendous Life Books.

Intimidation

Intimidation is effective insofar as the target is vulnerable enough to fear the possibility of aggression from the manipulator. Thus, intimidation is nothing more than a threat. The manipulator doesn't necessarily have to act on it, but they do have to be as convincing as possible (30).

Manipulators generally find out what the victim fears most, and proceeds to attack from that angle. Whenever the victim reveals their fears, the manipulator is able to latch on and take advantage of such a situation.

For example, it's common to see siblings bother each other with items they fear. Let's say that one of them is afraid of spiders. Then, another sibling will use this fear to get their brother or sister to do these dishes when it's not their turn.

While this may seem childish, it can be a very powerful tool when used correctly. However, there is a catch to it. The manipulator will have to eventually make good on their threats. Otherwise, the victim will soon realize that the manipulator is just talk and no action. In this case, the jig may be up, and the victim will rid themselves of the manipulator.

This is why intimidating others can backfire. When the victim is able to stand up for themselves, the manipulator may be in for a rough time. By the same token, if the victim is powerless to do anything, the manipulator may have an easy go at things.

It should be noted that intimidation is predicated on fear. As such, manipulators need to exploit the inherent fear in their targets. This can be achieved by making overt physical threats or utilizing psychological tactics, such as blackmail, to exert their influence over their targets.

Adelyn Birch, (2014) *30 Covert Emotional Manipulation Tactics: How Manipulators Take Control* in Personal Relationships

(30) Burg, B. (2011) – *The Art of Persuasion: Winning Without Intimidation*. Tremendous Life Books.

The Bait and Switch

In this tactic, the manipulator knows they have something that others want. It doesn't really matter what it is. So, the manipulator is perfectly willing to dangle it in front of others and then take it away. When this occurs, the manipulator lays down a set of rules and conditions the victim must meet if they want to have access to what they have. As long as the victim complies, everything is swelling. However, the real kicker is that the manipulator will never actually let the victim get what they want. They only string them along until the victim is eventually exhausted and gives up. Less sophisticated manipulators will give their victims a "taste" of what they want in the hopes of enticing them to continue complying with their wishes.

This type of technique is used to prey on the emotional needs of a person and is not limited to romantic relationships. This can also occur when a manipulator senses that someone is desperate to make money. The manipulator then uses this need to manipulate the victim with the promise of easy money or a steady income. The victim goes along only to be defrauded at some point.

This technique is predicated on a person pretending to be someone they are not until they get what they want. For example, a person who is interested in gaining something from another may pretend to be romantically interested in this person. The victim, who is desperate for love and affection, will go along with the hopes of entering a meaningful relationship. The manipulator then gets close enough to their target until they extract the benefit they seek. Once the manipulator gets what they want, they pull the bait and switch; that is, they revert to their true self.

The Blame Game

Guilt is one of the most powerful manipulation techniques known to humankind. Guilt can be used to manipulate people by making them feel inferior for the help and support they have received at some point, or can also be used to get others to feel inadequate for a condition they possess. Think of all those times you hear people say, *"things would be different if you weren't sick."* That is one of the most rudimentary means of making someone feel guilty, yet it is highly powerful. Also, you may hear others say things like, *"remember when you needed my help? Now, I need your help."* This is a clear attempt at coaxing someone to go along with the manipulator's intentions.

This is very common in the workplace. There are folks who are experts at pinning everything on someone else. For instance, when something goes wrong, the manipulator will find a way to shift the blame to someone else. The good manipulators can produce compelling evidence against others, thereby clearing their name of any responsibility.

Manipulators can play the "guilt card" or can play the "shame card" by using morals.

They may even go as far as condemning others for their actions in a preemptive attempt to confuse the rest. For instance, the supervisor on the production line of a company makes a mistake. This costs the company money. When questioned by upper management, the supervisor pins the blame on the employees by claiming a moral high ground. Statements like, "I am an expert in what I do" seeks to create this high ground. This automatically shifts the blame to line workers who may not be considered "experts" in that particular field. To take that one step further, the supervisor may choose to shame and lay guilt on their employees. Statements such as "you guys let me down after everything I've done for you" are rather overt attempts at getting others into taking on the blame for something they may not be responsible for.

The blame game can happen in relationships, business dealings, and politics. Politicians who find someone else to blame for the problems happening in their country often present themselves as saviors and heroes for their people. They are the ones who have a solution for everything, yet when you drill down on their track record, they really don't achieve much of anything.

Insinuation

Another devious technique used to exert undetected mental influence is referred to as insinuation. The "innocent" manipulator allows what is a deliberately crafted, insinuating statement to elicit an awkward emotional response. If you take offense, he will inform you that it is not what he said. The comment is generally presented as a "compliment," but not very encouraging. But it's enough veiled to assume you underestimated. The trainer understands what will annoy you, and he or she will be happy to launch such a grenade and see how the fault lies. Their comments are intended to have various possible interpretations that will cause a lot of hurt and doubt. You may sound plummy or left without a meaningful response if you hear it at first because it has so many possible interpretations. As an example, your partner smiles and says, "What do you know? As a prostitute, you can make a lot of money!" If you question him, he'll tell you he intended it to be a joke. But you may ask yourself for its real meaning during a long time to come. You might ask why, when your friend is with you speaking about prostitutes, how he first cares so much about prostitution; why he feels about you; and how much you should bring in the bill you're inclined to give. You'll also wonder whether he would praise you, like he said, on how good a lover he feels you are. Such remarks will operate on you and intensify anger, potential disagreements, and partnership instability. It is convenient for the manipulator to make it appear like a mistake, but therein is the clue: The manipulator insists that he or she intended it just as an unintentional compliment. Of course, you did; typically, a compliment does not hurt your emotions, nor makes you wonder what its true meaning is for years to come (31).

Triangulation

Another often-used technique of the controllers is that of triangulation. This is an effective tactic in a manipulator's arsenal, in which a partnership between you, him or her, and a third party becomes formed. The principal aim of this is to give the victim a feeling of confusion about the connection, causing the victim to have an intense love for the manipulator. That only makes her stay together for a long time thinking about the old lover she had, or simply bring up someone she always finds unexpectedly in the case of gyms. It is much worse if you create vague, negative correlations

---

(31) Adelyn Birch, (2014) – *30 Covert Emotional Manipulation Tactics: How Manipulators Take Control* in Personal Relationships

between yourself and the other man. Their targets are concerned primarily about fear. When you confront them and find out that your real problem is your depression and your low self-esteem, you will stop involving the other man. Where were you listening to before? It is also no exception for the manipulator when using him strategically, to view the other guy as his next target.

The Law of State Transference

The state is a term relating to a person's general mood. An example of a strong congruent state is when a person's thoughts, words, and acts are aligned. The law of state transference encompasses the idea that the person with the balance of power in any particular situation can shift their emotional state to the individual with which they are communicating with. When used by a dark persuader, this is a powerful concept.

If somebody tries to persuade people and understands the laws of state transference, a certain strategy may be used to manipulate their level of control over their target. In the technique, from the beginning, the influencer pressures their own state to suit the natural state of their subject. The influencer will force their state where the subject is feeling sad and talking slower than usual in the same format. Therefore, they establish a connection with their subject at a deep, subconscious level. This is another means of establishing rapport.

After a "state match" is done, the influencer begins changing their own state subtly to assess their victims' compliance. For example, the persuader can intensify their tone of voice slightly to see if their target is at the same pace as them. If the victim is showing signs of conformity, it clearly shows that the influencer has reached the hook point. Once a hook point is reached, the influencer is going to change the state of the subject to the state that they want. This could either be nice and positive or angry and negative depending on the situation that best suits the purposes of the influencer. This approach illustrates the effect of subconscious cues on the success or failure in the process of persuasion.

Chapter 7

Dark Seduction

Much is written about dark seduction. Most of the literature on this subject makes it seem as if there is some kind of art in which manipulators magically seduce their victims for their own devious sexual purposes. Sure, there are people who undoubtedly wish to manipulate others for their own sexual enjoyment. However, dark seduction goes beyond the mere act of sexual intercourse. It is a broader issue in which the manipulator seeks to use romantic overtures to extract some type of benefit from their victims. As a result, victims fall prey to the advances of the manipulator while the manipulator extracts the value they seek.

It should be noted that for the purpose of this book, we're not looking at any dark sexual practices. For instance, dark seduction may be confused with master-slave relationships, and so on. This is not the purpose of this chapter. The purpose of this chapter is to explore how manipulators use a romantic approach to gain the confidence of their victims and exploit them.

The Techniques to Make Dark Seduction Work

Seduction is about using charm and attraction to establish a romantic relationship with an individual. Regardless of gender, this type of practice works the same manner. Men react to certain tactics while women react to others. Yet, the underlying principles are essentially the same.

Physical Attraction

Physically attractive manipulators are by far the most successful. They can leverage their attractiveness to gain access to their intended targets. Often, these individuals seek out targets who are noticeably older or less attractive than they are. They use this difference to their advantage. Also, they prey on vulnerable individuals who are only seeking love and attention. By virtue of their physical attractiveness, victims lower their guard. This enables the manipulator to enter the victim's domain and gain a foothold.

Charm and Flirting

Skilled manipulators use their charm to get their way. If they happen to be physically attractive, this can be a very powerful combination. These kinds of manipulators are prone to use flirting as often as they can. They have no intention of establishing any kind of relationship with their victim. But just the fact that there is some kind of innuendo between the manipulator and the target is often enough to get the target to comply. Then, once the manipulator gets what they seek, the target is discarded (32).

Overt Sexual Advances

This tactic is generally employed by women as it is men who mostly respond to overt sexual advances. On the whole, women tend to become very defensive when a man makes an overt sexual advance. This is due to the social conditioning that women have as they grow. Women are taught to be guarded as men tend to be much more predatory in this regard.

---

(32) Chadderton, C., & Croft, R. (2006) – *"Who is kidding whom? A study of complicity, seduction and deception in the marketplace"*. Social Responsibility Journal.

When a manipulator is able to use overt sexual advances effectively, the target complies in the hopes of obtaining sexual favors. However, the manipulator will always try to get what they want without engaging in any kind of sexual activity. This is where the manipulation lies. There are times when the persuader must engage in sexual acts in order to keep the target motivated until the manipulator gets what they seek.

Why Are Dark Seducers So Dangerous?

Unless there is some kind of physical and sexual violence involved, dark seducers don't actually mean to cause harm beyond emotional distress. If the true intentions of a dark seducer are to engage in sexual acts against the will of the victim, then we are talking about a psychopath and not necessarily the average dark seducer. Seducers who use any means at their disposal to engage in non-consensual sexual acts are criminals and should be considered highly dangerous. Given the characteristics we described earlier, these people can be very hard to spot and would most likely use some type of coercion especially when victims don't comply.

Beyond the threat of actual physical violence, dark seducers are very dangerous because they are so hard to spot. After all, who would suspect of a very attractive man or woman? In fact, most victims would feel lucky to have such an attractive person be interested in them. And, that's where the danger lies. When people feel fortunate to have such attractive people notice them, they may end up losing sense of reality and give in to their emotional and even sexual desires. In the end, the manipulator gains control over the victim and begins to extract what they seek.

For some dark seducers, it may be simply a question of a power trip. They use someone just to get a rush. Once they've had their fun, they can discard the victim. The same can be said when there is a short-term gain to be made such as using one person to get to another.

On the flip side, there is a much longer-term approach. The manipulator may even marry their victim in order to gain access to something which the victim controls. For instance, it may be wealth or status. This is commonly the case when an individual marries the target and the divorces in order to gain access to their wealth. The victim is then discarded after the divorce. In the worst of cases, the manipulator makes sure that the victim does not recover at all, thereby leaving them in a state of complete submission.

Lastly, dark seducers are quite dangerous as they tend to hide behind a persona. This persona can be very neatly crafted to the degree that their true self is imperceptible. Yet, this persona only acts until they get what they want. Once they have control over their target, the true self will begin to progressively emerge until it has taken over completely. By the time the victim even realizes what has happened, they may have no chance of getting out of the situation they are in (33).

How to Avoid Dark Seduction

Act Quickly

It goes without saying that if you are in the grips of a dark seducer, you must act as quickly as you can. However, the downside to this is that it might be too late before you realize what's actually going on.

Nevertheless, there are some red flags to look out for. Most noticeably, beware of overly kind strangers. While there is no doubt that someone who was romantic interest in you may choose to act swiftly, if they are too persistent or too forward, then that would constitute a major red flag.

Also, be wary of anyone whom you've just met and begins to push ideas on you that make you uncomfortable in any way. Seducers go about things in this manner as they are in a hurry to get what they want. To them, taking longer than they absolutely should on you is a waste of time. So, they'll want to move as quickly as they can.

Get Help as Soon as You Can

Once you have realized something is going on, getting help becomes crucial. Often you may be unable to deal with it on your own. That's why asking family, friends, and a therapist of anyone else to provide assistance is of the utmost importance. Many times, others can step

---

(33) McMillan, Dina L. (2008) – *But He Says He Loves Me: How to Avoid Being Trapped* in a Manipulative Relationship

in to confront the manipulator. This will give you the emotional support you need to end the relationship.

There is no shame is asking for help. In fact, the worst outcomes in these types of relationships occur when victims don't ask for help. They think they can handle the situation themselves or think that things will work out on their own. Eventually, things may get out of hand to the point where the victim is overwhelmed.

Always Question Motives

You might come off as paranoid, but it's always important to question the motives that people have when they get close to you. It's important to keep in mind that most romantic relationships have a pattern in their development. Often, these types of relationships begin with some kind of contact before a romantic relationship develops. Other times, you meet someone new thus leading to a natural progression. But when you faced with someone who is rushing things, then you need to hit the brakes and question why they are so eager to move forward.

There are times when you need to ask some tough questions like, "what do you expect to get out of this relationship?" But it is these questions that may reveal far more than you would have otherwise known about this person.

Don't Let Your Emotions Get the Best of You

99% of the time, manipulators prey on their victim's emotions. This is why they seek vulnerable people, especially if they have been through divorce, bad relationships or are lonely. They prey on the need for love and affection these individuals have. So, they are likelier to fall for the manipulator's advances.

Ideally, we'd all maintain a balance of emotion and logic when approaching relationships. Again, if you feel that things are moving too fast, or there is a large amount of pressure on you, then it's best to take a step back and reassess your priorities. It could be that you are just getting ahead of yourself. If that is the case, then you should take a break and let things settle down first.

Do Your Homework

In a whirlwind relationship, it may be hard to come to grips with reality. Still, it's bet to do your homework. Please remember that when it comes to manipulators, the devil is in the details. If you neglect to do your homework, you might miss details that would otherwise tip you off that you are dealing with a manipulator. So, always ask questions, follow up with a simple online or social media search, and meet their friends and family. If you see they are overly mysterious and secretive, then you need to consider that as a major red flag. Someone who is genuinely interested in a romantic relationship will try to be as transparent as they can. Any hint of deception is always a red flag regardless of the circumstances (34).

---

(34) Buss, D. M., & Schmitt, D. P. (1993) – *"Sexual strategies theory: an evolutionary perspective on human mating"*. Psychological Review.

Chapter 8

The Dark Triad

The "dark triad" is a collection of character traits present in every person. However, these traits are more prevalent in some than in others. When they are predominant in an individual's personality, they can lead to inappropriate behavior, and in some cases, lead to criminal activity. They are the hallmark of manipulators. While it is not entirely known how they form, we do have a good understanding of how they can be fostered.

We will take a deep look into the dark triad in this chapter as we look to unravel the mystery that surrounds this type of behavior. Moreover, you will find detailed descriptions and examples pertaining to these traits and their corresponding behaviors (35).

---

(35) Jonason, P. K., Li, N. P., Webster, G. D., & Schmitt, D. P. (2009) – *"The dark triad: Facilitating a short-term mating strategy in men"*. European Journal of Personality.

When one of these traits is predominant in a person, you will find that they are generally disruptive in many ways, but highly creative and energetic in others. Moreover, people who exhibit dark triad traits in high order are generally more skilled and intelligent individuals who have a keen sense of the world around them. This is why they are able to make the most of their desires and push their agenda along.

In some cases, you'll see them as people who will stop at nothing to get what they want. Other times, you will see them as people who don't care much about the feelings of others, especially if that gets in the way of their achieving something.

If you are dealing with someone who exhibits any of these traits, or heaven forbid all three, then you really need to watch where you're stepping. Often, the best course of action is to get away from them. If you try to do battle with people exhibiting dark triad characteristics, you need to be several steps ahead of them. But, be warned that winning a war with these folks may turn out to be winning a war of attrition more than based on skills and tactics.

Manipulators are all around us. There is no question about that. Some are very easy to spot, while others may go unnoticed. Some manipulators act out of impulse, while others are perfectly aware of what they are doing. In such cases, manipulators may not spare expense to get what they want. Others may have a little more moral grounding, thereby enabling them to set certain boundaries as to what they will and will not do.

In the worst of cases, you may run into individuals who have no moral grounding whatsoever. In such cases, you may be in the presence of truly evil individuals. That is why we are going to dedicate this chapter to discussing the character traits which clearly identify manipulators based on their specific conditions or situations (36).

---

(36) Bursten, Ben. (1972) –"*The Manipulative Personality*", Archives of General Psychiatry, Vol 26 No 4, 318–321

Narcissism

Narcissism is broadly defined as love for oneself. This name comes from the legend of Narcissus, who was in love with himself. From this legend, narcissism is used to define a person who is extremely selfish. While it is true that we are all selfish to a certain extent, the average narcissist is so enamored with themselves that they will hatch whatever schemes they can come up with to place themselves in the spotlight (37).

Narcissism is typically associated with feelings of entitlement and conceit. These are individuals who seek to be the center of attention at all times while trying to get others to do their bidding. The most rudimentary of narcissists don't really care how they get others to go along with them. All they care about is that others must do what they want. End of story.

More skilled narcissists are able to use many tactics at their disposal to get others to go along. Often, these types of narcissists seem charming and very pleasant.

Yet, it's all a ploy. Their main objective is to get others to trust them and admire them. As long as they are admired and shown constant displays of affection, they are good with people. The problem occurs when they are not fed the feedback they seek. Often, it is a question of having their ego stroked.

For example, a narcissist will become livid if they get no recognition for the work they do. This is compounded if they feel they have put their best foot forward. As such, the lack of recognition will drive them up the wall like no tomorrow. On the contrary, if they are showered with praise and accolades, then all is good. They bask in their glory and seek to move on to the next display of affection and appreciation.

The biggest issue with narcissists is that they are control freaks. Since they feel that everyone must do their bidding, they need to control everything and everyone around them. Consequently, if a narcissist feels they have lost control of their environment, there are

---

(37) Behary, W. (2013) – *Disarming the Narcissist: Surviving & Thriving with the Self-Absorbed*. New Harbinger Publications.

liable to go to all means necessary to ensure that they regain full control. If this means destroying people along the way, they may not stop to ponder the effects of their actions on others.

A typical narcissist is formed in childhood, usually as the result of neglect and oftentimes abuse. Generally speaking, kids who go through abandonment and neglect in childhood tend to develop issues with control and lack of affection. If untreated, these conditions can develop into a full-blown narcissistic personality. In adulthood, a typical narcissist may have serious trouble being part of social groups leading them to isolation. While extroverted narcissists may have a lot of friends early on, they may end up becoming isolated as they struggle to form genuine relationships.

If you suspect that you are in the presence of a narcissist, be prepared for someone who demands a great deal of attention and affection. In addition, they will try to control every aspect of your life. In the end, you will have to either move away or play their game as best you can.

How to Spot a Narcissistic

The average narcissist is always seeking attention, power, or control. If any of these, or all three describe a person you are dealing with, then you can be confident you are dealing with a narcissist.

Narcissists are control freaks and micromanagers by definition. They insist on watching over everything while ensuring their orders are followed. They can be very competent in what they do. As a result, they seek the adulation and recognition that comes with being the best at what they do.

Highly intelligent narcissists will stand out on their own merits. The same goes for physically gifted individuals who excel as athletes. Those who have exceptional physical beauty may develop narcissistic tendencies as a consequence of the attention they constantly receive.

If you are dealing with a narcissist, then you can attest to the fact that they are always seeking attention and control. Narcissists also tend to be ruthless. When left up to their own devices, they will stop at nothing until they get what they want. However, once they get what they want, they often become bored and seek a new diversion.

Machiavellianism

Machiavellianism refers to the teachings of Machiavelli, a renaissance political thinker and strategist. His most famous work, The Prince, is a classic for all students of political science (38). In this book, he outlines what a prince, or any leader for that matter, must do in order to achieve power and control. Many famous phrases are quoted from this book such as "divide and conquer" and "it is better to be feared than to be loved." (39)

From this, psychologists have coined Machiavellianism when referring to a character trait in which an individual is cunning and calculating. Highly intelligent individuals can be Machiavellian in the way they act. They can be very methodical in their approach. In the worst of cases, they can be ruthless and stop at nothing until they get what they want.

This includes using people for their own purposes. Many times, Machiavellians see people as "a means to an end." As such, they want to use people, and when they no longer serve a purpose to them, they will discard without any regard for their feelings. Highly skilled manipulators may exhibit a considerable predominance of Machiavellianism in their personality set. If you suspect you are dealing with such a person, then you are in for a war of attrition as they will not back down easily.

The limits to which Machiavellianism can go essentially depend on the intelligence or support network of the person. There are cases, such as those of master criminals, who may be unable to figure out schemes for themselves but will employ those who can. This is a good example of how scruples and morals may be quite loose on some folks.

As such, if you are dealing with a Machiavellian person, you may have to choose if you want to be in such a situation or perhaps move away from it. Generally speaking, beating a Machiavellian involves

---

(38) Niccolò Machiavelli (2015) – *The Prince*. Zephyr House.

(39) Christie, R., & Geis, F. L. (2013) – *Studies in Machiavellianism*. Academic Press.

total defeat; that is, destroying them completely. For instance, if you're dealing with someone who is defrauding others, this may involve bringing them to justice. Even then, you might be involved in a complex legal battle that you may not have the will to see through.

How to Spot a Machiavellianism

In the definition, we underscored the fact that Machiavellianism refers to being cunning and calculating. Also, Machiavellianism is generally associated with individuals with higher intelligence. While it's not a requirement to have high intelligence to be a Machiavellian, it certainly helps.

You can spot Machiavellians as they are always scheming to get their way. The most intelligent kind come up with intricate schemes that often go undetected until it is far too late. The less skilled Machiavellians may hatch primitive schemes. Yet, their mind is always working, trying to find a way to get their way.

Another important way in which you can spot a Machiavellian is if they constantly talk about people as if they were objects. Whenever you hear individuals refer to other people as objects, and thereby treat them as such, then you know you are in the presence of a Machiavellian. This attitude is quite common in the military and in the business world.

Psychopathy

Another important element of the dark triad is psychopathy. In general terms, psychopathy is an absence of emotion. In particular, psychopaths are unable to feel empathy. This means they are unable to gauge what others feel. This is why they are incapable of understanding their actions hurt others. When you look at serial killers and other types of criminals, they genuinely believe they have done nothing wrong as they are unable to comprehend the pain and anguish they have put others through. Think about white-collar criminals who embezzle pensioners out of their savings. They have no remorse over their actions as they could really care less about those affected.

In some instances, psychopathy is associated with physiological issues in the brain. When this occurs, neurochemical reactions may not take place. As a result, these individuals may be unable to process their emotions leading to a condition of flat reactions to emotion.

In other cases, it may be a purely psychological issue as those psychopaths tend to have a dissociative personality. Dissociative personality is usually the result of prolonged exposure to abuse and trauma in childhood. Regardless of the type of trauma, a child may develop a dissociation between their feelings and the situations around them. This leads them to cut out their feelings from the mental processes they carry out. Consequently, a perfectly normal person can be developed into a psychopath purely through an abusive and neglectful environment.

If you are in consort with a psychopath, you had better get a good idea of what they are capable of. These individuals may be capable of just about anything. They may not have any sinister motives. Whatever they do, is purely for their pleasure and nothing else... even if it means inflicting grievous harm on others (40).

How to Spot a Psychopath

This is one of the toughest ones. It can be nearly impossible to spot a psychopath as some are extremely charming and polite. They are that nice neighbor that was always a bit too quiet or withdrawn. It can be a friendly shopkeeper that always goes the extra mile for their customers. It can even be a law enforcement officer that helps out in the community.

Yet, they hide shocking secrets in their closets... or in their basements.

Highly skills psychopaths use charm to lure their victims. After all, who would go running into the arms of a monster? Well, if they didn't look like a monster, lots of people would.

Psychopathic tendencies are rather easy to spot in the way that psychopaths treat animals, children and the elderly. In other words, the average psychopath is always looking for an easy target. They

(40) Aglietta, M.; Reberioux, A.; Babiak, P. *"Psychopathic manipulation at work"*, in Gacono, C.B. (Ed), The Clinical and Forensic Assessment of Psychopathy: A Practitioner's Guide, Erlbaum, Mahwah.

will never pick on anyone their own size as they know it would be too hard for them to inflict damage. Moreover, psychopaths lack self-control. As such, they will have a hard time controlling their urges. This is why serial killers generally fit the psychopath profile. Since they can't control themselves, they give into their animalistic desires and carry out their fantasies. If they exhibit high Machiavellianism, they can be quite sophisticated in the way they operate.

The Dark Triad in Action

Having just one of the dark triad traits fully developed is enough to foster an evil individual. When all three come into consort, even to a lesser degree, the individual may have no morals, scruples, and ethics. While they may not actually become serial killers, they may engage in activities that harm people in the pursuit of their personal aims and pleasures. This may lead to unspeakable acts of horror, crafty business schemes or even a relentless pursuit of power in which people fall by the wayside.

There is not a real way to deal with such individuals. It takes a lot of courage and energy to stand up to them. That is why the most common course of action is to get away from them. For example, people who grow up with narcissistic parents often leave home at a young age as they are unable to put up with the behavior of their parents.

In other cases, children of Machiavellian parents tend to have their parents concoct clever ways to run their life well into adulthood. And if someone happens to grow up with a psychopathic parent, they may be in for a childhood filled with abuse.

At the end of the day, the dark triad is present in all of us. We all have some type of manifestation of these traits, though most of us will never exhibit them to the degree that is quite harmful to others. If you happen to recognize the predominance of these traits in your own life, it is worth doing some introspection so that you can determine if you really need to get a better handle on your feelings and thoughts. After all, letting any of these traits run wild may end up consuming you to the point of emotional and psychological exhaustion.

Lawyers

Lawyers, like used car salesmen, are textbook manipulators. Lawyers, in particular, test the boundaries of what is moral in society. When they are tasked to defend a suspect who is clearly guilty, they may stoop to any means necessary in the pursuit of getting their client free of all charges. In many ways, lawyers are perceived to be unscrupulous and immoral. However, the truth is that lawyers are just representing a persona. Ultimately, it doesn't matter what they personally think. The only thing that matters is that they fulfill their client's wishes.

As for a lawyer's toolkit, they cannot openly lie as this would constitute a crime. So, they need to frame the truth in such a way that their client seems innocent. They also tend to mix half-truths in order to plant the seed of doubt in judges and jury. Please bear in mind that unless things are proven beyond a reasonable doubt, it is impossible to render a verdict. This is why lawyers will try to confuse the facts and pick holes in stories. They are masters at rephrasing statements and taking witnesses out of context. Trial lawyers are especially adept at confusing witnesses so that they end up contradicting themselves.

But perhaps the most valuable skill that lawyers have is to use evidence to prove their point. This is where facts and evidence are used to paint the picture they want others to see. In a manner of speaking, it's a type of gaslighting as they are attempting to replace the truth with a version convenient to them and their client.

Next time you watch a television show or movie in which lawyers are depicted in action, pay close attention to the way they bend the truth, switch contexts and make themselves out to be the bearers of reality. It's all a ruse to get those involved doubt the accuracy of the facts just enough so that they can plant the seed of their own version of the facts.

Politicians

Politicians, unlike lawyers, have the liberty to lie. In a way, it's a manner of taking creative license with the truth. Less skilled political players tend to make up facts and throw unfounded accusations against their opponents. Depending on their particular context, the media might fact-check their claims. When there is no one to hold them accountable for their remarks, they are basically free to say whatever comes to their mind.

As mentioned earlier, lies need to be credible to a certain extent. Outrageous claims will simply alienate voters. This is why skilled politicians do their homework so that their accusations are real and justified. That way, they can hold up to closer scrutiny.

Politicians are also known for their deceit. In general, deceit comes in the form of false promises. They often say they will do one thing or another only to end up doing something completely different. Also, politicians are known to be corrupt; that is, using their elected office for their personal gain. In some countries, corruption is more prevalent than others.

Overall, politicians are seen as individuals with very loose morals. While some are respected for their genuine leadership abilities, the majority are seen as liars and cheaters. At least that tends to be public perception, especially when scandals break open.

Salespeople

Salespeople are also seen as manipulators. Generally speaking, they will say whatever they have to in order to make a sale. This may include embellishing the features of a product or flat out lying about a product's quality or functionality.

The classic example of this is used car salesmen. But beyond that, salespeople will try to build rapport as quickly as possible so that they can get their potential clients to trust them. This, in turn, will lead to a sense of credibility.

Another common tactic employed by salespeople is the bait and switch. They may seem forthcoming and very approachable. But once they have earned their client's trust, they will revert to their true self and stick customers with a high price tag. Clever salespeople will recognize this and make sure that they don't screw over their customers. That way, they can ensure repeat business.

On the whole, the best salespeople are very outgoing and extroverted. In the worst of cases, they are narcissists who are out to flaunt their talents and abilities. If you happen to be in the presence of such an individual, be wary. It might be best for you to shop around first.

Public Speakers

Public speakers will use any and all tactics at their disposal to get their message across and position themselves in the minds of their audience. In order to achieve this, they must become master communicators, well versed in their subject matter and understand what makes people tick.

They can be very manipulative when they trigger emotions in people. Also, they are experts in non-verbal communication. This means that they pay close attention to their gestures and mannerisms in addition to their tone of voice.

When a public speaker is at the top of their game, they seem genuine and forthright even when they couldn't care less about the audience they are addressing. Some downright deceitful individuals will fabricate a persona that is presented to the public. Once the show is over, they revert back to their true self. This is especially true of religious cult leaders. They play the role of a messiah to their followers, but behind closed doors, they are truly wicked individuals.

Next time you see someone speaking in front of a large group of audience, look at the way they stand, they speak and handle themselves. That may provide you with enough contextual clues to determine if they are genuine or just putting up a front.

Chapter 9

How to Tell If You Are Emotionally Manipulated

Anyone who is in a manipulator's ultimate goal long-term or short-term relationship can attest to the fact that their interaction is dysfunctional to a lesser or greater degree. Sometimes the signs are obvious, but the victim chooses to ignore them. In some cases, the victim has no choice but to go along for the ride.

In a healthy relationship, there will be equal respect and commitment between partners. A poor relationship will be difficult to recognize since manipulation is subtler than compared to some kinds of toxicity. Psychological manipulation can happen when someone attempts to create or exploit someone else's power imbalance. Manipulation will be able to manifest a number of different ways, but one trend that appears to be commonly observed is that one of the individuals, the victim, tends to put in far more into the relationship than they are able to get out of it. It is often likely that someone ends up in a toxic relationship without even realizing it. The end result of this kind of relationship is exhaustion on the part of the victim. If the manipulator happens to completely exhaust all the resources from the relationship, then the likelihood of the relationship ending altogether is quite high.

It should be noted that toxic relationships can coalesce into a dysfunctional dynamics in which both parties are addicted to one another. That is, the manipulator is addicted to the power rush that comes from manipulation while the victim feels acknowledged by the manipulator's overtures. While this is by no means intended to justify the existence of such relationships, it does illustrate how such a dynamics can end up solidifying into a long-term relationship. Eventually, the relationship may find itself unsustainable. Nevertheless, there are examples of couples, or even entire family groups, that go on for decades under such a dynamics. In a manner of speaking, these relationships endure over a long period as no one is really willing to do anything to correct the situation (41).

If you are uncertain whether the relationship you find yourself in is toxic or abusive, it is important to examine the following indicators:

1. You are forced out of your comfort zone in many different ways. The manipulation goes physically, mentally, and emotionally so that everything is tilted toward favoring the other's wishes and desires. The manipulator should be the one with the upper hand at all times. When the power dynamics appears to shift, the manipulator will be swift to restore balance.
2. The manipulator will try to undermine your confidence. The logic behind this is that the manipulator always seeks to create a reliance on him or her. If the victim is confident and able to fend for themselves, then the reliance they place of the manipulator will be minimized. Naturally, this is not in the manipulator's best interest.
3. The silent treatment. The manipulator will be prone to silence as a means of punishing the victim for behavior that is unacceptable in the manipulator's eyes. This also extends to other forms of punishment, such as withholding affection

---

(41) Crawford, Craig (2007) – *The Politics of Life: 25 Rules for Survival in a Brutal and Manipulative World*

or withdrawing their attention until the victim complies with the manipulator's wishes.

4. Guilt trips. The manipulator will be quick to lay a guilt trip on the victim, especially when he provides material, physical or even emotional protection for the victim. For instance, the manipulator rescued the victim from a difficult situation as a means of developing this dysfunctional dynamics. Every time the victim acts in a manner that is not in accordance with his aims, the manipulator will be quick to lay a guilt trip on the target.

5. They dismiss unresolved issues and skip over them. Unhealthy relationships survive with many unanswered issues leading to problems festering beneath the surface. The manipulator will avoid dealing with issues at all costs. They will try their best to ensure that problems go unresolved, especially when solving the issue may cost them dearly.

The fact of the matter is that it is very easy to get into toxic relationship, either deliberately or inadvertently. Moreover, the manipulator, whether conscious or not, can quickly become accustomed to the power dynamics favoring them. By the same token, the victim can quickly become accustomed to being victimized, especially if this provides them with a benefit such as the manipulator's undivided attention.

Naturally, this is hardly something beneficial to either party. But for the most part, don't be surprised to find dysfunctional relationships to be far more common than you think. When unresolved issues are left to fester, the relationship can quickly degenerate into a dysfunctional one ultimately leading into a toxic relationship.

Here are some questions to ask yourself when evaluating your current relationships:

1. What kind of respect is there among us?
2. Are the expectations of this relationship being met? Are they reasonable or unreasonable?
3. Am I getting what I need out of the relationship?
4. Is the commitment equal on both sides? Is there anyone surrendering more than the other?
5. Do I really feel good when I am around this person?

By honestly answering these questions, you will be able to gain profound insights into the nature of your relationships. They don't necessarily need to be romantic ones. These questions apply perfectly well to any relationship you find yourself in. So, take the time to reflect on these questions any time you are evaluating the nature of a relationship.

How to Prevent Manipulation

Know Your Rights

This point kind of goes without saying. However, folks tend to get caught up in a toxic and/or abusive relationship to the degree they forget they have the right to stand up for themselves. In such cases, knowing one's rights is a fundamental element in ensuring that no harm comes to you. Naturally, no one has the right to cause any kind of physical, emotional or psychological harm to anyone. In fact, it is a crime punishable by incarceration. Moreover, inflicting such type of abuse on a person, regardless of circumstance, is downright cowardly and weak.

If you suspect you are in a toxic or abusive relationship, or anyone else for that matter, please bear in mind that we all have rights. So, there is nothing more important than to understand them and act upon them if need be. That way, you can get the support you need, or help those who may be unable to fend for themselves.

Stay Away

This is especially true in abusive relationships. Often, there is no way of repairing a relationship of this nature. So, the best course of action is to simply stay away. This may imply a divorce in the case of a marriage or quitting a job in the case of a workplace environment. Whatever the nature of the relationship, you might be faced with having to quit and move on for the sake of your mental and emotional health.

Also, there are folks who wish to "save" their relationship. That is certainly a valid argument. However, there may come a point where such efforts can go to no avail. Truth be told, once a relationship descends into abuse, there is really no way of saving it. After all, what guarantee does the victim have that the aggressor will not revert back to their abusive ways? These types of conditions make it hard for the victim to find a sense of normalcy. As a result, the aggressor needs to be put as far away as possible. In the end, the victim needs time and distance to put their life back in order.

In some cases, the relationship isn't quite as deep and meaningful. So, that makes it a lot easier to give the manipulator the heave-ho and move on. The main attitude to keep in mind is the desire and willingness to put the relationship to an end.

Do Not Let the Manipulator Proceed

There is a clear need to put a stop to the manipulator. No question about it. However, that is often easier said than done. Manipulators, especially when they are physically aggressive, can intimidate their victims to the degree in which they are unable to do much about the situation. So, standing up to the manipulator is no easy task. Nevertheless, there is a point in which the victim may have no choice but to do so. In some circumstances, the victim can seek help from others. As such, the intervention of others can help the victim put a stop to the abuse and eventually get away from the situation.

Learn How to Say No

Don't be afraid to say no. Plain and simple.

However, it's not always so easy. Manipulators have a way of coaxing their victims into agreeing with them. Many times, the victim is bullied into doing something against their will. Naturally, this is hardly a healthy dynamics. But when there is a credible threat on the part of the manipulator, the victim may find it virtually impossible to say no. That is why saying no from the beginning is a crucial factor in avoiding any possible manipulation.

When you set boundaries on people, you encounter right from the beginning, you will be able to protect yourself from future aggression. Often, this means having to put your foot down and standing your ground. Once the manipulator sees you are firm in your convictions, they will move on and find someone else they feel they can manipulate more easily. So, don't be afraid to say no when you need to. It will save you tons of headaches down the road.

Chapter 10
Neuro-linguistic Programming (NLP) for Influence

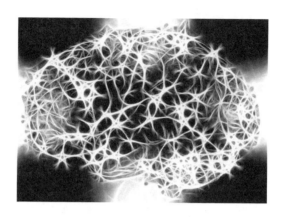

Earlier, we have discussed NLP and its application to dark psychology. In particular, we discussed how NLP could be used to fixate a message in people's minds. This is definitely the underlying purpose of NLP. In fact, it is commonly used in the educational field to help students remember content in a more efficient manner.

However, NLP was born out of research looking into human cognition, learning, and how knowledge is built into the human mind. This research led to the understanding that humans are creatures of habit. As a result, humans will never be able to internalize something at first glance. In fact, those individuals who are able to fixate content in their mind by taking on look at things are truly unusual people (42).

As such, we'll be taking a closer look at NLP in this chapter and the various ways in which it can be used to help manipulators advance their personal agendas. In particular, the use of NLP is centered on establishing a message in people's minds in such a way that the individual, or group of individuals, will not question the validity of

(42) Bandler, R. (1992) – *Magic in Action*. Meta Publications.

the information. In fact, they will eventually learn to take the information at face value, thereby accepting the manipulator's intentions and bringing down their own personal barriers.

A Brief History of NLP

Neuro-Linguistic Programming was born in 1970. Richard Bandler, then a recent graduate of the University of Santa Cruz in California and John Grinder, a professor at that University, began to study together the characteristics of communication used by some excellent psychotherapists, capable of producing changes and healings effectively and continuously.

Bandler and Grinder first met Fritz Perls (Gestalt therapist) at the Esalen Center in California.

After modeling (analyzing) Perls, the two began to analyze Virginia Satir's communication used in family therapy. Satir's great capacity for empathy and her unique style of therapy led them to study Virginia's language, from which many language models were drawn.

In the same period the anthropologist, Gregory Bateson advised Bandler, a great friend of his, to analyze the work of Milton H. Erickson, a doctor known as one of the greatest and most effective experts in clinical hypnosis. Also, from Erickson, communication models of extraordinary effectiveness in psychotherapy were extracted.

The result of the modeling of these three great therapists was the publication of two important books: "The Structure of Magic" (43) and "The Models of the Hypnotic Technique of Milton H. Erickson." (44)

As stated earlier, this approach was born out of research done on human cognition and learning. It evolved into a framework in which it seeks to encompass everything that can work on modifying human behavior through the use of sound and language.

---

(43) Bandler R., Grinder J. (1975) – *The Structure of Magic*, Science & Behavior Books

(44) Bandler R., Grinder J. (1996) – *Patterns of the Hypnotic Techniques of Milton H. Erickson*, Grinder & Associates

Consequently, behavior modification is possible without actively engaging the individual in a conscious activity that will lead to behavior modification.

While there is no conclusive scientific research done on the validity of NLP, empirical evidence has proven it to be rather effective. It has been implemented in a wide range of fields, though it must be said that the results have been mixed. This supports the notion that NLP is not a cross-cutting technique, but rather, it is more focused on getting messages across to individuals while looking to fixate them in their subconscious mind.

Core Concepts of NLP

"The overall meaning of any communication is found in the response it gets, not the original intention of the communication." What this means is that what matters most is what the victims of NLP understood to be the intention of a given communication and effectively what response they will give to that communication. It is important to know for anyone using NLP that it does not always matter what communication they put forth, but what matters most is the response they get from their listeners.

"The map is not the territory." This principle involves the relationship between an object and how that object is presented. This simply means that the description differs from what is described. Take an example of someone who is thirsty and he hears the characteristics of different types of drinks. He'll still be thirsty after the descriptions of the types of drinks because there is no actual drink. In the context of NLP, it used in psychotherapy, where patients are asked to describe their life and experiences, but these are only but a 'map' of their life.

"Behavior is inherently leaned towards adaption." This principle tells us that people change and they are meant to adapt, and this adaptation is easier than people would like to believe. This principle is often behind most behavioral changes in NLP models where a harmful behavior like regular consumption of alcohol is replaced with accepted behaviors like drinking water regularly because it is beneficial to the body.

NLP Modeling

Given the fact that NLP is a theory that looks to model the way in which the human psyche perceives the world, there is a clear effort in attempting to map the way the human mind can perceive the world. However, a universal model of the world cannot be represented since everyone experiences the world in a different manner. Therefore, it is possible to model how knowledge and experience are fixated in the mind, but the actual perception of the world is a truly unique experience for every individual.

Nevertheless, most NLP practitioners tend to offer people a "model" they can follow, which is intended to help them learn one thing or another or perhaps help them replace existing habits with new ones. As a result, NLP has become quite prevalent in the mainstream by affording individuals the opportunity to replace existing thoughts and ideas with new ones by essentially talking themselves into.

On the other hand, NLP has been proven to be effective in coercing others to do things or embrace ideas through the use of chants, slogans, songs, and visual imagery that reinforce a particular thought pattern. This is why NLP has become quite popular in the "dark" domain. NLP offers the possibility of communicating a message is such a way that individuals may not perceive it directly, but are subjected to it, nonetheless.

NLP as a Means of Communication

In the business world, it's common to see companies list their values and principles. This is done to give employees a frame of reference which they must follow if they want to be valuable and productive members of their organization. As a result, employees are often asked to cite the company's value through a series of chants and slogans disguised as motivational team-building practices.

However, the true intent behind this type of practice is to indoctrinate employees to perform in such a way that is expected of them. The reason why uniforms are used in the workplace is a glaring example of how individuality is discouraged in favor of universalization of behavior, dress, and attitude. When an employee does not conform to these established norms, they are generally cast aside. This is true of any social group in which members are expected to act in accordance with that social group's values and ideals.

Towards the end of the 1960s, Prof. Albert Mehrabian, an American psychologist, conducted some interesting research on the importance of different aspects of communication in getting a certain message across.

The result was shocking:

- The words, the verbal content, count for only 7%;
- - Para-verbal communication (tone, volume, voice rhythm, etc.) accounts for 38%;
- - Non-verbal communication (especially body and facial mimicry) has an influence of 55% (45).

Verbal Communication

Verbal communication is often misrepresented as words and language. And while that is the core component of verbal communication, the fact of the matter is that words, in themselves, are meaningless when faced with other components such as tone of voice, pitch, speed, and volume. For most individuals, picking up on these contextual clues is instinctive, that is, they are trained to recognize them from an early age though they don't really rationalize what they actually mean.

Therefore, verbal communication is an essential factor when it comes to getting a message across (count for only 7%). Even the most hateful comment can seem less damaging if it is delivered in a friendly tone. By the same token, the most beautiful words can be delivered in a somber tone, thereby ruining their intended effect (has an influence of 38%).

The fact of the matter is that verbal communication is tailored to suit the need of the manipulator. In some contexts, manipulators may be dismissed as hypocritical and false. Yet, they know when to smile and sound cheerful, especially when that means extracting some type of gain from their counterparts. A good example of this

---

(45) Albert Mehrabian, *Silent Messages: Implicit Communication of Emotions and Attitudes*, Wadsworth, Belmont CA 1981, e Albert Mehrabian, *Nonverbal Communication*, Aldine-Atherton, Chicago 1972.

can be seen in salesmen. They automatically turn on the charm when they want to woo a customer. Once they have made the sale, they can revert back to their real selves.

As such, skilled manipulators know how to use their voice and when to play with it. They will find the best way to get their message across while making sure they implant their true intentions. That way, the individual will react in the manner they seek.

Non-Verbal Communication

Non-verbal communication makes up the bulk of human communication. It is said that 55% of communication is non-verbal. This means that the way we dress, act, and gesticulate all points toward our true intentions. This means that you can betray your words by acting in a manner that contradicts what you are trying to outwardly portray.

This is why manipulators pay close attention to their gestures, body language, and mannerisms. They know that if they do one thing, or fail to do the other, they run the risk of blowing their cover. One of the most common actions that manipulators do is have some type of prop with them. This could include a cigarette, a cup of coffee, a phone, or anything they can use to diffuse any unconscious mannerism. Able manipulators are adept at smiling or feigning sadness when they have to. They are keenly aware of the way they are expected to act in a given situation and will do so, especially when they don't feel in that particular manner.

Building Rapport

What's rapport? Rapport is the ability to enter someone else's world to build a "bridge." It is created by mirroring the posture and language of the other person to create a resemblance and to get in tune with their deepest and most unconscious part (46).

---

(46) Miles, L. K., Nind, L. K., & Macrae, C. N. (2009) – *The rhythm of rapport: Interpersonal synchrony and social perception. Journal of experimental social psychology, 45(3), 585-589.*

It has been discovered that people who like or have a deep contact with each other adapt to each other in their expressive behavior. When one is in "relationship" with another subject, his distrust and resistance disappear.

The three elements to Building rapport: *Mirroring, Pacing, and Leading.*

Mirroring

Mirroring refers to the technique of physical adaptation of the other subject: reflecting posture, gestures, breathing, facial expressions...

Here one adapts to everything that can be seen as a mirror.

Calibration and Pacing

The calibration instead refers to the complete correspondence of the language style (example representation systems) and of the models (example meta-programs) used by the other subject you want to influence (47).

Leading

After adapting to the partner for a while and establishing a relationship, it is possible to move on to lead the interaction, thus changing the direction of communication and emotions. Being in "Leading" means guiding someone else based on the relationship they have established to lead them towards a specific goal or outcome.

NLP's communication-heavy approach is used by coaches and gurus in the art of building rapport. Rapport is a powerful manipulation tool as it consists of getting others to be comfortable around you so that they trust you. This includes a strong dose of non-verbal communication since most folks will automatically feel comfortable when confronting people that act and behave in a certain manner.

---

(47) Kinreich, S., Djalovski, A., Kraus, L., Louzoun, Y., & Feldman, R. (2017) – *Brain-to-Brain Synchrony during Naturalistic Social Interactions.* Scientific Reports, 7, 17060.

For example, rapport is predicated upon a cheerful tone of voice, smiling a lot and offering friendly, non-intrusive physical contact (a handshake is a good example of this).

When you are adept at building rapport, you will find that getting others to trust you is not hard. This is why you often hear that psychopaths tend to be very charming people. This is used as a lure to capture unsuspecting victims. Think about it this way: what would your reaction be if you saw a hideous monster? Naturally, you'd be frightened. Now, think of a hideous monster that wants to eat, but instead of having a gruesome outward appearance, they look like the most attractive person you could imagine. In this case, the trap would be far more effective.

This is why building rapport is a basic tool in the manipulator's toolkit. So, it's always best to be aware of a friendly stranger. You could be in the presence of a master manipulator.

The four <u>secret ingredients</u> to create a magical relationship are:

1. Smile
2. Eye contact
3. Active listening
4. Genuine interest
5.

Smiling

The power of smiling is seriously underrated. While you're generally taught that smiling is a great way to break the ice and so on, the fact of the matter is that a well-placed smile can go a long way toward connecting with someone. This goes back to our discussion on rapport. When you are able to build rapport with someone, the likelihood of getting them to go along with you is far greater.

It should be noted that there is smiling, and then there's a genuine smile. The difference lies in the fact that a fake smile can be spotted a mile away. When a person flashes a fake smile, they somehow seem uncomfortable when doing so. They don't seem sincere in the way they do it. To better exemplify this, think about people you meet at the grocery store or bank. You can tell they smile and say "good morning" simply because it's a part of their job.

So, pay attention to the people you encounter in all walks of life when you meet someone who flashes a smile at you, and they seem sincere while doing it, pay attention to the way in which they did it. You will notice that they make normal eye contact and do so under the right circumstances. For instance, a cashier will look at you and smile when they give you your receipt after paying for a purchase. Or, a waiter will smile at you while greeting you at your table.

You can use the power of smiling to your benefit when you meet someone, talk to them in a social interaction or when negotiating. However, you need to train your mind to do so when you are genuinely feeling the urge to smile. If you smile while thinking negative thoughts about this person, then you will find that your smile will be fake. Therefore, you have to get into character and at least tell yourself that you genuinely care about this person. This will be a great start.

Eye Contact

With effective smiling and positive interactions comes eye contact. This is a very tricky subject as a deep, penetrating stare will make people defensive. So, this may trigger a "flight or fight" response. In that manner, you may end up generating the opposite effect that you wish to create.

Positive eye contact is generally achieved when you are at a logical point in your interaction. For instance, eye contact, along with a pleasant smile and firm handshake when meeting someone, can easily trigger a "safe" response of the other party. This is essential when going into a job interview, for example. In a situation such as this, your interviewer will be relaxed and more open to hearing what you have to say.

If you reflect submission or even fear in your eye contact, the other party may be inclined to take advantage of this. By the same token, if you spot that your counterpart shows some type of reluctance, this may indicate that they feel uncomfortable in some way. This may be a signal to you to pounce on the situation and go for your particular objectives.

At the end of the day, eye contact can be a powerful weapon when you are able to make genuine and sincere contact while ensuring the other party isn't creeped out by your attempt to appear pleasing. So, if you find the other party is hesitant to meet your stare, then you are in a good position to take full advantage.

Active Listening

Listening is perhaps the most overlooked tactic when it comes to influencing others and getting them to comply with your desires. When you really listen, it will automatically give the other person the impression you care about them. As such, you will create the narrow ties essential to building trust capital.

Moreover, it's really easy to get others to see that you are truly listening. All you need to do is look at them and mirror some of their mannerism. Mirroring consists of doing the same things they do. For example, if they cross their arms, you can do the same. Or, if they place their hand below their chin, you can do the same.

Another great way to show that you are listening is to "echo" their words. This means that you can interject a comment in which you repeat what a person has said. For instance, if they say, "the weather is nice today" you can reply by saying, "yes, the weather is really nice." This is a great way of building rapport with others. While you may not necessarily agree with the other person's assessment of the weather, it doesn't matter as you are only going along with them for the sake of building rapport.

So, make a point of actually listening to people. You will find the results you are able to achieve by showing genuine interest will actually pay off in the end.

"Pleasure" and "Pain": Two Powerful Leverage

We have already said that our brain systematically leads us to make choices that avoid pain and possibly lead us to pleasure. But some are more sensitive to the "pain leverage" and those who are more sensitive to the "pleasure leverage." (48)

People "Towards Pleasure"

People drove more by "pleasure" are called in neuro-linguistic programming the "towards pleasure," in the sense that they go

---

(48) Bandler, R. (1992) – *Magic in Action*. Meta Publications.

towards actions; they are focused on what they want to occur; they are open to change.

For example, there are people to whom if (using the pleasure leverage) you say: *"Come to the sea and we'll have fun and stay cool,"* they don't move at all, but they are sensitive to the pain leverage and so if we say: *"Come to the sea with us instead of staying at home to get bored and suffer the heat."* They'll accept and they'll start.

People "towards pleasure" often ask themselves "what is there to gain?" and are focused on the positive emotions they will feel when they reach the final result.

If you know people "towards pleasure" and you want to persuade them, it is better to tell them about the "pleasures" or the advantages they will get if they do what you propose. These people are activated when there is something to conquer. They're motivated by the awards.

Here are some examples:

"If you want to make money, then you have to listen to me."

"If you want to win then you have to do what I say."

"If you want to be the best then you have to follow these directions."

People "Away from Pain"

People motivated by the leverage "pain" instead are called "away from pain" because they are focused on avoiding problems, running away from everything painful or annoying.

People "away from pain," ask themselves "what is the risk in this thing?" They prefer to think about the problem and how to avoid it, they tend to see the flaws in things. If you have to persuade a "way out of pain," it is better to describe to him the "pains" or the problems, the possible negative consequences that he might face if he does not do what you propose. These people are activated when there is a problem to be solved. They're motivated by threats.

Here are some examples:

"If you want to avoid a big problem, then you have to listen to me."

"If you want to be quiet, then you have to do what I tell you."

"If you don't want to make a mistake, then you must follow these directions."

Chapter 11

Manipulation and Conversational Hypnosis

Hypnosis is often depicted as a magical act in films and television. Classic Hollywood films show vampires using mind control power to hypnotize their victims in order to get them to comply with their wishes.

Of course, these are just mythical representations of a valid practice which has come to be used within the realm of psychotherapy in addition to manipulation. Hypnosis itself is not an evil or benign practice. It is just a practice which can be used in various ways. That is why manipulators have found practical uses for it within the realm of dark manipulation tactics.

In this chapter, we are going to be taking an objective look at hypnosis, what it is, and how it can be used by manipulators to help them get an edge over their victims. In addition, we'll be looking at ways in which you can ward off unwanted advances.

What is Hypnosis

The phrase hypnosis comes from the Greek that means "to rest," but hypnosis itself is very distinct from sleep. Over the course of history, hypnosis has had a couple of scholars try to give it a definition that best befits this concept. In short, hypnosis is the ability to lead someone in a transformed (this involves daydreaming) environment, utilizing verbal instructions, which ensures that they respond much more to suggestions. Once this condition is achieved, the hypnotist may offer direct and indirect recommendations to encourage the patient to break unhealthy and unpleasant behaviors, such as cigarettes, unhealthy diet, fears, etc.

Since hypnosis has been proven to be effective in modifying behaviors, it was turned into hypnotherapy. As such, it is commonly used to alter behavior in such a manner that people can break habits, or adopt new ones, by implanting "suggestions" in the subconscious mind of the individual.

Hypnosis then is a means of accessing an individual's subconscious manner in such a way that ideas and suggestions may be implanted, leading to the individual acting in a specific manner. This can also result in potential actions that go against the wishes of the individual. In a manner of speaking, hypnosis can be used as a means of controlling the willpower of other individuals.

What is Conversational Hypnosis

Conversational hypnosis is a term used to refer to "covert" hypnosis. By this term, it is understood to mean that the act of hypnosis occurs without the knowledge of the individual it is being practiced on. Naturally, this means that this event occurs without the consent of the target. This is why conversational hypnosis is considered part of dark psychology.

The reason for the practice of conversational hypnosis lies in the manipulator's wish to access the subconscious mind of the target without them being aware of their attempts. Manipulators resort to this type of tactic as they are aware that the target would not consciously agree to whatever scheming the manipulator is up to. Often, these schemes refer to getting the target to comply with actions that may not be in accordance to their beliefs or will.

Therefore, the manipulator needs to resort to underhanded trickery to ensure the target will follow suit (49).

Why Do You Need to Learn about Conversational Hypnosis?

Learning about conversational hypnosis has a two-fold intent. The first is to understand what it is and how it may be used against you. It's important to know how manipulators may go about using this tactic to compel you to act in their interest. The second is to gain insight into tactics which you could use in your own daily life. However, if you choose to use them, be wary that you are imposing your will on that of others.

The Ethics of Using Conversational Hypnosis

Generally speaking, anything that has the term "covert" attached to isn't exactly the most ethical practice. This means that conversational hypnosis is a controversial practice as it is not done with the consent of the target.

This is an important point to make as the target is not aware of the attempts being made on them during conversational hypnosis. As a result, the manipulator gains the upper hand before the target is even aware, if at all, of what's going on.

It should be noted that the effectiveness of conversational hypnosis largely depends on the mental strength of the target. Some people have a greater level of resistance to manipulation than others. So, when a manipulator attempts to use covert tactics, they are largely ineffective. Nevertheless, conversational hypnosis is not officially sanctioned by any organization and is deemed unethical even though it isn't necessarily illegal.

---

(49) Nathan Blaszak (2004) – *How to Hypnotize Anyone Without Getting Caught*. Life Tricks Inc. Kevin Hogan (2006). *Covert Hypnosis: An Operator's Manual*. Network 3000 Publishing.

NLP and Ericksonian Hypnosis

Neuro-linguistic Programming

Earlier, we touched on NLP and how it can be used to influence others, especially when looking to implant new behaviors or modify existing ones. The use of NLP is generally seen as a means of helping people overcome certain situations or perhaps improve their performance in certain areas. However, NLP can also be used without the consent of the target.

Now, it's one thing to use NLP in advertising such as seen in slogans and other types of gimmicks. But, it's an entirely different thing to use NLP to compel individuals to act against their will.

Consider this situation:

NLP can be used in conjunction with other practices such as subliminal messaging in order to implant ideas in the minds of people. Now, to further compound the situation, NLP practitioners use a series of "trigger" words to spur the individual to act in the desired manner.

That is why slogans are so effective. Slogans are trigger words that automatically signal the individual that it's time to do one thing or another. For instance, fast food chains use slogans on a continuous basis so that people feel compelled to consume this type of food.

Also, NLP can be used at an individual level. For example, athletes repeat certain mantras over and over as they seek to condition their mind and body to perform. Phrases and specific words can be used by coaches to train the athlete to perform a specific action. While this isn't necessarily covert or unethical, many times it's involuntary. So, the individual isn't fully aware of what the coach is doing.

Ericksonian Hypnosis

Milton Erickson is considered to be the father of hypnotherapy. As such, "Ericksonian Hypnosis" is named after the methods he developed in which hypnosis is used for therapeutic purposes. In this type of hypnosis, suggestions and indirect commands are used to spur the individual to do, or not do, something (50).

For instance, metaphors and stories are used to transmit meaning to targets. This is why children's stories are always wrapped up in a magical aura. The lesson that is contained within each story is made much more digestible to children when it is embedded in a fairy tale.

As for adults, the phrase, "sex sells" is a great example of Ericksonian Hypnosis. When advertising uses sexually appealing and suggestive material, it makes the mind more receptive to the type of message they seek to transmit. So, an attractive model presents a product, thereby reducing the likelihood that the consumer will reject the presence of the advertising itself.

Steps of Conversational Hypnosis

Rapport

The first step is to create rapport. Rapport is a powerful manipulation tool as it consists of getting others to be comfortable around you so that they trust you. This includes a strong dose of "non-verbal communication" since most folks will automatically feel comfortable when confronting people that act and behave in a certain manner and the right mix of "verbal" and "para-verbal communication."

Mirroring

On the subject of mirroring, one of the best ways in which you can create an effect that of being in sync with someone is to mirror their moves. If they cross their legs, you cross your legs. If they place their hand underneath their chin, you do the same. This is intended to send a non-verbal signal to the other party that both are very similar. This tends to reduce resistance from the other party and allows you to create a friendly environment. However, it's important

---

(50) Bandler R., Grinder J. (1996) – *Patterns of the Hypnotic Techniques of Milton H. Erickson,* Grinder & Associates

to be careful as to not seem so obvious. Otherwise, you'll come off as awkward thereby ruining the effectiveness of this technique.

Language

When looking to build rapport, your use of language is critical. The type of language you use will resonate with the people you are trying to win over. If you use the wrong type of language, you may very well alienate those you are trying to win over.

Volume, Pitch and Tone of Voice

When the manipulator starts using conversational hypnosis, it will adapt to the volume, speed, and tone of its target's voice to generate a feeling of relationship and "resemblance."

This is a mirroring technique that works particularly well during negotiations. On a social level, it works very well when you are looking to "sync" with someone else.

All of these elements are crucial to building rapport.

Secure Focus of Targets

This second step is the classic "you are getting sleepy" part. However, ensuring the focus on individuals doesn't necessarily entail this type of strategy. Many practitioners use less overt means of focusing targets' attention. For instance, they use music, images, scents, textures and so on, to capture the attention of the target. The main objective in this approach is to ensure that the target enters into a state of relaxation. Once that state of relaxation is achieved, it becomes a lot easier for the manipulator to begin the hypnosis process.

Induce a Trance-like State

Once the target has achieved a state of relaxation, it is possible to induce a trance-like state. Now, it should be noted that this isn't the type of trance seen in the movies. In fact, this state is mainly related to the brainwave pattern that can be observed in the target. Targets' brainwave activity tends to flatten, meaning that the brain is in a deep state of focus and concentration. The conscious mind doesn't put up much resistance, leaving the subconscious mind exposed. At this point, it is possible to introduce whatever materials the manipulator wishes to implant in the mind of individuals.

Implanting the Message

The last step is implanting the message that the manipulator wishes to "install" in the subconscious mind of the target. When the brain is in a state of deep focus and concentration, the subconscious mind is much more accessible. It should be noted than erratic brainwave activity, such as when a person is under a great deal of stress, is not conducive to hypnosis. The individual must be in a deep trance. Otherwise, the implanting of ideas won't be effective.

The act of implanting ideas can be as overt as needed. In some cases, manipulators may overtly say what they want targets to imbibe. In other cases, they may use suggestions and imagery to install their message. Whatever the means, a deep state of relaxation is needed to successfully implant the message. In the end, the manipulator gets away with instilling their material in the minds of their targets. Then, targets may feel compelled to act in a manner consistent with the manipulator's aims.

Anchoring in Hypnosis

Types

Have you ever been sitting in a car listening to a track you didn't hear in a long time? Has this album caused a kind of feeling from the past in you? The first time you heard this song or sometimes when you heard it, you went through these sensations, and this particular song was attached to your unconscious mind. The song would become an anchor of these sentiments through this process. Now, any time you hear this particular song, you cause the brain to enjoy it again. This is a great anchoring illustration.

Designs

Most hypnotists find that anchoring is a beneficial tool for their participants to be hypnotized. For example, when you recall getting punished for doing something good in the past, the hypnotist can get into a particular memory and allow you to replicate the emotions you felt. At the same time, during your recreation, the hypnotizer will have you take some sort of action, like touching your fingers together.

Installation

Now, you can have the same happy feelings again each time you touch your fingertips together. The anchoring process can work to motivate you to achieve something with good feelings. This approach is often used to help people find the strength to commit to weight loss and a diet. The hypnotist deals with the subject to create a positive focus, connected to the subject's mental image—in this case, the subject thinks of itself in a slim, sexy body. If the object re-images this picture, it stimulates the anchor and gets the optimistic push that it wants. The desire for weight loss in hypnosis is significantly dramatically increased compared with those who do not. In various instances, the anchoring process can be used to help the person improve himself.

Tips

You must be confident enough to know when someone experiences the feelings you want to evoke to use the anchoring of your sensory acuity. As the sensation rises to the top, you "fix" the anchor to bring in the atmosphere that you want to connect to. Consider how, in a romantic setting, anchoring takes place. A relationship is built up, and as you look at the person, hot and fuzzy emotions begin to grow. This alone puts the emotions into touch with the subject so that you only have to think and feel the face of the person. But you can use this to speed up these feelings by deliberately using the anchoring mechanism.

Conversational Hypnosis Tactics

Conversational Postulates

Conversational Postulates are a means of directing the conversation in such a manner that you are telling what you expect from the other party without overtly telling them to do so.

For example, if I tell a girl I just met if she'd like to go out with me tonight or tomorrow night, I'm assuming that she'll agree to go out with me anyway. Or if I tell a friend of mine if he would rather go to a restaurant or a fast-food restaurant, I am assuming that he has already agreed to go with me to dinner.

A statement like "you don't want that, do you?" is guiding the interaction in a certain direction. You are already implicitly telling the other party that they don't want something even though you open the door for their reaction by adding "do you." Nevertheless, you are already laying out what you expect them to respond well in advance (51).

Hidden Commands

A hidden command is a linguistic model in which an instruction, instead of being given directly, is hidden in a broader sentence. In this way it is received by the unconscious mind, going unnoticed by the conscious mind.

In the following examples, hidden commands—which represent what we want to achieve—are highlighted in italics:

"I wonder if you'd like to *collaborate with me*."

"I don't know when you'll be *buying our products*."

"If you want to *read my latest article*, go ahead."

An embedded command is a hidden order within a broader statement. The most common type of embedded command is known as a "call-to-action." In a call-to-action, the message transmitted contains elements that compel the target to act in a certain manner. For instance, "call now before it's too late" is a call-to-action which not only contains an embedded command, but also a threat. Given the context and circumstance of the command, the target may not even notice they are being commanded. Rather, they will simply take it as a means of convincing them to buy a product. So, if you

---

(51) Peliari S. (2009) – *The Art of Covert Hypnosis*. Life Tricks Inc.

Dilts, R., (2017) – *Sleight of Mouth: The Magic of Conversational Belief Change*. Dilts Strategy Group.

are looking to give out commands in a roundabout way, consider wrapping them up within a broader statement (52).

Analog Marking

The analog marking is used to identify words in a sentence by either using verbal or non-verbal means. Phrases and expressions can be marked by delays, changes in intonation or pitch in voice. The conscious mind hears the whole material, but only takes notice of the words which are marked. It makes a sensitive mind confused and enables direct access to the unconscious mind.

"Hidden commands" are particularly persuasive when combined with an underlining by analogy, which consists of using non-verbal language - tone of voice, expressions and gestures—to reinforce the message. The aim is to lead the interlocutor to give more importance to the instruction received, without consciously perceiving it as an order to be executed.

Negative Commands

Negative commands are a kind of reverse psychology. An interesting aspect of the unconscious mind is that, compared to its counterpart, it does not understand denial. This is because there is no mental representation of the word "not" and therefore the unconscious does not understand it.

This is very useful to us because we can use hidden commands in a negative form while stimulating a positive response in the recipient of the message.

To use the negative hidden commands it is sufficient to affirm what we want to occur by making it precede negation.

Some examples:

"I'm not asking you to trust me."

"You don't have to decide right away. Take all the time you need."

---

(52) Bandler R., Grinder J. (1996) – *Patterns of the Hypnotic Techniques of Milton H. Erickson,* Grinder & Associates

"I'm not here to list all the advantages of our proposal."

By denying commands we can prevent the conscious mind from blocking our messages—filtering them to check whether to accept them or not— because rationally it is not receiving them, unlike the unconscious mind.

Metaphor

With the use of metaphor, the manipulator tends to transfer in an object (or in a person) characteristics of another, with the effect of emphasizing the original meaning.

The persuader who uses metaphor triggers changes that emerge from the unconscious and emotionality rather than its rationality.

According to researchers at Stanford University, metaphorical language can condition the choices of the individual, as it "activates those areas of the brain involved in the emotional connotation of events," which affect our choices and our behavior, beyond awareness.

The use of metaphors is highly effective when you are looking to paint a picture in the minds of your interlocutors without actually saying what it is you are looking to say. This is a covert manner of saying what you mean. It leaves your words up to interpretation in such a way that only those who pay attention may pick up on your clues.

Often, manipulators make up funny situations and inspiring events to get their message across (53).

---

(53) Glenn Twiddle (2010) – *Advanced Hypnotic Selling*. Glenn Twiddle Publishing.

Chapter 12

Characteristics of Manipulative People

Thus far, we have discussed the main traits associated with manipulators and the ways in which they are able to control people around them. Moreover, we have focused on the ways in which personality traits that lean toward manipulation tend to manifest themselves in an individual. That's why we have gone into great depth in analyzing how and why the average manipulator acts the way they do.

On the whole, there is a debate as to whether being a manipulator is a question of in-born traits or whether it is a question of upbringing. In other words, we're referring to a nature vs. nurture debate. The fact is that there is no conclusive evidence linking specific genetic predisposition to acting in one manner or another. While traits such as psychopathy can be linked to actual physiological conditions in which the individual's brain may differ significantly, the fact of the matter is it is almost entirely an issue associated with the upbringing.

For most folks, manipulative traits, such as the dark triad, are fomented in early childhood and adolescence. When kids and teens are subjected to certain types of experiences, they generally develop coping mechanisms which grow into the personality traits that we associate with manipulation. For instance, narcissism is generally linked to abandonment issues which typically translate into a need for control. Of course, this isn't an iron law. But it does show that there is a clear correlation between the experiences that a child and teenager may go through, and how that translates into certain behavioral patterns down the road.

Therefore, it's important to analyze all aspects of a person's life in order to determine where one set of traits may emerge from. It can be rather foolish to dismiss the effects of the environment on a person's behavior. In fact, many folks make a rash judgment in saying that manipulators, or even psychopaths, are just "born that way." The fact of the matter is that while there may be a physiological component (mental illness has been found to be a hereditary issue), most of the time, manipulative traits are the result of a certain set of experiences that a person goes through from an early age.

How Manipulators Select Their Victims

One of the most important points to consider in this discussion is how manipulators select their victims. A victim, by definition, is the recipient of the manipulator's actions. Therefore, the victim suffers negative consequences from the behavioral patterns exhibited by the manipulator.

On the whole, victim selection is generally random. This means that manipulators will simply sniff around looking for someone they can take advantage of. When there is a greater amount of premeditation in the selection of a victim, then we might be dealing with a psychopath. As such, these individuals might make a more careful study as to the type of person they seek to attack.

Nevertheless, most manipulators will simply seek out those who are closest to them. This is why family tends to be the first target on a manipulator's radar.

Generally speaking, manipulators look for weak individuals whom they feel won't be able to put up a fight. This means that for one reason or another, the victim is powerless to stop them. When you think of physical violence, this is one of the main criteria that goes into the selection of a victim.

On a deeper, more emotional level, manipulators will seek out people who stand to lose quite a bit more than the manipulator.

Think about that for a moment.

Let's go back to the example pertaining to the workers who must deal with a manipulative boss. In the end, the workers need the job far more than the boss does. If anything, the boss manipulates the employees more for personal pleasure than a logical business reason. Consequently, the workers are faced with a dilemma: They either put up with the manipulation or find another job.

The ultimate objective of the manipulator is to subdue their victims to the point where they will offer resistance to the manipulator's tactics. This means the victim eventually becomes complicit in the manipulator's behavior. Sure, there are instances where the victim is unable to extricate themselves from the abusive situation they are in. In such cases, the victim can only hope to endure the situation until a time comes when they are able to finally get out.

Highly skilled manipulators will take the time to scout for potential victims. This occurs when a manipulator is able to identify the choice traits they are looking to find in their victims. As such, they will scout their surroundings and places they perceive will have the highest number of vulnerable individuals. That is why it's always a good idea to be skeptical of someone you don't really know in a place that you often go to. You never know who you might be dealing with.

Signs of a Manipulative Partner

One of the objectives on the mind of a manipulator might be to find a partner they can manipulate. This may occur either as a conscious behavior or an instinctive one. In the event of instinctive behavior, you can assume that the manipulator is not acting out of malice, but rather out of their own sheer desire. When you consider a conscious choice on the part of the manipulator, then you might actually be dealing with an evil individual who has a hidden agenda. So, it is important to recognize the warning signs before it's too late.

On the whole, manipulators can be easily spotted in romantic relationships by the subtle hints and lapses they show. For example,

128

they appear to be sweet and attentive, but suddenly change and appear to be disconnected. You can tell this by seeing in the way they pay attention to your conversation. Also, they might be very polite and caring but suddenly react abruptly when something that they don't like happens.

These are very subtle signs that you are dealing with someone who might not be entirely forthcoming. But the red flags get worse when you're dealing with someone who is jealous and possessive. This can begin with incessant text messages and calls. It's a progressive matter; they start off by increasing the number of calls and texts until you find that they are controlling everything you do. Eventually, they expect a tally and report of all the things you do.

In addition, a manipulative partner will strive to find out things which are negative, embarrassing or even traumatic about your past. Then, they will use that every time they can. For instance, a manipulator may use their partner's weight as a means of shaming. They will use this to coax their partner to comply; after all, "no one will love you as much as I do." These types of statements are a clear indication that there is a manipulation attempt.

These red flags are important to keep in mind as they can quickly degenerate into an abusive relationship. Highly skilled manipulators will make the transition so subtle that the victim won't even notice the relationship is degrading to that level. In the end, all the victim can feel is the effects of the abuse.

How to Know You Are Being Targeted

It can be hard to know if you are being targeted by a manipulator. Perhaps the easiest way to go about this is to confront the manipulator. If you happen to run into someone who is overly friendly, then this should be a red flag for you. Also, if you happen to be surrounded by people who only remember you every time they need something from you, then you know you're definitely being targeted.

Unless you know a person well, it's always a good rule of thumb to keep an eye out on everyone. While this may seem like paranoid behavior, the fact of the matter is if you are able to be alert, the chances of being nabbed by manipulators are rather slim.

Here are some practical tips:

1. Be wary of overly friendly strangers.
2. Watch for offers and deals that are "too good to be true."
3. Keep an eye out for sudden mood swings.
4. Watch out for contradicting behavior and words.
5. Pay attention to the moment in which people approach you.
6. Avoid responding to unsolicited advice.

These situations are all indicative of a manipulator trying to "test" you. If they find you are responsive, then they may feel compelled to continue their advances until you give in what they want. In the end, it's usually best to just get away from these people. You may never have to openly engage them; all you may have to do is just move away from them.

How to Deal with a Manipulator

If you happen to find yourself dealing with a manipulator, here are three very important steps which you can take to help you better deal with this type of individual.

1. ***Try your best to get away from the situation.*** While there are circumstances in which getting away from a manipulator may be virtually impossible, it is the most recommended course of action. This will take away their opportunities to manipulate you. Moreover, if you can completely extricate yourself from a situation (such as finding a new job), then all the better.
2. ***Find out what they are using to manipulate you and then take it away from them***. If you can identify what they are using against you, then you will be able to take that weapon away from them. In fact, you may even be able to use it against them. That will be a clear indicator to the manipulator that they can't have their way with you any longer.
3. ***Know your rights***. If you happen to be in an abusive relationship or situation, you have the right to seek help. This can be any form of help that may be available to you, but you must act on it. If you know you are being affected by a manipulative and even abusive person, but fail to say

anything about it, you may never get the help you need. So, it's important to speak up.

4. ***Avoid the blame game.*** Do not think for a second that this situation is your fault. Also, there is no need to blame the manipulator even though they are responsible for their actions. When you play the blame game, you are hurting yourself by making it seem that you are directly, or indirectly, responsible for what's happened. So, even if you are the victim, it's not your fault that this has happened to you. By the same token, the manipulator is not at fault for being a manipulator. However, they are responsible for their actions.

5. ***Know when to quit.*** If you choose to confront the manipulator, you need to know when you may need to get away from them. There is only so much energy you can spend on a person like this. Often, dealing with a manipulator becomes a war of attrition. So, your determination to win that war may leave you more spent, both physically and emotionally, than what you stand to gain.

Behavioral Traits of Favorite Victims of Manipulators

Certain characteristics and behavioral traits make people more vulnerable to manipulation, and people with dark psychology traits know this full well. They tend to seek out victims who have those specific behavioral traits because they are essentially easy targets.

Emotional Insecurity and Fragility

Manipulators like to target victims who are emotionally insecure or emotionally fragile. Unfortunately for these victims, such traits are very easy to identify even in total strangers, so it's easy for experienced manipulators to find them. People who are emotionally insecure tend to be very defensive when they are attacked or when they are under pressure. That makes them easy to spot in social situations. Even after just a few interactions, a manipulator can gauge with a certain degree of accuracy, how insecure a person is. They'll try to provoke their potential targets in a subtle way, and then wait to see how the targets react. If they are overly defensive, manipulators will take it as a sign of insecurity, and they will intensify their manipulative attacks. Manipulators can also tell if a target is emotionally insecure if he/she redirects accusations or negative comments. They will find a way to put you on the spot, and if you try to throw it back at them, or to make excuses instead of confronting the situation head-on, the manipulator could conclude that you are insecure and therefore an easy target. People who have social anxiety also tend to have emotional insecurity, and manipulators are aware of this fact. In social gatherings, they can easily spot individuals who have social anxiety, then target them for manipulation. "Pickup artists" are able to identify the girls who seem uneasy in social situations by the way they conduct themselves. Social anxiety is difficult to conceal, especially to manipulators who are experienced at preying on emotional vulnerability.

Emotional Fragility is Different from Emotional Insecurity

Emotionally insecure people tend to show it all the time, while emotionally fragile people appear to be normal, but they break down emotionally at the slightest provocation. Manipulators like targeting emotionally fragile people because it's very easy to elicit a reaction from them. Once a manipulator finds out you are emotionally fragile, he is going to jump at the change to manipulate you because he knows it would be fairly easy. Emotional fragility can be temporary, so people with these traits are often targeted by opportunistic manipulators. A person may be emotionally stable most of the time, but he/she may experience emotional fragility when they are going through a breakup, when they are grieving, or when they are dealing with a situation that is emotionally draining. The more diabolical manipulators can earn your trust, bid their time, and wait for you to be emotionally fragile. Alternatively, they can use underhanded methods to induce emotional fragility in a person they are targeting.

Sensitive People

Highly sensitive people are those individuals who process information at a deeper level and are more aware of the subtleties in social dynamics. They have lots of positive attributes because they tend to be very considerate of others, and they watch their step to avoid causing people any harm, whether directly or indirectly. Such people tend to dislike any form of violence or cruelty, and they are easily upset by news reports about disastrous occurrences, or even depictions of gory scenes in movies. They also tend to get emotionally exhausted from taking in other people's feelings.

Sensitive people also tend to be withdrawn. They are mostly introverts, and they like to keep to themselves because social stimulation can be emotionally draining for them. Manipulators who are looking to control others are more likely to target people who are introverted because that trait makes it easy to isolate potential victims. Manipulators can also identify sensitive people by listening to how they talk. Sensitive people tend to be very proper; they never use vulgar language, and they tend to be very politically correct because they are trying to avoid offending anyone. They also tend to be polite, and they say please and thank you more often than others. Manipulators go after such people because they know that they are too polite to dismiss them right away; sensitive people will indulge anyone because they don't want to be rude, and that gives malicious people a way in.

Emphatic People

Emphatic people are generally similar to highly sensitive people, except that they are more attuned to the feelings of others and the energy of the world around them. They tend to internalize other people's suffering to the point that it becomes their own. In fact, for some of them, it can be difficult to distinguish someone's discomfort from their own. Emphatic people make the best partners because they feel everything you feel. However, this makes them particularly easy to manipulate, which is why malicious people like to target them. Malicious people can feign certain emotions, and convey those emotions to emphatic people, who will feel them as though they were real. That opens them up for exploitation. Emphatic people are the favorite targets of psychopathic conmen because they feel so deeply for others. A conman can make up stories about financial difficulties and swindle lots of money from emphatic people. The problem with being emphatic is that because you have such strong emotions, you easily dismiss your own doubts about people because you would much rather offer help to a person who turns out to be a liar than deny help to a person who turns out to be telling the truth. Emphatic people have big-hearts, and they tend to be extremely generous, often to their own detriment. They are highly charitable, and they feel guilty when others around them suffer, even if it's not their fault and they can't do anything about it. Malicious people have a very easy time taking such people on guilt trips. They are the kind of people who would willingly fork over their life savings to help their friends get out of debt, even if it means they would be ruined financially. Malicious people like to get into relationships with emphatic people because they are easy to take advantage of.

Chapter 13

Toxic Relationships and What to Do About Them

Toxic relationships are everywhere. They can be overtly toxic in the way that people treat each other, or they can be covertly toxic in a subtle manner. Regardless of the actual nature of the relationship, toxic relationships can undermine a person's confidence and destroy their peace of mind. We will look at the definition of what a toxic relationship is, the types of toxic relationships, and what you can do to avoid them.

What is a Toxic Relationship?

Roughly speaking, a toxic relationship is any kind of relationship that causes harm to at least one of the parties involved. This is an important distinction to make as some toxic relationships affect only one of the parties (there needs to be at least two parties involved), or they may hurt all of the parties involved.

The type of harm that occurs in this kind of relationship can be physical, emotional, or both. Most of the time, one type of harm is more prevalent than the other. In some cases, there may be a combination of both. Be that as it may, a toxic relationship will inflict harm on the parties involved in such a manner that it can leave lasting effects (54).

Consider this example:

In a marriage, one spouse is physically abusive to the other. The victim generally puts up with the abuse for any number of reasons. For argument's sake, let's assume that the victim does not leave the relationship out of fear. As such, the victimizer takes full advantage of this and looks to further submit their prey. In the end, the physical harm endured by the victim may lead to grave consequences such as death and serious bodily injury.

In this example, one of the parties is the recipient of the abuse and thereby bears the brunt of the harm. The victimizer may suffer from emotional distress as a result of their action. For instance, the victimizer may feel guilty after inflicting the abuse upon their spouse, though such cases aren't always the norm.

Now, let's consider a situation in which both of the spouses are in a toxic relationship and in which both suffer harm.

In this scenario, there is no physical harm inflicted upon any of the spouses, but rather it is emotional harm. Both spouses are verbally abusive to one another. They frequently engage in shouting matches in which they say very nasty things to each other. The end result is emotional distress beyond anything either spouse has experienced.

In this case, both parties play a dual role; that is, victim and victimizer. This naturally leads to a breakdown in the relationship which, most of the time, is irreparable. This means that the pattern of abuse will continue until the relationship itself ends. However, both partners may be so set in their ways that the thought of ending the relationship may seem inconceivable to them. The end result may be a pattern of abuse that lasts for years on end.

---

(54) McMillan, Dina L. (2008) – *But He Says He Loves Me: How to Avoid Being Trapped* in a Manipulative Relationship

How to Recognize a Toxic Relationship

Generally speaking, you are most likely in a toxic relationship whether it's romantic, professional, family or friendship, when you are suffering any type of harm, that is, you are hurt in any way, at least on a consistent basis.

Some of the signs may be too subtle to tell. But if you consistently feel bad, in any way, then you may have to take a closer look at your relationship. Perhaps things aren't so bad on the surface, but beneath the visible surface, there may lie a deep pattern of abuse.

Let's consider your workplace.

If you find yourself working with colleagues who drag you down rather than spurring you to be your best, then you are most likely in a toxic workplace environment. If you add to that a boss who is demanding, overbearing and domineering, then you might as well get a new job.

Think about it in this manner.

If you get home absolutely tired at the end of your workday; if you feel like you have run a marathon; if you feel that you are emotionally drained, every single day, then you might very well be the victim of toxic relationships. Now, it's one thing to have a tough job which is demanding and requires a high degree of physical and emotional conditioning. You can tell the difference because you feel that your job gives you a sense of purpose beyond the paycheck. But if you would rather go through a root canal rather than go to work, then it's a safe bet that you are not in an ideal environment.

Another telltale sign that you are in a toxic relationship is when you feel you are giving more than you are getting. While this may be the manifestation of unfulfilled wishes (for instance, a narcissist may feel they are not getting what they want in a relationship), an honest assessment of both your actions and those of the other parties may reveal that you are in a toxic relationship. It could very well be that others are simply taking advantage of you.

Furthermore, toxic relationships are manifest when there is a clear benefit for one party as compared to other parties. For example, parents clearly derive a benefit from their children while the children themselves don't receive the love and attention they need. This is generally seen in child stars. The parents reap the benefits of their child's success while the child is neglected and forced to work.

On the whole, toxic relationships are fairly obvious once you begin to peel back the onion. This assessment begins when you see that you are hurt in some manner, or you are not receiving any kind of benefit in the relationship. Moreover, if there is any kind of physical harm in a relationship, then it's time to end it.

Types of Toxic Relationships

While the term "toxic relationship" tends to be seen as an umbrella term encompassing any kind of harmful relationship, the fact is that there are multiple variants of this type of relationship. The difference generally lies in the way the relationship is set up. Some relationships that are focused more on a romantic interest, whereas others are focused more on a professional setting.

Toxic Romantic Relationships

This type of toxic relationship can take on any number of facets. It is the only one we are going to explore in isolation as it is the one which is the most vulnerable to degenerating into a toxic, abusive interaction among both parties.

In general terms, toxic romantic relationships tend to be broken from the beginning. As such, the foundations of the relationship are set up in such a way that there is hardly any semblance of what a normal romantic relationship would like.

In theory, romantic relationships involve two individuals who profess affection and fondness for one another. This means that there is an affinity between both of them in such a way that they commit their time and energy to care for each other.

If a relationship is set up under those pretenses, then the chance of it surviving over time is far greater than if they are set up under any other type of objectives. The situation now shifts dramatically when one of the parties in the relationship enters it with a hidden agenda. When this occurs, the relationship may be broken from the beginning. Then, there is the case in which a relationship deteriorates over time, thereby leading to its toxicity.

Roughly speaking, one, or both, parties in the relationship are somehow hurt by the dynamics that ensues. When this happens, resentment brews leading to potential animosity between the parties. At this point, the relationship may be beyond repair. In fact, the only solution may be to break up and move on. The situation gets further compounded when there is some type of physical harm involved. Natural, physical harm is extremely difficult to deal with as it could lead to serious injury or even death.

That's why it's important to note that abuse in a romantic relationship can range from verbal aggression to physical harm. Everything that happens in between can be a sign that the victimizer, whether acting consciously or unconsciously, is looking to extract as much benefit for themselves as possible. As a result, the manifestation of blackmail, gaslighting, guilt or blame can be evident. As the abuse deepens, one or several of these phenomena may emerge. The victim may be left broken with their self-esteem shattered in a million pieces. The victimizer may end up resenting themselves though unable to break the pattern that they have become accustomed to.

Dependence

Dependence is especially toxic when the victim is the party who sustains the dependency of the victimizer.

To clearly exemplify this, think about a drug addict or alcoholic. The addict becomes dependent on their spouse, parents, siblings or friends, especially when they are under the influence. When addiction takes over a person's life, they may be unable to function in a traditional social context. For instance, they may depend on financial support as they are unable to work. If we assume an adult child who is financially dependent on their parents, the addiction may perpetuate this dependency on the parents. The relationship then becomes toxic for the parents, especially if they are older and no longer able to work. In addition, the emotional toll that such a relationship can take on a person is truly exhausting.

Dependence can also be seen at an emotional level. For instance, a person is completely dependent on their partner's attention and validation. In this case, the dependent individual may be unable to function properly without having the full attention of their partner. This can be seen in jealous types (regardless of whether they are male or female). The jealous types will strive to control their partner's every move so that they can feel safe and secure. Naturally, the relationship becomes toxic for the victim as they tend to feel suffocated and smothered by the relentless desire for attention from their partner.

Narcissism

This is one of the most toxic relationships you can be in. A narcissist will generally stop at nothing when looking to take full control over their partner's life, or in the case of narcissistic parents, their children's lives.

Let's explore narcissistic parents a bit further.

Narcissistic parents are the kind that seek to control everything about their children's lives. They will be eternally vigilant and overprotective. This attitude is not the product of genuine concern for their children's wellbeing. Rather, it is a manifestation of their own insecurities. As a result, they need to be in full control of their children's lives so that they can feel more at ease. Furthermore, narcissistic parents have a tendency to live vicariously through their children. This means that these types of parents will push their children into activities and areas in which they, the parents, failed in their own lives. As such, the parents are looking to realize their own dreams through their children. Hence, the support that these types of parents put into their children's development is done more out of the desire to realize their own dreams rather than pursuing their children's wishes and desires.

Lastly, dealing with a narcissistic boss can be a terrible experience. A narcissistic boss is generally a micromanager and very slow to delegate any kind of responsibility or decision-making power to anyone else. Thus, they are totally committed to supervising everything that is done while centralizing all decisions. Needless to say, this can be extremely frustrating while leaving employees with a deep sense of powerlessness. In the end, these types of bosses manage to alienate their employees to the point where they may no longer care about the work they are doing. The boss, on their end, may end up feeling completely exhausted, both physically and emotionally, as all of their energy is spent on trying to maintain control of everything around them. This type of relationship is completely toxic for all of those involved.

Manipulation

Manipulation in relationships can be subtle or quite overt. In some cases, manipulation occurs when the manipulator has a hidden agenda that they act upon. In other cases, the manipulator simply acts out instinctively without really being aware of what they are going to their victim.

Regardless of the case, the manipulator uses their victim for whatever purpose suits them. In some of the most sordid cases, the manipulator may choose their victim out of sheer pleasure and enjoyment; that is, they take sadistic satisfaction in victimizing a vulnerable person.

As discussed earlier in this book, manipulation can occur through blackmail, guilt, lying or even mind control techniques. The level of sophistication on the part of the manipulator may end up determining how well these techniques can work on their victim.

Furthermore, when the victimizer gets bored or fulfills their purpose, the victim may very well be discarded. This is the type of attitude that manipulators with psychopathic tendencies might take. They may not have the slightest amount of compassion for their victim. As such, they will see their victims are disposable.

One other thing about manipulation: when a victim becomes aware of the manipulation but does nothing to stop, they become complicit. In a manner of speaking, they become an enabler as they do not attempt to put an end to it.

When this occurs, the victim may take pleasure in being victimized. This is a masochistic response that may evolve as a result of prolonged periods of exposure to the abuse and even torture. So, don't be surprised if you happen to find people who actually enjoy being subjected to painful experiences.

How to Avoid Toxic Relationships

There are two ways of going about this: first, what to do when you are already in a toxic relationship, and second, how to avoid getting one in the first place.

If you are in a toxic relationship, you need to assess how toxic the relationship really is. If you believe it may be repaired, then it would be wise to talk with the other party to see if there is a possible solution. However, if you feel that the relationship is seriously compromised, then you may need professional help in order to restore a healthy balance (55).

On the other hand, if you believe the relationship is beyond repair, then there may be no other way but out. Often, professional help may be of benefit, but repairing a toxic relationship requires the commitment of all parties involved. If one of the partners is reluctant to work on the relationship, then there may be no solution to it.

In addition, it is important to spot the red flags as they emerge. Here is a list of red flags to look out for:

1. Excessive control
2. Jealousy
3. Insecurity
4. Emotional dependence
5. Physical violence
6. Guilt
7. Hurtful comments
8. Passive-aggressive attacks
9. Name-calling
10. Constant blaming
11. Constant reminder of past mistakes

If you spot any of these red flags them, it should indicate you might be in a toxic relationship. The sooner you spot them, the sooner you may be able to get out, or in the best of cases, repair the relationship. If you realize you are, in fact, the manipulator, then you might be able to make amends and restore balance to your relationship.

---

(55) Murphy, Christopher M.; O'Leary, K. Daniel (1989) – *"Psychological aggression predicts physical aggression in early marriage"*

Chapter 14

Mind Control Techniques

When you think about "mind control," what comes to your mind? Chances are it conjures up thoughts of a mastermind controlling their minions like puppets. In a roundabout way, that's true. Some folks seemingly have a magic power the enables them to compel others to do their bidding (56).

The fact of the matter is that there are no such powers. If there were, whoever could develop them would be incredibly powerful. So, that begs the question: what is mind control?

To answer this question, we need to focus specifically on how free will among humans works. In general, a human being possesses free will. This means that a person is free to choose whatever they want to do. However, this ability can be more or less enhanced depending on the circumstances surrounding a person.

Think about that for a minute.

---

(56) Dantalion, J. (2008) – *Mind Control Language Patterns*. Mind Control Publishing.

If you happened to find yourself stuck in a concentration camp during Nazi Germany, there wouldn't be much that you could do to exercise your free will. Any type of manifestation of your freedom of choice would have been quickly crushed by those in charge of keeping prisoners in line.

What this implies is that free will can be negated to a certain extent, though not completely extinguished. So, mind control, with the context that we are focusing on in this chapter, can be influenced in such a way that a manipulator can motivate a person to do one thing or another. Now, this isn't your traditional "influence" or "persuasion." We're talking about powerful techniques in which you can play with a person's reactions and natural instincts so that they are compelled to do what you want them to do.

This is powerful stuff indeed. This chapter will delve into the ways in which you can use such techniques to get others to go along with your plans and your ideas without having to resort to coercion or any other type of underhanded trickery.

Blame, Guilt, and Shame

Manipulators assume that "the best defense is a good offense." What this means is that the average manipulator will proactively find a way to make their victims feel like they are the aggressors rather than the victim. For instance, abusive spouses may blame their partner for their own abuse. Statements such as "you deserve this after the way you acted" are commonly utilized to make the victim feel as if they are responsible for the abuse inflicted upon. It goes without saying that even when a person is responsible for misdeeds, there is no reason in the world to justify abuse.

Manipulators also love playing the "blame game." This is especially true when they feel cornered. A great example of this is the workplace. Manipulators in the workplace will find ways to shift the blame for their shortcomings on their co-workers, even when it's clear that they were at fault. When this occurs, manipulators can twist situations to their favor thereby avoiding responsibility. If left alone, manipulators can make a routine out of shifting blame on others. Needless to say, this can be devastating to the people around them.

Shaming is another common tactic that manipulators use to bend their victim's will. In shame, the manipulator finds something in the person and uses it to their advantage. In romantic relationships, manipulators can use a partner's physical or emotional flaws against them. For instance, statements such as "no one could love you as much as I do" is a thinly veiled shaming tactic which really means, "I am so generous in loving you, especially when no one else could love someone like you." When you read the subtext, it is a horrible way of treating a romantic partner. Nevertheless, it happens all the time.

Good Cop, Bad Cop

This technique alludes to the common movie plot in which two detectives question a suspect in a variety of ways. However, the technique takes shape when one cop is overly aggressive while the other is more condescending and friendlier.

What you see in this case is not a struggle between various types of personality. What you are seeing is a clear attempt at confusing the suspect. You see, when you are faced with an overly aggressive person, your natural instinct is to go into a defensive position. Then, when you are immediately confronted by a "nice" person, your psyche is thrown out of whack. You really don't know how to react. You may be fearful or suspicious.

Playing the Victim

Some skilled manipulators opt to play the role of victim rather than aggressor. This may be convenient for those who don't have greater physical strength or find themselves in a position of power. When manipulators play the victim card, they are putting others in the role of aggressor thereby exerting influence in a covert manner.

Consider this situation.

Two cars collide in the middle of the road. One of the drivers is a tall, muscular individual while the other is a short and frail-looking individual. In this example, the "weaker" individual is to blame for the accident. However, they automatically play the victim card indicating that it wasn't their fault and so on. When police arrive, they seek the protection of the officers by claiming that the larger individual is threatening them. Whether or not this is actually true is beside the point. What does matter is the fact that the police will side with the individual who appears to be weaker than the other. And while that may be true on a physical level, the "weak" individual is nothing of the sort. They are clever enough to exploit an apparent weakness for their own benefit.

Conscious Misrepresenting of Feelings and Thoughts to the Level of Absurdity

This type of tactic is used to reduce someone's feelings to the lowest possible expression. For instance, when someone is feeling hurt or upset about something, a statement such as "oh, it's no big deal" is intended to belittle this person's feelings especially when it really is a big deal. Of course, there are cases in which people really do overreact. Nevertheless, the systematic downplay of people's feelings can lead to a genuine sensation of emptiness. The end result may be a complete and utter feeling of disappointment.

Also, manipulators enjoy taking importance away from people's feelings and emotions. There is a simple reason behind this: if you are empathic and looking to foster people's feelings, you are actually empowering them to build themselves up. When this occurs, it's hard to control and manipulate them. The end result is someone who has a strong sense of being and togetherness. This is why manipulators look to do away with any semblance of unity within a person.

When you are in the presence of a skilled manipulator, you will find that they strive to create rifts which can, at some point, turn into a gaping chasm that cannot be easily filled with anything else. This creates a reliance on the emotional "support" that the manipulator can provide. Eventually, the manipulator is able to isolate the victim. All of this begins by belittling the victim's emotions to the point of absurdity.

The "White Knight"

This game is used by skilled manipulators. In this game, the manipulator purposely creates a problem and then rushes to the rescue. The intention is to create emotional dependency among those around them as the manipulator is the only one who can solve the problems they encounter. However, the victims may not be aware that the problems are artificially fabricated by the "white knight" to make themselves look good.

This is an expression of the problem-reaction-solution technique. With this technique, manipulators create a problem or exacerbate an existing one, then get people to react in a certain manner so that they can come to the rescue with the miracle solution.

So, the next time you ask yourself where certain people get these miraculous solutions in desperate times, don't be surprised if you happen to find yourself in the midst of a master manipulator.

Chapter 15
Ways to Protect Yourself from Mind Control

Don't Fall into Their Trap

Individuals can use any kind of strategy, such as misunderstanding, guilt, or coercion, to play with others' feelings to really get into their heart. When, like at the office, you often have to contend with these kinds of people, overlook and ignore them by saying something nice rather than struggling against them. Emotional manipulators succeed when you fall for their tactics. But when you don't let them get to you, they fail as you clearly sidestep their attempts at emotional manipulation (57).

Steer Clear Whenever Possible

This completely removes the chances of getting caught up in their games. When you are able to spot manipulators, or better be lucky

---

(57) Crawford, Craig (2007) – *The Politics of Life: 25 Rules for Survival in a Brutal and Manipulative World*

enough to have others warn you in advance, you can sidestep these individuals. Often, you may be compelled to be polite to them while keeping a healthy distance. This can save you a great deal of heartache down the road. In this type of circumstance, it's always the best to live to fight another day.

Ignore Everything They Do and Say

Whether you have clearly identified that you are dealing with a manipulator or not, it's always best to ignore people who act like bullies. Oftentimes, they lash out in this manner because they are seeking attention. In order to do this, they may take on brash attitudes or aggressive stances. Also, they may look to intimidate others just to satisfy their own inadequacies. So, it's always best to ignore them. They will eventually get tired and move on. As long as you don't get sucked into their game, you should have no more aggravation than you need.

Try Not to Be Suckered In

Don't deal directly with their issues. The average manipulator will never openly confront you. Instead, they'll look for less covert means of engaging you. They're passive-aggressive, and they seek subtle ways to back you into a corner. For instance, they make general observations which are clearly aimed at someone. Statements such as, "it's such a mess in here, why doesn't anyone clean up?" are intended to draw a reaction. Someone who is caught off guard may take offense to the statement and fall for the trap. These passive-aggressive attacks are often aimed at the victim so that they can react and essentially become the aggressor. At that point, the manipulator can play the role of victim once the target fires back.

Do you see the manipulation here?

That's why it's best to think twice before reacting to any snide comments, sarcastic remarks or insinuations made by anyone around you, especially when it's clear they don't have your best interest at heart.

Stop Compromising

When folks are trapped in an abusive relationship, they tend to compromise. Often, they believe that this is the best they can do. For instance, they are in a toxic workplace but choose to remain there as they believe this is the only job, or the best one, they can get. So, they allow the abuse to continue even when they are cognizant of it. Many times, this happens out of fear, that is, the fear of going out and getting another job. At a personal level, people can settle into a routine and consequently find it hard to get out of it. If you are compromising for whatever reason, please reassess your values and your goals. You don't need to settle for any reason whatsoever.

Create a Greater Sense of Purpose

Many times, it's easy to get lost in the hustle and bustle of life. When this happens, it can be quite complicated to find the true meaning of life, which is not simply some epic quest where we must traverse the depths of the Earth. In fact, it is a matter of making a commitment to a greater sense of purpose. By this, we mean committing to a higher value, for instance, empathy. When you make this commitment, it's difficult for others to bring you down. Moreover, if you are in a relationship such as this, making this commitment can help you climb out of it and make the most of your time and efforts.

This means that if you happen to see that there are others around you looking to sabotage your growth, then it may be time to move away. This might mean making some painful decisions; but you need to do whatever makes you feel good about yourself and the circumstances you find yourself in.

Bet on Yourself

Toxic relationships have a habit of undermining your self-confidence and self-esteem. In particular, your self-confidence can be completely shot when a manipulator takes hold of your psyche by playing mind games. When this happens, you might find yourself completely at odds about what to do and how to handle your larger projects. The fact of the matter is that that's exactly what manipulators want you to do. They want to sow confusion inside of you so that you can't find your bearing. Otherwise, it's virtually impossible to manipulate a clearly focused individual who has their feet on the ground and a good head on their shoulders. When you make a commitment to improve yourself, you will find that betting on your abilities will always pay off in droves.

Avoid Emotional Attachment with Them

Easier said than done; especially if they don't instantly show their true colors. Pay attention to their first warning, as there are always red flags. This is particularly true in the case of romantic relationships. While you may not realize what the manipulator is up to until after you have made an emotional investment in them, try your best to avoid attachment until you are reasonably sure. Emotional manipulators always scan the horizon for their next victim. But if you haven't invested too much in the relationship to begin with, it's much easier to break away. If you can pick up on those early red flags, you can move on before letting them hurt you in any way.

Develop a Strong Mentality

Mental strength seems like a buzzword as many gurus out there claim to have the recipe for building toughness and resiliency. The truth is this process usually involves a great deal of trial and error. By this we mean that you will go through a lot of negative experiences before you can arrive at a point in which you know what to expect out of a myriad of circumstances. As you develop your strength, you will notice that many of the actions that once negatively affected you won't become as important anymore. Moreover, you'll be able to let negative feeling wash away without inflicting the damage they once did. In a manner of speaking, a strong mindset is the product of maturity and experience. Always try your best to look at the negative experiences in life as a lesson learned.

Chapter 16

Brainwashing

When most people think about brainwashing, they tend to think about the depictions seen in films.

In Hollywood films, it's commonly depicted that victims undergo a series of treatments in order to have their will essentially subjugated to that of their master's. As a result, the victim stops thinking for themselves. Instead, the victim ends up acting and behaving in the manner the master or manipulator orders them to do.

Almost always, brainwashing involves some type of force or trauma which causes the victim to essentially fear the consequences of not complying with the manipulator's orders. A good example of this can be seen in the film "A Clockwork Orange" in which an inmate is subjected to a series of tortures. Each torture increases the level of violence to the extent where the test subject's will is broken.

In this film, the entire purpose of this process is to "rehabilitate" a convicted criminal into a model member of society. So, what you are seeing is the replacement of one set of behaviors for another. Of course, there are many more meaningful ways in which this can be done. However, the effectiveness and overall success of replacing a habit by means other than violent ones cannot necessarily be guaranteed.

While this type of situations do happen, we are not talking about using trauma-based mind control in this book (58).

What we are discussing is how brainwashing generally takes place as part of a broader social situation.

For example, children are raised in a certain set of value as part of their community. As they grow up, they may be faced with various scenarios in which they may be compelled to change this mindset. This is where you have seemingly normal kids become terrorists after joining a political organization. Also, you have people who join a religious cult and suddenly become "brainwashed" into believing that the leader is a god.

All of these situations underscore how brainwashing can be a "gradual process" in which the individual doesn't realize what it being made to them. They just go with the flow only to realize they have been deceived when it's too late. In some cases, they may never get out of it.

It should be noted that the way these cults and political groups operate is by altering a person's perception of reality. As long as you are out of touch with the reality, you can be manipulated. When a person has been removed from the environment that grounds them to their personality and their reality, they are susceptible to being brainwashed.

The Brainwashing Process

The term "brainwashing" is used to refer to the fact that a person's set of beliefs and ideas is replaced by another as implanted by the manipulator. This is important to note as all humans have a set of thoughts, ideas and beliefs programmed as a part of their upbringing. Naturally, this means your social, cultural, economic and religious context will determine the type of programming you have as an adult.

---

(58) Dennis M. Kowal (2000) – *Brainwashing*, Oxford University Press, pp. 317–447

This is what makes brainwashing so difficult. After all, how can you change this programming, especially if the victim is reluctant to do so? As such, a mechanism is necessary by which the victim is able to accept the change in programming thus leading to a change in behavioral patterns.

The most common device used to achieve this shift in programming is violence. Violence can be used to get a person to accept a change in behavioral patterns due to the fear of negative consequences. In short, effective brainwashing occurs when a person is subject to a series of negative consequences when they fail to comply with what the manipulator demands.

Let's consider this situation.

A person wants to quit smoking, but is unable to. The manipulator is insistent on getting the victim to quit smoking by any means necessary and will beat the victim every time they smoke. By the second beating, the victim will become afraid of negative consequences that come with smoking. As a result, the victim will think twice about smoking lest they face the negative consequences. Eventually, the victim will be perfectly clear on what they can expect every time they smoke. In the end, the victim is so fearful that they will stop smoking.

While this type of technique may sound barbaric, the fact of the matter is that it's quite common. Throughout society, we are faced with negative consequences every time we do something that transgresses societal norms. Think about criminals. They face negative consequences when they break the law. These criminals are put into prison as a result of their transgressions. The main purpose of this is to create a deterrent so that other members of society will observe the laws lest they also face similar consequences.

Negative reinforcement is just as powerful as positive reinforcement. The difference lies in that positive reinforcement looks to praise appropriate behavior while negative reinforcement seeks to punish unwanted behavior.

When positive reinforcement is used, behaviors are encouraged through conviction. The individual understands that what they are doing is good and pleases society as a whole. On the other hand, negative reinforcement seeks to create a culture of fear in such a way that anyone who does not comply will have to face a series of harsh consequences. Ultimately, fear is much more effective than praise as fear play with instinctive reactions in humans.

Steps of Brainwashing

Breaking Down of Self

The breaking down of one's self is the first step of the brainwashing process. The agent wants to break through the old identity of the subject, making them more fragile and open to the desired new identity during this process. This step is needed for the process to proceed. If the subject is still firmly in his determination and his old self, then the agent is not very successful with his efforts. Breaking this identity and making the subject question themselves and their surroundings will help change identities more quickly in the subsequent steps. This is accomplished by several steps, such as an attack on the subject's identity, using guilt, self-betrayal, and then breaking point (59).

Possibility of Salvation

Once the agent has been effective in breaking down the self of the subject, the time has come to move to the next step.

In this step, the subject can only be saved if they are prepared to turn away from the former self and their beliefs and instead embrace the new one that is offered. The subject has the chance to understand what's around them, and they are assured that everything will be okay once they follow the desired path.

In this phase of the brainwashing phase, there are four steps: leniency, compulsion to confess, channeling of guilt, and release of guilt.

---

(59) Taylor, K. (2006) – *Brainwashing: The Science of Thought Control.* Oxford University Press.

Rebuilding of Self

The subject has experienced several steps and emotional disturbance by this step. They are convinced they are wrong, and have to be fixed, and that their belief system is created by their mistake and that it needs to be changed. They have been put through a lot actions designed to rob them of their old identity. After all, this has been done; the subject must learn with the guidance of the agent how to repair themselves.

This stage offers the agent the opportunity to introduce new ideas or concepts because the subject is a clean slate and very willing to learn how to feel better and be better.

The Impact of Brainwashing

The overall impact of brainwashing can be found in the individual's personality. When brainwashing is successful, the overall result is a fragmented psyche in the victim. By "fragmented psyche" it is understood that the person does not actually have a fully integrated being, that is, a being totally in control of their emotions and actions. An individual with a fragmented personality may end up losing touch with reality. This is the main aim of brainwashing.

When a person loses touch with reality, it can be hard to distinguish what is real and what isn't. The end result is an opportunity for the manipulator to implant their version of reality into the psyche of the victim. In this way, the victim may find themselves struggling to find any type of meaning in their life. As such, it can lead to episodes in which the individual panics. This is where brainwashing techniques need to be reinforced. For example, the individual needs to be subjected to torture once again in order to reaffirm the negative consequences that come with non-compliance.

As horrendous as brainwashing may sound, the truth is that negative reinforcement can happen at a variety of levels. For instance, parents can set up boundaries for their children whereby a transgression of the family norms can lead to a negative consequence. These consequences may include grounding the child for a certain period of time or perhaps taking certain privileges away. As a result, the child will comply with the house result lest they face the consequence of their actions.

Now, this opens up a very important caveat. Often, the threat of negative consequences may be enough to get an individual to comply. But there is a point in which the manipulator needs to make good on their threats. This means that if the manipulator may have to actually carry out their threats in order to prove they mean business.

This is seen in the world of crime on a consistent basis. When a drug lord or mob boss issues a warning, they need to make an example out of someone so that others "fall in line." While this is resorting to violence, the example stands alone. So, if a parent warns their child that failing to complete their homework will lead to a loss in television privileges, then the parent had better go through with it when the child fails to comply.

In the end, making good on threats serves a psychological purpose: it creates consistency in the mind of those around the manipulator. It is exactly the same result when a person offers positive reinforcement. If people are encouraged to do one thing or another in exchange for a reward, then the offer must be made good when it is called for. Otherwise, people will feel cheated and will fail to comply in the future.

Brainwashing Tactics

So far, we have established that brainwashing involves some kind of violence, or at least the threat of it, in addition to negative reinforcement. This can ultimately lead to a fragmentation of the psyche, or at the very least, the discouragement of undesired behavioral patterns. Now we will take a look at some of the specific tactics that can be used to provoke a "brainwashing" reaction in an individual. It should be noted that these tactics are all varied in the degree of force and should not be practiced without a full understanding of the outcomes they may be able to produce.

Undermining Self-Esteem

One of the most effective ways in which a person can be brainwashed is by undermining their self-esteem. When a person is

158

fully integrated and confident in their abilities, they won't feel as though they need to depend on any external source for validation. They have all the validation they need as a result of their own perceived value. It is when this perceived value drops that the individual needs validation from outside sources.

Undermining a person's self-esteem can be as simple as constantly telling they are not good enough, pointing out their mistakes and ensuring that they are criticized at every turn. This type of attitude will ensure that these individuals never get off the ground and thereby become emotionally dependent on the manipulator.

Isolation

One of the textbook tactics that manipulators like to look for is isolation.

Now, isolation can happen in a literal sense; that is, a person is essentially kidnapped and extracted from their usual life.

When this occurs, the victim is physically removed from any context with which they are familiar.

Manipulators will do much to isolate victims from their families, friends and other support networks. This is because they want to be the only source of information for the victim. Caring family members will tell the victim they are in a cult or an abusive relationship because clearly, the manipulator does not want the person to realize this. Once the victim has been cut off from their family and community, they don't have any real place to go. So, they become overly reliant on the manipulator. It is at this point where the manipulator can gaslight the victim. The victim, now alone and without any support from any source, will depend emotionally, financially and even spiritually on the manipulator and their network. This is why runaway teens almost always end up becoming part of these groups. Also, people who have been through serious traumatic experiences end up falling prey to these schemes.

It becomes difficult to change your mindset if you are fully entrenched in your comfort zone. So, be wary when people suddenly urge you to drop everything and follow a radical new behavioral pattern. This is how cults get their victims. They convince them that they need to forego their current lifestyle and adopt the beliefs of the new cult. In the end, the cult replaces the victim's current life with an altered perception of reality. For instance, cults make victims believe they are now in touch with the Supreme Being and have no need to mortals. This is where isolation occurs and the victim is at the mercy of the manipulator. This is why a kidnapping experience can be so traumatic for a person.

However, isolation can also take on <u>another tone</u>. It can occur when the manipulator latches on to their victim and alienates from their friends, family and social groups. This is very common in romantic relationships. The manipulator increasingly demands more and more attention from the victim to the point where the victim no longer goes about their usual life (60).

The intention behind this is to isolate the victim from any support mechanisms which could serve as a counterweight for the manipulator's advances. The end result may be a profoundly confused victim which, of course, serves the manipulator's purposes very well.

Furthermore, such experiences can be seen in military and police training. When a recruit goes through this type of training, they are sequestered from their usual surroundings, indoctrinated in a new set of values and beliefs, and then returned to society as a changed person. While military and police training do not involve brainwashing per se, they do involve a fundamental change in beliefs and values, especially if the individual's original values somehow contradict the values instilled by the police and military.

Fear and Dependence

We have discussed at length how fear is a valuable resource for manipulators. Fear is one of the primal instincts that humans cannot easily discard. If anything, fear is an instinct that evolved as a means of helping humans survive. This is evidenced by the "fight or flight" mechanism. Without this mechanism, early humans would

---

(60) L.J. West (1989) – *Persuasive Techniques in Contemporary Cults: A Public Health Approach*, Washington, CULTS and New Religious Movements American Psychiatric Association

have been unable to distinguish danger. As a result, the survival of the human species may not have been assured.

Consequently, fear can be triggered by any number of stimuli. In general, fear can be the result of an imminent threat or exposure to unknown situations. To further compound the issue, fear is generally triggered by the possibility of physical harm (more than emotional harm) and death. Death, in itself, is the ultimate fear that all humans face. Any time a person is confronted with the possibility of death, their survival instincts start setting off desperate survival instincts.

Skilled manipulators are able to recognize what causes people to feel especially fearful. When they are able to recognize these aspects, whatever they may be, they can use them against their victims. This opens up two distinct possibilities.

In the first possibility, the manipulator uses their victim's fear to manipulate them in such a way that the persistent threat "keeps them in line." As we have mentioned earlier, the point comes where the manipulator must make good on their threats. If the manipulator follows through, the fear is reinforced.

The second possibility is quite the opposite of the first. In this possibility, the manipulator emerges as a hero. Consequently, the manipulator "saves" their victim from the perceived threat. Highly skilled manipulators are able to fabricate threats so that they can emerge as saviors. In the end, the unsuspecting victims grow to admire the manipulator without really thinking about the fact that the threats don't really exist.

When looking at fear on a deeper level, dependency can emerge as a result of the manipulator's "heroism." You can see this in social groups and organizations in which there is one person who is always responsible for making sure things work in the same manner. Think about the government, for instance. People have become so accustomed to the government solving all their issues that they become overly dependent on what the state can provide them. Ultimately, reliance on government is a type of drug from which people may never be able to get away from.

This is the reason why drugs are used in brainwashing programs. Once a victim is hooked on a certain type of drug, they will become complaint so long as they are able to maintain access to the drug. In the end, the manipulator uses this to torment victims unless they are fully compliant.

Us vs. Them

This is the typical "divide and conquer" scenario. The manipulator will create a perception of reality in which the victim believes the world is against them and the only solace is the manipulator. This ensures that the manipulator has full control over their victim. Often the "us vs. them" rhetoric is intended to create animosity among people. It is a divisive measure used to drive a wedge. The more the manipulator is able to drive that wedge, the better their mind control tactics become. It should be noted that this tactic is not often in isolation. It is generally combined with other tactics so that they all produce the desired effect (61).

Blind Obedience

Total compliance is one of the aims that manipulators seek to achieve in their victims. However, gaining full compliance, that is, total obedience from someone is rather hard to do. This is due to the fact that people have free will. While there have been countless attempts at controlling a person's free will, the fact of the matter is that the best that manipulators can do is influence people's emotions and thoughts. Blind obedience is generally the result of having people's core values replaced with others the manipulator wishes to instill. The most common examples of this are found in religious cults and in the military. When people adopt a core set of values, they are willing to give their life for them. By the same token, people will resist complying if they believe certain actions are not in accordance with their value set. That's why manipulators must try their best to ensure that they can supplant their victims' core values.

---

(61) Schein, Edgar H. (1971) – *Coercive Persuasion: A Socio-Psychological Analysis of the "Brainwashing" of American Civilian Prisoners by the Chinese Communists.*, New York, W.W. Norton

Physical Activity

The adage that says, "humans are creatures of habit" is as true as it has ever been. Human behavior emerges from a pattern of behavior that cannot be easily changed once it has been instilled.

Think about that for a minute.

When you hear that someone is "set in their ways" it means that they have a certain way of doing things and will become reluctant to deviate from that pattern. Therefore, making significant changes can become virtually impossible at this point.

On the whole, physical activity can be used to change behavioral patterns in people. For instance, someone who is looking to adopt a healthier lifestyle will embark upon a new exercise regimen. In this manner, the individual needs to be consistent in their new regimen. Otherwise, the changes will not stick. Thus, we can infer that physical activity leading to a change in behavioral patterns is scaffolded by consistency.

When you translate consistency into brainwashing, there needs to be a pattern in which the victim is subjected to physical activity which can reinforce this new conditioning. This is why Special Forces soldiers are subject to grueling physical activity. It serves a dual purpose: one is to create soldiers who are in peak physical condition, and two it reinforces the core set of values instilled in these soldiers. The end result is a highly skilled and trained soldier that has a set of core values that resonate with those of the military they belong to.

Repetition and Routine

This section harkens back to the point about humans being creatures of habit. It is impossible to assume that a person can learn something new instantly. No matter how clear and effective the teaching and learning process may be, humans need practice and repetition before they can internalize new information. When this occurs, then the knowledge is fixated until new habits are formed.

In brainwashing, there is a clear need for routines and repetition. Otherwise, the victim will be broken beyond repair. This occurs when the "good cop, bad cop" tactic is implemented. When victims simply don't know what to expect, they may become so profoundly confused that their psyche begins to shut down. The victim may be unable to function properly simply because they don't have the slightest clue of what to expect. The end result is a person who is unable to function in the real world. Naturally, this is not the aim of brainwashing.

A good example of this is an experiment conducted by lab mice. The experiment consisted of a mouse approaching a buzzer. When the mouse pushed the buzzer, it would either get a food pellet or an electric shock. Since the point of the experiment was to have the buzzer produce random results, the mice became so anxious at the thought of pushing the buzzer that they simply avoided it altogether. Even though the mice knew there was a chance they could get a food pellet, they would rather go hungry than risk being shocked once again.

This is a clear example of how devastating it can be to confuse a person. That's why consistency is the name of the game in the world of brainwashing. In this manner, the manipulator can ensure the new habits and behaviors they seek to implant in their victim will stick without rendering their victim into a useless and broken soul.

When considering brainwashing, it's important to note that these tactics have produced mixed results. While no clinical studies can prove its effectiveness (brainwashing is considered unethical), an abundant amount of literature proves the damaging effects these types of techniques can have on a person. In the end, brainwashing is the type of technique that is reserved for the dark underworld of spy training. On the whole, this type of activity has no practical purpose in the real world.

Moody Behavior

Moodiness is a type of "good cop, bad cop" manipulation. The point of being constantly moody is to confuse the other party to the point of exhaustion. Once the subject has been exhausted, the manipulator can do as they please. So, if you are dealing with extremely moody individuals, it is best to distance yourself from them. They will suck you into their game. In fact, many get a sick kick from keeping others guessing. They feel a total power rush when others cannot find a foothold. Be careful not to fall under the guise of "unpredictability" as this could just be a nice term to say that these individuals are emotionally unstable.

The "Love Bomb"

While this technique is generally seen in romantic relationships, it is not exclusive to them. The "love bomb" consists of a significant effort early on in a relationship with the purpose of wooing a potential romantic interest. Once the romantic interest has agreed to engage in a relationship with the manipulator, the manipulator is then free to essentially be themselves. However, the love bomb approach will persist until one of two things happens: one, the manipulator gets what they want and no longer has an interest in the victim, or two, the manipulator gets tired of the love interest and essentially becomes bored.

The love bomb can be a devastating technique when applied to someone who has very little experience in romantic relationships or is particularly vulnerable. For example, if a person is on the rebound after a breakup, they may be especially susceptible to the love bomb. In that case, the victim may end up completely devastated once the effects of the love bomb wear off and are left empty following the manipulation (62).

A variant of the love bomb can be seen in the workplace. A new employee makes strides to have their peak performance early in their tenure at their new job. Once they feel entrenched in their new position, they can gradually revert back to their usual self. Another variant can be seen in politicians once they are first elected into office. They carry the momentum they built during their campaign into the first few weeks in office. Once the honeymoon effect has worn off, they can safely revert back into their traditional way of acting.

In any of these cases, the love bomb proves to be nothing more than a ruse until the manipulator gets what they want. Once this occurs, then the manipulator is free to act in the manner they please. Often,

---

(62) James, O. (2018). *Love bombing: Reset your child's emotional thermostat*. Routledge.

this means leaving the victim behind and moving on to their next target.

Testing the Effectiveness of Brainwashing

Most of the above described tactics are the result of ample testing on real human subjects. It should be noted that these tactics are not part of mainstream psychological testing as they are rather unethical. As a result, you cannot expect to find academic literature on how to brainwash people. Nevertheless, there is ample academic research into the effects of trauma and personality modification by various means and tactics.

Also, numerous case studies have dealt with this topic in rather extensive detail. If you are curious and would like to pursue this research further, a number of scientific papers are based on case studies involving brainwashing and other mind control tactics. Please bear in mind that they are all addressed from a psychological perspective while also focusing on biological responses.

How to Prevent Brainwashing

Gain Control over Any Situation

Staying in control of your thoughts and emotions is essential. When you are willing to surrender control over your consciousness, in particular your emotions, you are a sitting duck. Sure, it's alright to cry when you are sad and laugh when something is funny. But it's a completely different story to allow others to control the way act and think. When you find yourself in a group setting in which you are being compelled to act in a certain way, then you need to head for the door. Peer pressure is a significant way in which this can be done. You might be bullied into doing something you don't want to do.

Don't Do Anything You Don't Feel Compelled to Do

Many manipulators will try to bully you into doing one thing or another. There is no need to succumb to this. If you feel you cannot stand up for yourself, it's perfectly fine to leave and get help. After all, anyone who tries to force you to do something you don't want to, is just looking to exploit you. The best attitude to keep in mind is that you have full control over who you are. No more, no less.

Don't Put the Cart Before the Horse

Often, manipulation occurs when our emotions are triggered, such as in the case of an epidemic or a natural disaster. When the media is looking to trigger your feelings by creating an illusion of panic, you need to sit down and think things through. When you succumb to panic, fear or hysteria, it's easy to make mistakes.

This is what manipulators want.

While it may be hard to do, keeping a level head at all times is the best way in which you can nip any manipulation attempts in the bud. That way, you can avoid some of the worst effects, especially during times of crisis.

Be an Action Taker

You have to understand the truth of things. It is good. Yet protecting against these dark techniques of deception is so much more critical. It's often painful and thrilling at first as you try to protect yourself against the hands of such manipulators. Slowly, this frequency can contribute to negation. The slower you behave, the sooner the delusion continues, and if it does, it is highly likely you will be stuck in the same network and fall back. You can stop it by acting as soon as you know that somebody is trying to manipulate you.

Being proactive in this regard is one of the best ways in which you can protect your mental health. Try your best to disconnect from the world through practices such as meditation and mindfulness. Also, limit your consumption of television and social media. The contamination produced by these sources is considerable. They tend to overwhelm your mind and your senses.

Lastly, always keep a critical mind. If you question everything you see and hear, you'll often find that people are well-intentioned. Yet, this will enable you to catch that individual who is trying to exploit you. You'll begin to see the rather overt attempts made by the media while also being able to pick up on other attempts at controlling your mind and your reactions. In the end, you will be better off for it. With time and experience, you'll be able to automatically detect when someone is trying to take advantage of you.

Chapter 17
How to Analyze People

Several skills are important in analyzing people. The first and perhaps most important is having an understanding of human nature and normal human behavior. If you do not have a sense of how humans behave under normal circumstances or what motivates most people, then you are unlikely to correctly interpret the actions and intentions of others. Just as a judge relies on their sense of how people typically behave and what motivates them in their judgments, so you too must develop an understanding of the normal spectrum of human behavior in order to properly analyze someone. Of course, human beings can behave in highly original ways, which makes the process of analyzing them difficult at times. Although human beings frequently behave in typically human ways – like being jealous at the success of others, or envious of a colleague who just married a beautiful wife – sometimes people can surprise you. Indeed, some people never feel jealous or envious of others. Most poor people do not steal even though they may need this or that because it just is not part of their character to do so. Indeed, frequently the greatest, most flamboyant thief is the person who already has all that they need. That being said, in order to analyze people, you will have to start with knowing how humans behave generally. This includes understanding the spectrum of human emotion, the behaviors linked to these emotions, and the forces that motivate people to do this or that. Everyone wears a mask, which means that sometimes the intentions of others are not always clear. But even with this mask, people can reveal to you their emotional state, the events that make them happy and the actions that make them sad. We all wear a mask, but perhaps only FBI agents are so skilled that they never give you some sort of clue. A spontaneous laugh, a twinkle in the eye, a giddy tapping of the foot: these are unconscious signs that men and women give of how they feel. Analyzing men and women appropriately will require taking a basic understanding of human behavior and using it to interpret the things that people say and do.

What is Nonverbal Communication?

This is a process where you send and receive a message without the use of words, either inscribed or spoken. It can also be referred to as manual language. Nonverbal behavior will usually exist within parts of a spoken message.

This term was brought about in 1956 by a psychiatrist Jurgen Ruesch and author Weldon Kees in their book Nonverbal Communication. The publication had notes about the visual perception of human relations. There were observations that the contours of the body disclose the disposition and inclination of the brain. The motions of expression reveal the current humor and will describe the state of mind and will (63).

Types of Nonverbal Communication

There are a variety of nonverbal dimensions:

1. Body movements or kinetics include facial expressions and eye contact.
2. Vocalists entails volume, timbre, pitch, and rate.
3. Individual appearance.

---

(63) Pease, Allan & Barbara (2004). *The Definitive Book of Body Language.* Orion House, London: Orion Books

4. Your physical surroundings and the objects that comprise it.
5. Personal space.
6. Haptics or touch.
7. Time.

Signs created by a distinct movement of the hands or body will encompass all the gestures that constitute words, numbers, and punctuation marks. They can vary from monosyllabic responses to some complex systems like American sign language for the deaf (where nonverbal signs will have a direct translation). Meaning is prescribed to these gestures with the help of facial expression and intensity.

Many of these motions depend upon the culture of the audience. The thumb and forefinger gesture (the thumb touches the forefinger while forming a circle) is meant to look like an "a" and means "okay" in the United States; this is an offensive interpretation in some Latin American countries. When interpreting physical signs from others, it is imperative to understand their background.

Importance of Nonverbal Communication

While interacting with others, it is vital to understand unspoken sentiments. Learning about nonverbal communication may explain the cues that others use in conversation. This knowledge could also improve skills in the area of public speaking. These signs can include eye contact, glances, blink rate, gestures, facial expressions, and postures among many others.

There are some motions that you can use in conversation that allow others to feel at ease. Mirroring someone's actions can subconsciously communicate to them that you are on the same wavelength. Using these tools during a presentation could ensure that your audience is open and receptive to the information that you are conveying.

Nonverbal Abilities

1. Repetition will help in reinforcing what has been said.
2. Contradictions may be seen as untruthful when it contrasts the message being relayed.
3. Substitution can replace or take the place of words.
4. Complementing can enhance a verbal message.

5. Accenting can highlight a certain point in a message.

Be Presentable

Your image will act as part of your nonverbal message to others. Dressing well and taking care of yourself will give an appearance that you are organized and in control of yourself. Your audience will automatically associate your aesthetic with your work or your ideas.

Being casual has its place. When you are trying to convince others to follow your lead or allow you to make a change, a tidy appearance can be encouraging. Next time you are in a public place, pay attention to the snap judgments that you form about others, based on the way they dress.

Work on It

When preparing for a presentation, it can be an interesting experiment to film yourself. You will be able to see what your facial expressions communicate with your audience. Is it happiness, anger, fear, anxiety, surprise, or boredom? You could make note of your posture to make sure you don't look like an uninterested speaker.

You could try and film yourself on more than one occasion. Pay attention to where you will place the nonverbal patterns and where to have a steady delivery of your speech. You should also rate yourself in the following areas: facial expression, tonal variations, posture, gesture, and eye contact.

Plan

60% of human interaction is nonverbal, and 30% is your tone. This means that 90% of what a human being says isn't in the contents of their words. Presentations consist of two different elements that must be interwoven together; showing and telling. You must tackle both sides with care.

Allow yourself to come up with a plan for your speech patterns and nonverbal cues. Imagine the way that you will stand and the words that you will emphasize. With conscious effort, you will be able to inspire trust within your audience. Their ability to retain information is based upon their relationship with you.

Effects of Nonverbal Communication on Verbal Discourse

Paul Ekman and Wallace Friesen are psychologists involved in the discussion of the interdependence that occurs between nonverbal and verbal messages. They have explained the different ways in which gestures affect oral discourse. Tone and inflection can be used to emphasize your words.

An experienced speaker can use devices (like forced pauses, changing vocal rate or volume, etc.) to maintain the attention of their audience. A motion may even be used to repeat what you have said. You can *say* yes, while nodding at the same time. Repetition can be used to place emphasis on your message. You can also substitute your words with gestures to add intensity.

There are times when nonverbal communication can contradict what you say. Someone can tell you they had a great time out swimming, but their facial expressions look flat and unemotional. When you are upset, these signals can assist you with relaying your actual message to others, even though you may not be saying it outright.

Deceiving Studies

Experts have traditionally come to an agreement that nonverbal communication has an impact on the message it carries. This claim was supported by 93% of people; 7% of the participants only considered verbal information to be valid. This data is not infallible.

A study was done on two occasions that compared vocal and facial cues. Other research doesn't support the 93% claim, though they agree that children and adults mostly rely on nonverbal cues. Your reliance on unspoken signs could vary greatly from that of other people.

Nonverbal Miscommunication

Some people believe they can expertly read body language, like airport agents, for instance. Security administrations have spent a lot of cash trying to train "behavior detection officers" to recognize the nonverbal cues that can identify terrorists. There have been so many critics claiming the operation has never been successful in stopping even a single criminal, among the thousands of passengers in a year.

Principles of Nonverbal Communication

Studies have shown that nonverbal elements of interaction have a crucial impact on the overall message you're trying to impart. Understanding these devices will allow you to take control of your own information. You can present exactly the data that you wish to convey. You can establish trust within the audience or the individual that you are speaking to. This is a powerful skill to possess both in business and in your personal life because it can change the way that others relate to you. You need to learn some principles of these cues as you start to hone your skills.

1. **Age, Geographic Location, Gender, and Culture are Vital**
   Gestures can have different definitions in various places or regions. Culture and family rules can also have some effect on the way you handle and react to nonverbal signals.
2. **Put Things Into Setting**
   When you see someone with crossed arms, it may mean they are chilly. Before you come up with any conclusions, try and place the interaction and the person into the setting of the topic, timing, and external inspirations.
3. **Combine Signals**
   You may agree with me that it's challenging for the whole body to lie. Someone may find it hard to hide their intentions, and this is because the true meaning will come out through other channels.
4. **Incongruence Will Have Several Implications**
   There are situations where words and nonverbal signals won't be in alignment, and your instincts will be necessary to judge the intent behind the interaction. When you have psychological discomfort, this can be an indication of distrust. That uneasy feeling could have a different meaning in another situation. When you ascertain a person's ability to

be attuned to nonverbal signals, then this can increase the chances that you will understand their communication.

5. **Trust Your Intuition**

   Intuition is an insentient process during which information is demonstrated through physical feelings. You should be authentic as people will pick up on insincere communication. When you are aware of the spoken and unspoken, then you will be able to heighten your people-reading skills.

Zones for Nonverbal Cues

Different areas of the body act to manifest these unspoken cues. To master nonverbal communication, you must learn about the function of these regions. Placing all of this knowledge together will allow you to get an accurate picture of the intent behind the words.

Face

This is the zone that gives the most noticeable and overpowering cues. The face expresses countless emotions without any word being said. Unlike the other zones influenced by cultural customs, it is considered to be universal. There are specific expressions for happiness or joy, being sad, angry, surprised, anxious, and disgusted.

Eyes

One look can display complex cognitive functions. You should note that too much eye contact is considered aggressive and will cause others to glance away with an inaccurate impression of your words. The eye can also assist in monitoring situations and the feedback of others.

Gestures and Hands

These are the indicators that will be affected mostly by cultural or geographic norms. In cases where you are working with international clients, be warned that gestures can have a different meaning. For instance, in Texas when you hold up your index and small finger to create a horn symbol, it stands for the "Hook 'em Horns". In Spain, this is considered an offensive signal. You should realize that hand movements and signs convey vastly unique impressions.

Posture

A person's position will define their attitude, confidence, and personality. The way you conduct yourself matters, and so does your posture. Sitting or standing up straight can convey that you are proud and sure of yourself or your work. Slouching may appear lazy or disconnected. The way you move can insinuate so much about you to your audience.

Head Position

How you hold your head will paint a picture of your disposition. Lowering your face can suggest insecurity. This movement will, most of the time, accompany a weak or closed posture. Raising your head can be a sign of interest. These behaviors can impact the message you wish to send.

Proximity

This will be all about your positioning and your space in relation to other people. Different factors will determine how close we sit or stand, next to someone. The distance will be established by social and cultural norms and the unique relationships of those communicating. Violating these standards can leave others feeling uneasy or as though you are communicating aggression.

Feet and Legs

How you position your feet and legs will be an accurate indicator of your relationship with your audience. These both act as a turning cue that will allow you to ascertain the interest of another party. The direction of someone's feet will indicate how eager and ready they are for you to move. You can look at the trajectory of the shoes of two people engaged in intimate conversation; they should be pointed toward one another.

You may also observe a group of people: feet that are positioned towards the inside of the circle indicate that the person is engaged. When the direction faces outside the ring, then the person is ready to move on. Paying attention to these body language cues will allow you to read the emotions of the people that you are speaking with.

Defining Verbal Communication

When people think about the word *communication*, all they think about is talking. Many of us depend upon verbal interactions to share information with others. The workplace is filled with such conversations. Written word falls under this domain also.

This book you are reading is written communication meant to shed light on human interaction, in general. There are different components of our definition of verbal communication and how it has impacts on our lives. This is the most direct form of data-sharing.

Verbal communication entails language that is both written and spoken. It is the use of words, whereas nonverbal is the use of other means such as body language, gestures, and silence. Both forms can be spoken and written.

A lot of people believe verbal communication only describes spoken dialogue. You will come to learn that this is not the case. When you joke with your friends, and they laugh, that is a form of verbal communication. Verbal communication is used to share agreed meanings with different components.

Incongruence Between Verbal and Non-Verbal Information

When you have experienced an emotion, it will be manifested in your facial expression. Due to this reason, many people will try to read someone's feelings by looking at their visage. The eyes, nose, and mouth all give away clues to someone's mood.

Recognizing facial expressions can be a crucial element in smooth human communication. Studies have examined brain activities and connected them to changes in the visage. The results show that people can trust or reject others based only on verbal interactions and facial expressions.

Your Mind and the Way You Communicate

The nature of the mind is very difficult to understand as it has hidden elements. It has been defined by psychologists in different manners. Since Sigmund Freud stated that the structure encompasses the conscious, the unconscious, and the preconscious, several psychologists have been able to understand the framework and how it influences our behaviors. These components include:

Engaged Mind - This state emerges when we is fully immersed in what we are doing at the present moment. When you cry about a sick friend or ski down a mountain, or when you eat a delicious slice of pizza; basically the attention or thoughts that are fully connected to the current happenings are the engaged mind. Those who are absorbed in their daily routines are always more satisfied and generally happier with their relationships and lives.

Automatic Mind - The brain impulsively performs a range of tasks. We, for instance, experience shifts in our environment, such as movements, changes in light or new sounds as well as bodily sensations and pains that are noticeable. During this mental state, we can make judgments or evaluations about things being negative or positive. We make decisions about things and categorize our experiences. The content of the automatic mind is influenced by atmospheric conditions, instincts, prior learning, and perceptions. This is essential for human survival and aids in adaptation, among other things.

Analytical Mind - Since humans possess self-awareness, this frame of the mind helps us to intentionally step back from our current feelings, experiences, and thoughts. We mentally observe and manipulate this information. This process includes all the complex reasoning that the brain is responsible for (64).

(64) Bradbury, Andrew (2006) – *"Talking Body Language"* in Develop Your NLP Skills Kogan Page

How the Unconscious Mind and Limbic Brain System Influence Behavior

The limbic system is responsible for your unconscious behavior. It influences your actions in a pattern of emotional response such as pain and pleasure. Experiencing joy usually results in a feeling of inner calm. When faced with threats it reacts by an instinct for survival mode. The common languages of this structure are either fear or peace.

The limbic system also feeds on your emotions. When you have a strong feeling towards certain situations or experiences, it tends to react with intensity. Human action can be manipulated easily by training the behavioral aspect of this part of the brain.

Important Aspects of the Limbic System

The limbic neurons are buried deep within the cerebrum. They influence your daily meditation and how you express your emotional, sexual, and social behavior. It also controls and monitors body processes such as your internal homeostasis and some basic needs such as hunger and thirst.

The limbic system is made up of many different regions of the brain that all play their part in our function. The hypothalamus is responsible for hormones, appetite, and sexual desire. The amygdala allows us to interpret emotions. The hippocampus, septal nuclei, anterior cingulate, posterior cingulate, thalamic nuclei, reticular activating system, orbital frontal lobes, and certain nuclei of the cerebellum are also part of this structure.

Of specific importance to unconscious human behavior are the hypothalamus, amygdala, hippocampus, and septal nuclei. They influence the emotional and psychic functions of your brain, such as meditation. The above regions come together to allow us to feel, experience, and express our desires.

The limbic system is also responsible for memory and emotions, which includes how you respond to rewards and punishment. The following are responsible for some of your unconscious behaviors:

1. The amygdala is responsible for regulating how you perceive fear. It also decides how you react to nervousness and

179

aggression. This area of the brain also has connections to other systems related to feelings and anxiety. It influences your facial responses and displays your unconscious perception of different emotions. It is connected to neurotransmitters related to stress and aggression.

2. Under the amygdala is the hypothalamus. This region helps in the regulation of your hunger, thirst, and sex drive. It also gives responses to the satisfaction of the mentioned needs by creating feelings of pleasure.
3. The hippocampus is critical in storing information in long term memory. Any damage to this area could result in amnesia.

The Old Brain

There is an area in our brains that has been present within the heads of our ancestors for hundreds of thousands of years. Before humans developed the complexity of consciousness that we are now studying, this was the mind that we used to navigate our world. This region sits in the innermost area of our brain and includes the stem. It is (and has always been) responsible for our most basic survival instincts. This structure is made up of:

1. **The Medulla** - This is designed to control your heart rate and intake of air. It influences how you eat, breathe, and move, thus sustaining your life.
2. **The Pons** - This is the part of the brain that helps to control your movements and balancing.
3. **The Reticular** - This formation has the primary function of filtering the stimuli coming from your spinal cord. It then relays the remainder of the signals to other relevant parts of the brain. Its other functions are influencing your walking, eating, sexual activity, and your sleep. Severing this part of the brain results in a coma.

Chapter 18

How Can Anyone Read People?

Mind-reading is essentially knowing what other people truly mean without them saying it out loud, or even despite them stating otherwise. Anyone has the potential ability to analyze others, with the right set of skills and training. It is, however, time-consuming and requires focus and patience. An open-minded approach cannot be overstated. The reader needs to be completely receptive to the subject's thoughts and nuances, far removed from any prejudices that they may have about the matter at hand or the environment in which the reading is taking place.

Particular attention should be paid to the subject's eyes, as they are said to be the window to the soul. A person's general personality should be noted too, which includes but is not limited to, appearance, overall behavior, physical movements, and, not surprisingly, the gut feeling you have about them. Listening to your intuition can be valuable with such matters.

Context

There are many reasons why you want to read someone's mind. Empathy is the most common reason because we long for a close connection with other people. Humans are social beings and this need is natural.

Most of the basic emotions, sadness, joy, fear, anger, surprise, and disgust are expressed in the same way across all cultures and races. This makes it easy to read such emotions in another person. The subtle nuances remain much harder to decipher, and it takes a dedicated person to learn how to interpret each person correctly.

We all seek ease when it comes to communicating with others. Reading someone's mind can help adjust how we react to any given situation. Relating also makes it possible to respond suitably.

This skill may also aid in lie detection. Being able to look past words to ascertain the truth is a valuable ability. This is most useful in criminology and law enforcement professions, where it is essential to know when and what information a perpetrator may be withholding. For example, a suspect who has an accomplice may not want to give them up. A terrorist with a bomb hidden somewhere may not want to reveal the location of the incendiary device. It is, therefore, necessary to have such analytical skills to decipher information that may not necessarily be spoken. Speed and accuracy are imperative in these instances.

The situation or the environment matters at the time of understanding any nonverbal cue. The same action done in a different setting or as a reaction to various circumstances could have a different meaning. For example, a cough in a draughty room could be just that, an innocent cough, whereas a cough after an especially awkward comment could be a sign of discomfort.

One should always be careful not to pay mind to stereotypes as a mind reader. People and their body language are as diverse as the fish in the sea. One person's 'tell' may not necessarily be another's. This is well evidenced by high stakes poker players who take time and resources to research their opponents and figure out their weakness to gain a competitive edge.

Considering More Than One Sign

Communication is done through multiple distinct channels; there is verbal, non-verbal, written, and visual. These are all used differently, according to the message you want to put across. For example, someone who is angry at someone else may text or write to them in capital letters to express their anger, which would be equated to shouting if the person re actually speaking their thoughts. It is essential to understand the subject's thought process and how it applies to all these.

More often than not, it takes a combination of signs to bring the intended message out clearly. A mind reader needs to learn by constant practice how to correctly interpret a combination of signs in the subject. For example, eyes downcast could mean that someone is ashamed. The same motion while continually looking outside or away from you may mean that they have something to hide, or that they are not interested in the current topic of discussion.

Signs are also vital because, for someone who may be living with one kind of challenge or other, they may need more than one way to understand a statement or concept. Likewise, they will also communicate with more than one sense. Examples include people with failing vision, the hearing impaired, and even people within the autism spectrum, especially those who may not necessarily understand typical social cues and need help interpreting them.

Not Knowing the Person

Reading a person unknown to you can pose a challenge, but it is still possible. Meeting someone for the first time is a whole new experience that registers as a 'new file' in the brain and sets the tone for consecutive meetings. Hence the adage "first impressions are very important."

Reading a stranger's mind may require more patience and more intense focus, so as not to miss out on subtle cues. One should be careful not to make the subject uncomfortable, though, and it is recommended not to stare for too long. An initial fifteen seconds should be enough to get a general understanding of someone without making them uneasy.

A short series of basic questions, like name and address, should elicit truthful answers. These inquiries can help establish a baseline for that person's facial expressions, tone of voice, and eye contact when they are telling the truth. Another generally accepted 'tell' is the firmness of one's handshake. A firm handshake may denote confidence, while a weak handshake may denote a non-committal attitude.

One should also consider other factors that could determine a person's responses. These include age and cultural background. For example, someone born in the forties or fifties may be more conservative on subjects to do with sexuality or religion than a millennial might be. Also, in some cultures, handshakes are not appropriate, especially between individuals of different genders. Being unaware of such a seemingly trivial matter could lead one to misread a subject who does not want a handshake or who gives only a fleeting one.

When reading a stranger, it is best not to make assumptions. Such haste can lead to misunderstandings. Take the time to learn the basics of an individual. A current mood may not be that person's usual disposition. For example, maybe they had a hard time finding parking and seem flustered, which is just a momentary state. Their real character should be evident once the agitation is over.

Biases

We should also be particularly careful about applying our own judgments and perceptions to the person whose mind is being read. These are referred to as cognitive biases. On the contrary, we should consciously strive to observe or listen to the other individual objectively and rationally.

Understanding these biases helps us to avoid the pitfalls of misunderstanding or wrongly interpreting the other person's responses or intended meaning. Being objective toward others is also a wise way to conduct oneself, in general. These preconceived notions are the halo effect, the confirmation bias, the actor-observer bias, the false consensus effect, and the anchoring bias.

The Halo Effect

The Halo Effect is also referred to as 'the physical attractiveness stereotype.' It is the tendency to let our initial impression of a person influence what we think of them overall. It has the potential to cloud our vision on the person's other characteristics just because we judged them at first sight. The more physically appealing someone is to us, the more favorably we are disposed to them, and vice versa, without taking into consideration the person's other character traits.

For example, a well-dressed person on the street would gain more of our attention and possibly admiration than a shabbily dressed person, yet the well-dressed person may be a ruthless grifter who preys on retirees while the shabbily dressed one could be an honest person down on his luck. This is also very much evidenced at job interviews, where one is encouraged to attend well-groomed to give a positive first impression. We associate attractiveness with benevolence.

The Confirmation Bias

The Confirmation Bias is when people lean towards information that seems to confirm previously held beliefs. It is a polarizing pitfall. People may listen to the same story but only pick from it what confirms their opinions, to the exclusion of all others. For example, a presidential campaign usually has supporters and opponents, and whatever a candidate says or does is sure to be interpreted to suit either side. It will be praised and touted by supporters, while the same action will be vilified and discredited by opponents. We should be careful not to let our own long-standing ideals determine what we hear and understand from the person whose mind we are reading. Instead, we should listen logically and rationally to reach an informed conclusion.

The Actor-Observer Bias

The Actor Observer Bias is when we perceive others and attribute their actions to several variables, influenced by whether we are the actor or the observer in a situation. That is, when it comes to our actions, we are more likely to explain ourselves by attributing faults to external influences while blaming other people's actions to their internal causes. For example, imagine being late to a meeting and saying the traffic was unbearable yet blaming another person who comes in a few minutes later by saying that they are just lazy. This kind of bias should be far from a mind reader's modus operandi. Otherwise, the exercise would only be clouded with endless blame games.

The False Consensus Effect

The False Consensus Effect refers to our tendency to overestimate how much other people agree with our own beliefs, behaviors, attitudes, and values. It stems from the fact that we spend most of our time with the same people, who tend to share our opinions. This leads us to believe that our thoughts are the same as the majority, even outside of our circle. Those who think like us are good and normal, while everything else is not. This is a dangerous attitude for anyone because it can easily foster intolerance.

Thinking this way limits our understanding of the subject's opinion if it differs from our own. For example, a spirited defense of the benefits of eating meat or animal protein may be unacceptable or repulsive to a vegan, who would thereby miss the subtle nuances of how the other is expresses sincerity and conviction. We must remember that the world is full of people from different backgrounds.

The Anchoring Bias

The Anchoring Bias occurs when we allow ourselves to be overly influenced by the first piece of information that we hear regarding any subject. This is a tricky cognitive device because it has a significant bearing on how a conversation or negotiation will proceed. For example, imagine hearing that "there is Ebola in Africa." This is a blanket statement, as Africa is a continent, not a single country, and the disease may be confined to only one country or one region, and the rest of the continent is Ebola-free.

An over-cautious European government may issue a travel advisory to Africa, thereby affecting many other countries that are reliant on tourism, though they may be Ebola-free. It also affects serious matters like medicine. A doctor can create an anchoring point, where his first impression on the symptoms a patient may present could lead to them giving a wrong diagnosis. This is the reason for the recommendation of a second or even third opinion, giving the new doctor a complete history of the problem, despite it all being in your medical file. Anyone trying to get to the bottom of a problem should be keen to take in all the information presented, and not be tempted to overlook important data based on the initial utterance. One who can do that will have overcome the anchoring bias.

Mirroring Body Language

This is a nonverbal and intuitive tool used to form a bond and establish a rapport between two or more persons. It helps to build a connection of mutual trust and understanding. Mirroring applies to all aspects of body language, including posture, gestures, accents, voices, and intonation. The most common forms are smiling and yawning.

Smiling when you see someone else smile immediately improves your mood. It is also very common to yawn within thirty seconds of seeing or hearing someone yawn. Even a fake yawn can elicit a real yawn in someone else!

To be perceived as being on the same wavelength or vibe as the person whose mind you are reading, it is advisable to mirror their body language. Be careful to copy only the positive gestures. For example, speak at the same tone and pace that they do. Talking too fast may make them feel intimidated or under pressure while going too slow may make you seem disinterested. Similarly, sitting upright is a positive body expression. You should not slouch, even if your subject is slouching. It could come off as lazy or unprofessional. It is also not advised to presume someone's feelings and use that to inform your behavior, as this can lead to miscommunication.

It is a documented fact that assuming a specific body language position identifiable with a particular emotional state makes you start to experience the said feeling. For example, steepling your fingers, which is connecting the fingertips of both hands and pressing them together, is a sign of authority and confidence. Doing this during meetings makes you feel more confident about the message you are putting across.

Men and women have also been shown in studies to have different ways of mirroring body language, generally. A person interested in reading minds should be aware of this in order to apply it successfully. Women tend to be more astute at picking up and interpreting psychical signals. They are able to flow more easily with a conversation through multiple changes in voice, gestures, and facial expressions.

Men, however, prefer to keep a mask-like appearance, which makes them harder to read. They do experience the same range of emotions but prefer not to show it on their face or with too much movement. This allows them to feel in control. Therefore, the more effective way to mirror a man is by matching his body language as opposed to trying to imitate his facial expressions.

Another important factor to consider when mirroring body language is your relationship with the person you are following. A subordinate mimicking the boss's dominant body language may be interpreted as arrogance. Matching the movements of someone who is trying to intimidate you, may disarm them and make them more agreeable. All in all, mirroring makes the other person see their own reflection in you, making them instantly comfortable and more receptive and trusting.

Chapter 19

Body Language: How to Interpret Non-Verbal Communication in Different Parts of the Body

In addition to speaking, we interact using body language. Nonverbal communication is significant in your everyday life. You can use these movements in addition to speaking, or on its own. It is, therefore, essential to look at people when they talk to us so that you see what they do as well as what they are saying.

Although your ability to communicate well using the spoken word is the key to passing or receiving messages to others or from others, it is your nonverbal cues that usually speak the loudest. So, what is body language? Body language is internal communication using your physical behavior, mannerism, and expressions. These are the movements that indicate our intentions to those whom we are speaking to.

This communication is done instinctively as opposed to consciously. Whenever you meet other people, you continuously display wordless signals with or without your awareness. You send messages using your nonverbal behaviors through the gestures you make, your body posture, the tone of the voice you are using, and the way you maintain eye contact with the ones you are interacting with.

The way you use your body language when communicating can result in different feedback from those receiving your messages. Your nonverbal cues can put people at ease, get them to trust you, offend them, bring confusion, or undermine the message you are trying to pass to them. You should note that unlike verbal communication, nonverbal messages don't stop once you stop speaking. You are sharing information even when you are quiet.

There are instances during which the messages you communicate verbally and the ones you convey through your body language conflict. When you are saying something, but your body language displays a different meaning, then whoever is receiving your message will feel you are not honest. For example, if you say "no" while you are nodding your head, then you only succeed in giving a mixt signal.

Importance of Nonverbal Communication

Your body language is essential in telling the listener whether you are honest or not. Your nonverbal communication should, therefore, match with your spoken word. When these signals agree, you not only enhance the message you are trying to pass, but also increase the trust, rapport, and clarity of the word.

If you are interested in becoming an efficient communicator, then you need to be very sensitive to your nonverbal communication skills as well as the body language of those you are speaking to:

Roles of non-verbal communication skills

1. **Retention role** – Your nonverbal communication is essential in repeating the message you are passing. The ability of others to understand your message is based upon the way you pass along information.
2. **Role of contradiction** - Your nonverbal communication cues can also contradict the message you are trying to pass to others. It will indicate to your listener that you are not honest.
3. **Role of substitution** - You can use nonverbal cues to substitute your verbal message. Your physical cues often create a more precise, stronger signal than your spoken word.

4. **Complementing** - You can use your nonverbal cues to add or to complete the verbal message you are conveying to others. For example, if you receive a pat on your back from your boss, then it sends a message of praise.
5. **Accenting** - Some nonverbal cues are used to emphasize the importance of your message. For example, you can pound the table to emphasize the urgency and importance of the information that you are passing to your audience.

Nonverbal Communication Cues and how to Interpret Them

Conscious vs. Unconscious Nonverbal Cues

Whether you are speaking or not, chances are you are always interacting with other people throughout the day. Most of your communication is through nonverbal cues sent via body language. So, if you are keen on what someone is honestly thinking, then you need to pay attention to their movement. Once you are adept at reading other people, you will gain an advantage over them because you get useful clues at what they are thinking about as they listen to and speak to others.

You will know how to react and respond to others appropriately. Nonverbal cues usually operate at an unconscious level. The messages are generated automatically and unintentionally by your brain. To be an excellent communicator, you need to train yourself to spot the gestures which others are displaying while they are interacting. In most cases, they don't know they are doing so, and that is why they are referred to as unconscious body language. Their motions will betray their feelings.

The unconscious signals can be released in the following situations:

1. When you first meet the other person.
2. When you are spending time with the other person.
3. When you are about to leave each other.

These signals fire off automatically and are common to all human beings, whatever the race or culture. The following are some of the universal unconscious body language indicators and how you can learn to identify and interpret them.

Interpreting Facial Expressions

Your head and visage are very expressive and effective instruments of communication. Faces express feelings such as anger, surprise, fear, disgust, happiness, and sadness. Indeed, these movements, more than any words, reveal a person's true feelings.

Your face conveys several messages unconsciously, even without you uttering a word. As compared to other non-verbal communication cues, this is universal. For example, the features that imply happiness, fear, disgust, and anger are collective across all cultures.

Learning the skill of reading other people's emotions, as expressed in their faces, is an essential aspect of human communication. If you can effectively recognize change in other people's features, then you can easily sense what these inner feelings are. You should learn to interpret several major types, among them:

How to Read Happiness - A face that displays the emotion of joy or happiness will always show a smile. With genuine pleasure, teeth will be exposed. You can also notice a line running from the nose to the corners of the lips. The person's cheeks should also be raised with their eyelids becoming tense or wrinkled.

You can easily recognize a smile that is not genuine by keenly observing the person's eye muscles. A mock smirk usually doesn't involve the muscles in the eyes. This is also common in any expressions, which aren't fueled by real joy or happiness.

How to Read Sadness - If you want to interpret a visage that displays sadness correctly, then observe the eyebrows of the other person. A forlorn face usually has brows that are drawn in and up. Moreover, the features should include triangulated skin just below the forehead. The person's face should also come up with the bottom lips pouting out. Upset is one of the hardest emotions to fake.

How to Read Contempt - A contemptuous or hateful face should have one corner of the mouth rising. This gives an impression of a half-smile, which is commonly interpreted to mean a sneer.

How to Read Disgust - If the other person has a face with downcast eyebrows and raised eyelids which causes the eyes to narrow, then that person is disgusted at someone or something.

How to Read Surprise - A surprised face should have their eyebrows raised in a curved way. The features should also include the skin below the brow stretched. Horizontal wrinkles should also be running across their forehead.

How to Interpret Fear - If the face of the individual has raised eyebrows, then the person is displaying the emotion of fear. The face should also have wrinkles between the brows, and such a person's upper eyelid should also be raised while the lower eyelid is drowned up in a tense way. The person's mouth can also be open with flared nostrils.

How to Read Anger - An angry person should have a face with lowered eyebrows that should also be drowned together. Their eyes should be bulging out with lines running between the brows. Such a person's eyelids are usually tense. Their mouths should be firmly pressed together with their nostrils flared (65).

How to Interpret the Expressions Eye Movements, Eye Signals, and Eye Contact

Popular society believes that the eyes are the "window to the soul." You can know other people's hidden emotions by looking at these features. You should know several different eye behaviors and cues, such as:

Blinking - Although this is natural, you can learn a person's inner feelings by observing the way their eyes blink whenever the individual is faced with different situations. When a person is feeling distressed or uncomfortable, they tend to blink their eyes more rapidly. When someone is attempting to control their emotions, they tend to do so less and infrequently.

Eye Blocking – When people don't like what they see, they usually cover or shield their eyes. This can also happen when people are faced with a threat, or when they're repulsed. This is usually interpreted to mean they are uncomfortable.

Pupillometry - Your pupils tend to dilate whenever you are exposed to low lights or when you come to the view of stimulating images. This happens to allow you to take in more of your

---

(65) Fast, Julius (2014) – *Body Language*. Open Road Media

environment. You can quickly tell if someone's interest is aroused by looking at their pupils.

Squinting - Squinting eyes express a strong dislike of what is before an individual. It can also be indicative of a dislike of something they are hearing.

Eyebrows - Raised eyebrows are used to draw the other person's attention to their faces to send clear messages. This often happens when the other person wants to be understood or whenever they are emphasizing a point.

Gazing - Gazing is used to communicate powerful messages, such as disagreeing with the opinion of someone. When you hold your eyes longer than usual, you send a signal that your views don't match up with what the other person is saying. On the contrary, this can also be used to communicate messages of love or intimacy. This happens when someone looks at you from your eyes, then mouth, and then the rest of the body.

Sideway Glances - This usually conveys the message of uncertainty and the need for clarification. If a person you are talking to makes this face with a furrowed brow, it could indicate they are suspicious of you. While a sideway it could interest, it is usually accompanied by eyebrows that are raised.

Darting Eyes - A person with darting eyes conveys a message of insecurity or discomfort.

Maintaining Eye Contact - It is important to look directly at the person you are talking with. Eye contact is essential when you are seeking to stress a point, or you want to show that you feel strongly about something. Whenever you maintain their gaze, you send a message that you are confident in what you are saying.

How to Interpret the Expressions of the Mouth

The mouth expressions and movements can give out several messages. For example, you display the feelings of worry and insecurity whenever you chew on your bottom lip. Moreover, whenever you cover your lips, you may be trying to hide your disapproval of someone or their actions. The following are some areas you should use to interpret the expressions of the mouth:

Pursed Lips - Pursed lips are indicative of disproval or distrust. It could also signal feelings of distaste.

Biting of the Lips - People tend to bite their lips whenever they are worried or anxious.

The Mouth Turned Up or Turned Down- Whenever you have feelings of happiness or optimism, you tend to turn up your mouth. On the other hand, if you feel sad or you don't disapprove of something, then the corners of your lips point downward.

Interpreting Body Gesture

You could be familiar with some of the most common gestures you use to communicate daily. Such as waving or pointing. You are also familiar with how to use your fingers to indicate numerical amounts.

However, there are many unique gestures used all over the world and across various cultures. You should note that many of the movements have different meanings in other parts of the world. It is crucial then, that you learn what signals mean to different people or societies.

The following are the most common gestures and their interpretation:

A Clenched Fist - A clenched fist is usually indicative of anger. In some cases, it is used to send the message of solidarity with your team or colleagues.

Thumbs Up and Thumbs Down - Thumbs up are commonly used to give your approval or consent. While thumbs down indicates disapproval.

The V Sign - This is a sign created by lifting your index and middle finger to come up with a v shape. The v-shaped sign is indicative of peace or victory.

How to Interpret the Arms and Legs

You can also get valuable signals from the extremities of others. For example, whenever someone crosses their arms, it may give a message of defensiveness. If someone crosses their legs when they are quite away from where you are, it could mean they dislike you, or they are not comfortable with you. The following are some of the other arms and legs body language:

Crossed Arms - Displays the messages of self-defense or self-protection.

Standing with Hands Placed on the Hips – Sends a message that the person is in full control or is ready for an undertaking. It could also be a subtle sign of aggressiveness in that individual.

Clasping of the Hands behind the Back - Indicates boredom, anxiety or anger.

Crossed Legs - Indicative of a person who is exceptionally closed off and needs their space and privacy.

Interpreting Body Posture

You can send several messages depending on how you carry yourself around others. Body posture can also give clues about your inner feelings and your personality traits. It can even be used to determine character traits like confidence level or submissiveness.

A person who is always standing or sitting straight indicates they are very confident, focused and attentive. Moreover, a person who does so with a hunched posture conveys a message of indifference or boredom.

The following are some of the signals you can use to read a person's body posture:

Open Body Posture - When an individual keeps the trunk of their body open and exposed. This posture sends a message of friendliness and willingness.

Closed Body Posture - Occurs when a person hides their body trunk by bunching forward. They also tend to keep their arms and their legs crossed. Such individuals display the message of anxiety, hostility, and unfriendliness.

Interpreting Touch as a Form of Body Language

You communicate plenty of messages through your touch. You should pay close attention to the handshake you receive from others as they can use this express their inner feelings. A firm hand shake tells the other person genuinely likes you or is interested in you and vice versa. There are also hidden messages in warm hugs, patronizing pats, or a controlling grip on the arm.

Interpreting Their Voice

Take into consideration not only what people say, but the way in which they do so. You can interpret the person's inner feelings by reading the tone they are using to communicate their messages. Pay close attention to such aspects as their timing and pauses whenever they are speaking. You should also notice their inflection and how loud they speak. These devices may be used to convey sarcasm, anger, confidence or affection.

Personal Space

You tend to feel quite uncomfortable whenever someone, usually a stranger, comes too close to you. This can feel aggressive or even creepy. Personal space refers to the agreeable distance between people as they interact. The distance you keep between you and another usually depends on their relationship with you.

Physical space between individuals usually conveys a wide range of nonverbal information. There are four levels of the standard social distance you may find yourself in, in the course of your interactions with others:

Personal Distance of 6 to 10 inches - This is a measured distance of between 6 to 10 inches from one individual to the other. Individuals who can comfortably maintain this length, usually share a closer relationship. This is often practiced by those who enjoy intimate bonds, such as those who are dating or are in romantic partnerships. It also occurs during intimate situations such as when hugging or touching or whispering.

A Personal Distance of 1.5 to 4 Feet - This level of distance usually occurs in family members or people who are close friends. When people keep a short length of 1.5 feet between each other, it indicates they are very close in their relationship. The higher the distance, the less likelihood of them being intimate.

The Social Distance of 4 to 12 Feet - This level of distance is often typical with close acquaintances. This is common with people who know each other well and who regularly interact with each other, such as colleagues at your workplace. In case you are communicating with an acquaintance whom you don't know well or whom you don't often meet, the length increases to between 10 to 12 feet.

The Public Distance of 12 to 25 Feet - This is the distance commonly used in speaking events. Some good examples of public distance are the distance between the teacher and their students during lessons. This is also practiced by the members of the clergy whenever they are performing their sermons. It is also common with politicians and other figures when they are campaigning or giving lectures.

Vocal Dynamics

Your vocal skills are crucial in effectively communicating with others, especially where you want to persuade, sell, reassure, or inspire others. What is essential is not what you are saying but how you do so. Words pass information, but it is the nonverbal communication that lends meaning to the message.

This means that you should always use color and emotion in addition to your body language. You must use your voice skillfully to encourage more influence. The following are some of the deviations that you can employ to engage your audience effectively.

Deep Breathing and Projection of Voice - Whenever you are speaking, ensure you are breathing deeply because your speech needs a sustained sound which you must control. When you can steady your voice, you can create your desired effects through your delivery of the words. To sound powerful, you should have enough air in your lungs to allow your voice to reach every corner of the room and reach everyone.

Pitch Inflections - This refers to the highness or lowness of your voice. Avoid speaking in a monotonous voice. You need to vary the pitch of your tone to sustain your audience's attention. This can also be used when you want to emphasize some points.

Voice Quality - You can use expressive voice quality to interest and persuade your listeners. Your sound could be harsh, pleasant, soft, loud, reasonable, demanding, assertive or passive.

Paralinguistic Communication

Paralinguistic communication deals with your voice and how you say your words. The way you speak reveals a lot about you. You need to study other people's paralinguistic signals and cues to understand their hidden emotions, which often can't be shown with the words of the speaker alone. For example, a person may speak in a loud, booming voice that conveys aggressiveness or a firm voice that conveys conviction. The following are some of the paralinguistic cues:

Rate or Speed

When someone speaks with rapid rates of speech, they display a trait of composure or self-assurance. Such persons also give out quick responses during the conversations. If you want to establish rapport with a person, learn to speak at the same haste they are taking.

Rhythm

Rhythm in international languages like English can be used to establish a person's language of origin. For example, a Frenchman tends to speak with a different flow as compared to someone from Singapore. The pacing of their first words often influences the way a person speaks English; for example, the French usually use rhythmical pace similar to that of their native French language.

You need to match the rhythm of your speech to that of the slowest person speaking, to communicate effectively.

Volume

A person who speaks in a loud voice often conveys some level of confidence, assertiveness, or boldness. If you want to appear confident, then you should raise your voice when speaking with others.

Pitch

A person with a low pitch often conveys greater credibility, authority, and maturity, while high pitch voices can sound squeaky or childlike.

Personal Appearance Skills

Personal appearance is an essential part of your communication and presentation skills. This is because the first impression matters a lot if you want to gain the acceptance and attention of your audience. The first impression can be about how you dress or your attitude.

People often make assumptions based on their appearance. They judge you based on your facial impressions, how you dress, your grooming, and generally your body language. The following as some of the personal skills you need to learn for success:

Clothes and Grooming

You must pay close attention to the clothes you wear and how well-groomed you look. You need to dress appropriately as each occasion demands. Looking put-together can give you an edge in any situation.

Some organizations have specific attire they expect their associates to wear when they report to work. Others are fine with casual dressing, while some expect a more professional standard. You should also groom well. Proper hygiene and a tidy appearance will help you to project a more clean-cut look. Respect is easily earned from strangers by looking like you know what you're doing.

Facial Expression

You need to appear jovial when performing your speech. Avoid a gloomy, disinterested look if you want others to take you seriously. Learn to convey a calm, friendly, and professional exterior whenever you are giving presentations. Project an image of confidence, capability, and enthusiasm.

Body Language

Body language is an essential part of personal presentation. Your movements help you to support and enhance your verbal message. You need to adopt the appropriate posture, gestures, and facial expressions if you want to be an effective communicator.

Factors that Influence Body Language

Having excellent communication skills is the key to effective interactions, whether at a personal or professional level. The following are the factors that may influence how well you connect with others. These factors are also vital in determining whether you interpret other people's messages correctly.

Nonverbal Signals - You must pay a lot of attention to nonverbal signals such as gestures, eye contact, and facial expressions whenever you are interacting with others.

Different Behavior – You should pay attention to the nonverbal behavior of others to determine if they are telling the truth or not. The expression should always match the words of the speaker.

The Tone of Speech - When someone speaks, focus on their tone. This must be able to convey a message similar to their words. Moreover, you can use inflection to know the speaker's inner emotions and feelings.

Eye Contact – This is another critical component of communication. When you maintain eye contact when speaking, you convey a message of confidence and interest. However, if you avoid it, this could mean you lack confidence or are dishonest. Too much eye contact conveys confrontation or coercion.

Context and Situations - Certain scenarios demand formal and crisp communication, like in business meetings. This is the opposite of informal occasions like parties. It is essential to match your nonverbal communication with the situation and context.

Practice – It's essential to monitor your nonverbal communication and identify the areas you can improve on. When you practice regularly, you will be able to improve your nonverbal interpretation signals in a better way.

Chapter 20

Our Bodies and the Way They Talk

Body language, also known as kinesics, is a nonverbal communication whereby physical behaviors are used to convey or express the information. Elements that are commonly used are body posture, facial expressions, eye movement, gestures and the use of space. Interpretation may vary from one country to another, but there are agreed-upon meanings behind specific.

Body language should complement verbal communication during social interactions. As a matter of fact, some researchers concluded that unspoken cues account for a significant part of the information relayed during interpersonal interactions. Our posture and movements play a vital role in conveying our feelings and emotions.

Nonverbal communication plays a major role in conjunction with spoken words. Our body language can reiterate our message, reinforce our statement or contradict our words. Therefore, it is important to keep these cues in sync with our emotions, since body language can either disagree with or emphasize the message. The conflict between our voice and body can make us appear deceptive and untrustworthy.

It is important to know the difference between open and closed body language when trying to understand the feelings, thoughts, and disposition of our audience (66).

Open Body Language – People with receptive personalities are better able to process information. Individuals with open body language tend to use their hands when speaking and are interactive and expressive. We rarely huddle up and cross our arms in the comfort of our own living room.

Closed Body Language – Displaying a closed posture has been tied to being unreceptive to new ideas. Closed personalities have hidden motives, and they tend to cross their legs and arms, keeping their hands close to their body. Monotone voices are used to express the same discomfort.

Positive Bodily Gestures

How we carry ourselves is important not only during usual conversations but also during interviews, formal discussions, panel meetings, group discussions, etc. It is hard for one to survive in a professional arena without positive body language. Our posture can convey the right information to the recipient or others.

Allowing yourself to seem open and willing to learn has an impact on the way others view you. Imagine you have just completed a job interview, feeling as though you aced every question. When the company picks another candidate, you are left wondering what you did wrong. The answer could be in your posture or gestures. Mastering your message will give you the power to control the way that others perceive you.

Below are movements that are generally understood to indicate positive body language:

Relaxed or Uncrossed Limbs

Relaxed limbs rarely cross one another, except as a position of comfort. They hang loosely.

---

(66) Fast, Julius (2014) – *Body Language*. Open Road Media

1. **Arms** - Tense arms are held close to the body and are rigid, but relaxed arms move smoothly or hang loosely. Crossing can indicate tension while folded may just be comfortable.
2. **Hands** - During the conversation, and we are anxious, most of the time we use our hands to hold ourselves or fidget to show tension. Allow yourself to find a natural stillness. Jerky movements are distracting and show your fear. Gestures are not tense or sudden, but are generally open.
3. **Legs** – Legs may casually be flung out or sit gently on the floor when sitting. They may move to a rhythm while you tap your toes. They may also be crossed, but not wound around each other.

When a person is controlling the upper part of the body and arms, legs can convey tension. On top of the table, one may appear relaxed, but the legs may be wrapped and held tense. It can be helpful to consciously relax your extremities before a professional meeting.

Open Palms

Palm gestures are commonly used in conversations, but do people really understand what they are doing or why? There are three positions one can form: closed fist, palms down, and palms up. Each of these gestures can relay a different attitude. Therefore, it is important to master and use them appropriately.

1. **Palms Down:** Palms down shows dominance, it is used to establish authority and superior attitude. It is a way to tell people you are in control and you are doing the talking. Intensity depends on how forceful the motion is or how inclined your hand is.

   This can also be a good device to prevent other people from interrupting your speech. You simply raise your hand when someone is about to interrupt, and you ask them to wait, non-verbally. Another example is when you raise the hand with your palms towards someone; by doing this, you are asking for patience. This can also mean you are creating a wall between you and the other person.
2. **Palms Up:** When someone places their palms up, they tell us that they are honest, trustworthy, and have nothing to hide. Our subconscious has accepted this as a credible way to show

sincerity. This explains why people who hide their hands during conversation appear a little suspicious.

This can also signal submissiveness. This is a way to gain trust and support by giving up control. For instance, with your palms up, you ask someone to do something, there is a high chance he or she will accept the request, not as an order but as a favor.

3. **Pointing:** This gesture can be annoying or useful. When we were growing up, we used it to point at stuff and to learn to count or name objects. As grownups, we also use it as a tool in teaching. However, pointing at people, especially with the thumb, is rude. It is considered as a sign to ridicule or a way to accuse someone. It is best to avoid this gesture unless your goal is a provocation.

The Speed of the Speech

The speed of your speech is a significant factor in how your audience will perceive the meaning, intent, credibility, impact, and emotional state of your words. If you want to capture the attention of others, you need to find a proper speaking pace to pass along the information. Effective speaking takes these factors into consideration.

In some situations, you may have to slow down your speech. For example, regional or ethnic accents can create barriers during communication. If you have a strong inflection, people from different areas or countries may struggle to understand what you are saying. Therefore, it is important to slow the haste in your voice to allow them time to process your words.

If you are a fast talker, you could be losing your audience. A good pace of speech ranges between 140-160 words per minute. Any rate higher than that can make it difficult for the audience to absorb the material. There may be countries or regions that speak at a faster speed but going slower is preferable.

However, a too slow speech speed can give a listener an impression that is incompetent, slow in thinking and being uneducated. Although, if you are a foreigner, measured speaking is important since it may be a challenge for the listener when it comes to your pronunciations. There is a comfortable average that suits most situations.

Pupil Size

During our conversations, we mostly look at the other person's face. The signal people send out with their eyes can reveal a lot about their attitudes and emotions. The Pupils react unconsciously to stimuli and, therefore, cannot be manipulated or controlled. Your eyes are the means of seeing what is going inside of you. This is why when people meet for the first time, they make judgments based on what they see.

When an individual holds a gaze, he or she is telling you one of these two things. First, they find you interesting or attractive or they are feeling hostility or anger. You can ascertain this by looking at their pupils. In the former case, the pupils are dilated, while in the later have constricted pupils.

Pupils will dilate or contract as mood and attitude change from negative to positive and vice versa. When one gets excited, their pupils will get dilated to up to four times the normal size. Conversely, negative moods or anger causes the pupils to contract. There is an easy way to remember this information: when the person wishes to take in more of the world (because they are pleased) the pupils expand. They shrink when the person wants to limit the flow of information.

Another example is the eyebrow lift, which is a long-distance equivalent of "hello" When they rise briefly, the purpose is to draw attention.

Leaning Forward

To establish trust and allow others to open up to us, we need to show them that we don't fear them and that we are not a threat. You do this by showing the willingness to cooperate. Leaning forward is a sign you are engaged and attentive to the conversation.

When people are involved in an interaction, they lean in to signal that they are listening to the information. This is a universal sign that the other party is consciously respecting your words. Use this device when listening to others, to encourage their trust in you.

Negative Bodily Gesture

If you have studied body language, I am sure you have come across this term before. Negative gestures are body movements that could give a bad impression to others. Even when an individual does not know how to gesture, he or she can still manage to get an inaccurate perception of your movements, because the subconscious will detect them.

Here are some of the postures that are related to negative body language gestures:

1. **Leaning Away:** Also can be referred to as leaning out, which signals people that you are not interested in them, what they have to say, or/and their ideas. This movement is important in dating, business, and friends. For example, propping yourself toward conversation when you are on an outing with your partner can show her or him that you wish to gain some intimacy, whereas doing the opposite suggests that you are not paying attention.

   During a business meeting, when you sit at the edge of your seat and lean in towards a person presenting, this shows you are keen to gain the information. While with your friends having lunch, when you sit leaning forward as you engage, you portray interest. These gestures all work in reverse to show the opposite.

   This action is still valid, even when standing. Leaning away can portray that you are closed off to the interaction. Do this when your goal is to communicate disinterest.

   Leaning back can also be used as a display of dominance. You can observe a pair of partners, to understand who is in control. Pointing your body toward the conversation can be a signal of submissiveness.

2. **Crossed Limbs**: People always, either knowingly or unknowingly, read our body language. Crossed limbs have a significant role to play in non-verbal communication.

   Crossed Arms: Crossed arms can be read by others to mean you are insecure, distant, defensive, anxious, or stubborn.

   Crossed Legs: It shows dominance and confidence when you sit with your legs crossed, ankle over the knee.

This is predominantly male body movement, but it is being used increasingly by women. Ankle lock is crossing your legs at the ankle while seated. This can mean that you are uncertain, holding back, or fearful.

3. **Tight Shoulders:** Tension can be telling for a person's state of mind. Anxiety and distaste can cause a constriction of the muscles around the neck. Stiffness is a sign that someone is apprehensive.

   Shoulders hunched up, usually with arms folded or crossed tight and holding the body, this can be a sign that the person is feeling cold. It can also mean the person is extremely uncomfortable. When an individual fears attack (actual or virtual), he or she raises shoulders and lowers the head to protect the neck. Our instincts dictate some of our movements without our knowledge.

4. **Feet Turned Away:** People rarely notice the secret messages their feet are sending to others. They have the ability to reflect our feelings. If a window to your soul exists in the eyes, then legs must be the signpost to what you are thinking or feeling.

   People do not pay much attention to how they position their legs when having a conversation. Therefore, if you are building up your body language, then perhaps it is best you add this positioning to your cluster of cues. Control the message that you share with others while also accurately reading anyone around you.

   When you are having a conversation with someone, if his or her feet are pointed towards you, then it is most likely that he/she likes you, interested in what you are saying, and agrees with you. However, if his feet are turned away from you, this can mean that he wants to leave and need to be somewhere else. It almost feels like they are already walking away. Being cognizant of what you wish to convey with aid in the smoothness of interactions.

5. **Leaning on Two Hands or Head Resting on One Hand:** It is possible that you have noticed people leaning on two hands, or perhaps you have found yourself doing it and you've wondered why. There are some physical reasons as to why our bodies react this way. Maybe you have been in the same position for a prolonged period of time, or you are tired, and this serves as a refreshing stretch. But that aside,

we want to understand why people are doing this, and what they are unconsciously saying when they assume this position.

Placing your hands behind your head while leaning backward can send two different messages. The information sent is dependent on the placement of the palms where the arms are placed. These two positions are referred to as the cradle and the catapult. Cradle can mean insecurity and a need for comfort, whereas catapult suggests dominance and aggression.

Resting your head upon your hand is another common behavior. This posture is telling us that the person is uninterested in the current situation and is a sure sign of boredom. Our movements will always give away what we are thinking about.

Torso

The torso is the trunk of the whole body and it contains all the major organs. The word is derived from the Latin "thyrsus", which means stalk. This area is also flexible. It can turn, twist, bend forward and backward. This is an area of the body that people have limited control over. Perhaps, that is why we have vital organs there. In simple words, it works without our conscious involvement.

Lack of our conscious control makes this a good indicator of our body language signals. When one turns their torso away, it could be an unconscious signal that they want to leave. It could also mean they are feeling threatened and are just trying to protect the vital organs. It could be an indication they don't like you and don't like to engage with you any further.

In a business setting, people turn their torso for different reasons: they are defensive or feeling insecure, or they are in a hurry. It could also mean they are hiding something, but no matter the reason, when it happens, it's a sign they are no longer engaged with you and are not entirely comfortable with you. These situations call for acting with care, so as not to offend the other party.

You can also send signals using individual parts of the body. Here are details of some of the contributions of each of those parts:

Neck Body Language

The neck is used to rotate and support the head, so it controls some body language. The neck can also relay few signals of its own, including:

Hiding - Neck is where a predator will aim, either to rip out the windpipe, or penetrate the jugular artery. When people feel an imminent threat, they will react by protecting this sensitive region. Some people can do this by pulling down the chin to protect the throat, and others may raise their shoulders to defend the sides. This is often not a conscious behavior on behalf of the acting party.

Turning – The neck can be rotated to enable us to look in many directions. This is useful to extend our range of vision. It can also be used to deliberately send a signal that an individual is removing or giving attention. The neck can also be rotated to exercise it which can signal tension or indicate boredom.

Shoulders Body Language

Shoulders too can be used to convey a variety of signals, including:

Raised Shoulders – Raised shoulders and the lowered head is used to protect the neck when the person fears an attack. This can signal that someone is uncomfortable or uneasy. Imagine someone approached and tapped on the shoulder by a stranger, this movement may happen as a way to recoil from the unwanted advance.

Curved Forward – This happens when one folds the arms. When shoulders are curved forward and hands down, it reduces the width of the body and, therefore, can be a defensive posture. The goal of this movement is to reduce the amount of space the person is taking up, as though they desire to be unseen. This is another demonstration of discomfort.

Pushed Back – When shoulders are pushed back, it forces the chest out, exposing the torso to potential attack. This shows the person is not afraid of attack, and it demonstrates power. This is dominant stance that people assume, right before they face a challenge.

Circling – This is done backward or forward, with both shoulders or one. This is a way to exercise a stiff shoulder which may have resulted from tension, indicating anxiety.

It can also signal that the person is preparing themselves for action, perhaps combat, and, therefore, can mean aggression. When done while the other person is talking, not minding to listen carefully, can be a signal of power.

Shrug – Classic shrug is a one-off raising and lowering of shoulders, which usually means "I don't know" and can be done with raised eyebrows. A quick shrug performed subconsciously may indicate a lack of understanding. It can also mean uncertainty. When a person shrugs instead of speaking, this can indicate that they are lying, as they fear their words may give themselves away. An animated and prolonged shrug can indicate preparing for aggression and thus signaling a threat. It can also indicate frustration or irritation in a smaller form.

Turning – If a person turns their shoulders while still looking at you, it probably means they want to leave. Perhaps because what you are saying is beginning to sound uncomfortable for them. Even when this gesture isn't meant in an offensive way, it signals that the other party is done with the conversation.

Chest Body Language

The chest can be used to send non-verbal body language signals, including:

Thrust Out - This movement attracts attention, and can be used to display romantic gestures. Women, for example, are aware of the fact that men are aroused when they see breasts. When they push forward their chests, they may be inviting intimacy or just teasing.

Men also push their chest forward to display their strength. They do this both for attraction and aggression. In the case of a mate, the man is saying, "I am strong and can protect you." In relation to a peer, he is suggesting "I am strong and had better not cross me."

Withdrawn – The chest cavity contains very vital organs and is vulnerable to attack. When pulled back, it indicates the person is attempting to hide or appear inoffensive. This can either be protective or a sign that someone is insecure and ill-at-ease.

Leaning – Leaning toward another person can have two meanings. Doing this can show interest in the other person. It can also indicate a more romantic attention.

Secondly, it can invade the space of the other person, thus posing as a threat. This is aggressive and often shows in dominant body language.

Hips Body Language

Hips are at the base of the body trunk. Without any doubt, they do signal certain messages in nonverbal communication. They aid in the movement of the torso when reacting to stimuli.

Thrust Out - Hips have primary sexual organs, and trusting them out is a provocative and suggestive gesture. The same movement may be used to mock and taunt others.

Held Back - This is the opposite of thrusting them forward, it hides the genitals, to prevent them from being noticed. This can be a defensive position indicating that someone is uneasy.

Moving - Hips moving from side to side is a common dance move. Any movement that is in tandem with a musical rhythm can show someone to be carefree, fun or sensual. Movement also attracts attention to that part of the body and hence inviting flirtatious actions. Moving hips back and forth, simulating sexual intercourse and can be considered arousing.

Hands Body Language

Hands are the richest source of non-verbal language, after the face. Some of the most commonly experienced gestures include:

Holding – Cupped hands symbolize holding a fragile idea. The movement can also be used to give an object to another by utilizing the bowl-like shape of the palms. Gripping can indicate ownership, possessiveness, and desire.

People can also use their own touch to comfort themselves every now and then, for example holding their own hands. Doing this can also be seen as an act of restraint, letting the other person talk. It is used when the person is angry, to stop them from attacking. The more forceful the gesture, the more intense the emotion behind it.

Control – Hands are used to greet people, and the most common way of greeting is shaking. For example, prolonged holding, using more strength can be an assertion of dominance.

Submission is revealed with a floppy hand, the palm facing up, and a quick withdrawal. Most of the handshakes are done with vertical palms, which indicates equality. Both partners withdraw from the action at the same time.

When Asking - Palms upwards is commonly used as a plea gesture, while facing downwards can mean asking the other person to calm down. Pressing one's hands together, with fingers upwards—the prayer position—indicates a more anxious pleading. Touching the chin while doing this can indicate thoughtfulness or unease.

Rubbing - Rubbing the hands can indicate the person is feeling cold. Massaging hands together is an indicator of anxiety and stress when the hands are tense. This movement occurs when a person is fidgety. Touching the chin can signal the person is evaluating, deciding, and thinking.

Leg Body Language

Our legs can tell a lot without us realizing it. This is because people normally focus on the upper body when they want to concentrate on their movements. Legs conflicting with the rest of the body show deliberate control and thus signaling what they are thinking.

Open Standing – Standing with feet open about the width of your shoulders is a relaxed pose and normal. A wider stance makes one appear bigger, hence signaling dominance and power.

Closed Standing – A person standing with feet put together displays some anxiety. This is related to the previously mentioned desire to take up less space.

Crossed Legs – Crossed legs while standing can mean shyness, especially when hands are held behind the back and the head is lowered. When sitting, this movement can take many forms. For example, an ankle cross while tucking your legs under the seat can show concealed anxiety.

Moving – A crossed leg that moves up and down, can indicate impatience. A leg might also swing to music, meaning the person is enjoying the vibe and is relaxed.

Walking – A person with a fast walk shows he or she is in a hurry while slowing down indicates that the person has time to kill. However, an unaffected walking speed indicates self-consciousness; the person is not concerned with how others perceive them.

Our bodies display these cues depending on how we are feeling and what we are thinking. People do this either consciously or unconsciously, based upon the setting of the conversation. Looking for these signs can allow us to assess what the person is feeling, even when it contradicts their words. We can also connect with others more effectively by learning how to use our non-verbal communication cues to complement our words.

Chapter 21

The Intricacies of the Face

Analyzing human behavior is much easier when we are speaking in-person to the individual we wish to analyze. When communicating with others, the face and head display some of the easiest to follow nonverbal cues. This chapter is going to break down common emotional displays that we can decipher using the visage and other body parts.

The Head

In human anatomy, this part of the body consists of a skull and other attached outer bone and cartilage components (including a lower jaw). The head is connected to the spinal column by a cervical vertebra, atlas, and attached to the body muscles, blood vessels, and nerves that establish the neck. This area of the body serves to protect the brain.

The term "head" can also be used to explain the anterior of animals and not only humans. It weighs 5 to 11 pounds (2.3 to 5.0kg). The face sits on the front and consists of the eyes, nose, and mouth. The mouth has a fleshy border to the oral void. Ears are present on either side of the skull.

Blood supply to the head is accomplished through internal and external carotid arteries. "Internal" refers to the inside of the skull, while "external" is on the outside. Areas in the scalp receive blood from the vertebral arteries that go up through the cervical vertebrae. Twelve pairs of cranial nerves provide mainstream nervous control to the head. Face sensation is given via branches of the trigeminal nerve. The cutaneous innervation of the head is like this:

1. Maxillary nerve.

2. Cervical plexus.

3. Ophthalmic nerve.

4. Dorsal Rami of Cervical Nerves.

5. Mandibular Nerve.

The head consists of two eyes, two ears, one nose, and tongue inside the mouth. The skull houses the brain. All of these previously mentioned organs are the processing center for the human body. Data is collected through the various orifices and then interpreted in the brain. Humans are capable of processing data so quickly, with the help of the central nerve cluster.

The Face

The human face is considered to be a distinctive feature that helps in the identification of others. We have short and retracted faces underneath a huge braincase. We will resemble those to whom we are related, but every visage is different.

The facial skeleton is formed by fourteen solo bones that consist of respiratory, digestive, olfactory, and visual systems. A vital understanding of the evolution of the human face in the hominin clade in the past 6 million years can be gained through the study of ancient bones. As more fossils are being unearthed and many more hominin species are discovered, there are still doubts about how the current human face came about (67).

---

(67) Ekman, Paul (1993) – *"Facial Expression and Emotion"*. American Psychologist.

By looking at the re-created faces of our ancestors, we can begin to understand their connection to us. Ancient civilizations survived through the same social interaction that we are learning about today. They lived their own lives in pursuit of happiness and partnership. Human communication has changed dramatically throughout the eras, yet we are the same at our core. Our civilization is still full of drama and intrigue. We are still fighting for the things that matter to us.

Our faces are now, as they were then, a window to deeply complex creatures. What is in a visage? We memorize the look of those we interact with, so that we are able to recognize them later. We use our own to show others when we are elated and when we are repulsed. These emotions radiate from us like a ripple through a disturbed lake.

Standard Facial Signals for Different Emotions

Reading the facial features of another can allow us access to their innermost thoughts. Learning this skill will be incredibly helpful in both a profession and a personal context. It is imperative to remember that, while you may know what someone else is feeling, you don't necessarily understand why.

You could interpret someone's movements as being closed-off without knowing anything else about them. They could have had an awful day. This individual could have received terrible news just before your interaction.

Learning about these displays can give you a massive insight into your own interactions. You can watch others react to your professional pitches, in real-time. Being cognizant of the impact you have upon others, can allow you to ace tough situations. We will be learning about deciphering the emotions of others.

Universal Emotions

Research says that there are worldwide facial expressions that bound across cultural borders. Even blind people will use similar facials to show their interpretation of emotions such as:

6. Surprise.

7. Disgust.

8. Anger.

9. Fear.

10. Contempt.

11. Sadness.

12. Happiness.

By practicing these various expressions that coincide with their respective emotions, you can be in a better position to read them from other people.

Micro-expressions

Not all the feelings stick around for an extended period of time. Emotions that seem to blink in and then immediately out of existence are referred to as micro-expressions. These can be instinctual blimps on your radar. The subconscious will interpret threatening behavior in others, even when you would rather not know.

Eyebrows

Others can't help but react to stimuli using their eyebrows; they may be raised and arched to show surprise or lowered and knit together to show anger. The inner corners of the eyes may be drawn up to express sadness.

Eyes

The eyes will tell you even more about an individual than the brows. When they are wide open, they will be expressing surprise. If you are staring intensely, then you are angry and when you have crow feet crinkles, then you are happy. Many people show fear or romantic feelings by blinking, and when they blink rapidly, it's an extension of being dishonest or being stressed.

Mouth

This is another essential instrument in the quest to understand the thoughts and feelings of others. When the jaw has dropped open, a person is reacting with surprise. Fear is displayed through an open-mouthed gasp. When one side of the mouth is raised that's a sign of hatred.

The corners of the mouth will turn up to indicate happiness and down to show the opposite. Anxiety will manifest through lip and cheek biting. People often purse their lips to show distaste. Covering the mouth can show you are keeping a secret.

Common Facial Signals for Different Emotions:

Finding Happiness

Happiness comes in various forms, and so many people may not know how to look for all of the signs. Some people will take pleasure in being pesky. You should know that you have everything you need to be joyful around you. So, learn to appreciate all of your resources (68).

1. Live your life with integrity.

To invite happiness into your life, try and live within your limits, beliefs, and opinions. The things you do and your values can allow you to be joyful. For instance, you can have a love for the environment; thus, you can keep in mind your carbon footprint. If you have a family, are you happy having them, and do you create time for them? Find out what matters most to your life and live your life appropriately.

---

(68) Ekman, Paul (2009) – *Emotions Revealed: Recognizing Faces and Feelings to Improve Communication and Emotional.* Life Malor Books

2. Enhance living in the moment.

You should focus your energy on living in the current and don't worry about the past. Enjoy the present moments and stop worrying about what happened in your before now.

3. Show gratitude every day.

When you always show appreciation, this will lead to feelings of being satisfied and being happy. When you show kindness to someone or compliment someone positively, then a feeling of pleasure will grow inside you. Show gratitude more often.

4. Satisfaction with your work.

When you are satisfied with the things you do, then it's a sign of being happy. The more you believe that what you are doing is meaningful, the more you can be satisfied with the changes that you make in the world. The passion may not even necessarily be linked to your career. As long as you are participating in activities that you find meaningful, you will find a sense of calm within yourself.

Common Signs of Sadness

Many people will try to hide depression, but they won't be able to hide the signs that indicate sadness. Many people may even fail to realize that they are dealing with this struggle. Various symptoms show someone is forlorn or exhausted.

1. Changes in weight and appetite

When you find yourself eating too much or too little, then depression is always a likely cause. You may find yourself turning to food to comfort yourself, but others may lose their appetite due to a change of moods. Variations in your meals may cause you to either loss or gain. Changes in your weight may also cause mental distress.

2. Changes in your sleeping pattern

Mood and sleep are linked very closely. When you don't have enough rest, then you can quickly become depressed. Sadness can also lead to a lack of sleep. A study from the national sleep foundation says that individuals with insomnia are ten times more likely to be depressed than those without the condition. Too much slumber can also create these problems.

3. Use of drugs and alcohol

You can find yourself taking alcohol or abusing drugs to cope up with feelings of being sad, lonely, or desperate. In every five people, there is one person that uses drugs to cope with depression, according to a study from the Anxiety and Depression Association of America. This is a Band-Aid fix for a long-term issue.

4. Fatigue

When you are chronically tired, there are high chances of being depressed. Research shows that 90% of individuals with the condition will also experience fatigue. Some people will be bored much of the time, but severe lethargy comes along with other symptoms and both can point toward mental distress.

Common Signs of Anxiety

There are various signs of anxiety disorder, namely:

1. You worry too much

When you find yourself worrying so much, then you are probably experiencing anxiety. Fear occurs in our day to day lives. Studies show that those around the age of 65 are exposed to anxiety disorders. Nerves can cause debilitation for some individuals, making it difficult for them just to live their lives.

2. You feel agitated

Your nervous system goes into overdrive when you are anxious. This can bring out a lot of negative effects within your body: sweaty hands, dry mouth, racing pulse, lightheadedness, depersonalization and shakiness. These intense reactions are caused by your system's "fight or flight" response. You are drowning in adrenaline, because your brain is sending out distress signals all the time. This makes you feel as though you are always in an immediate and deadly danger.

3. You are restless

This will be experienced in children and teens. You will feel like you are on edge or it can even be uncomfortable to move. A study done to 128 children with anxiety disorder showed that 74% of them were restless. Feeling an overwhelming nervousness, chronically, for six months can be a sign of disorder.

4. Fatigue

Being easily fatigued is a symptom of anxiety disorders. Your system is exhausted from the feeling of near-constant threats. In some cases, being worn out can allow panic attacks, while in others, the feeling can be chronic. You should note that this lethargy is a sign of depression and many other disorders.

Common Signs of Fear

Many signs of anxiety go unheeded because they could mean nothing on their own. The following symptoms indicate that you are fearful:

1. Heartburn

When you are experiencing anxiety, your body will manufacture too much stomach acid that can bring about heartburn. The solution could be found in therapy, instead of inside the antacid bottle. It can be a good idea to research the medical history of your family so that you can better trace the origin of this condition.

2. Lack of sense of humor

You will find it difficult to view anything as funny. This is because your heart is racing, and your palms are sweating. Humor is one of the best ways to calm your fears. You can assist others with anxiety by allowing them to have more recreational time. Finding a good escape from reality can be vital to calming the symptoms of chronic fear.

3. Skin rashes

Sometimes this is referred to as "hives". You may produce this symptom and never be aware of it, as it generally appears on the back. These rashes are a sign of fear. The next time you are experiencing an intense attack, find a way to check your skin for a reaction.

4. Exhaustion

Sleep is fleeting and hard to capture. Waking up in the morning is the most difficult part of your day. You dread the activities to come and feel drained all the time. This is related to lethargy and sometimes it can seem like it doesn't matter what you do, you will always feel worn down. These issues must be addressed with a psychiatrist or a doctor so that you can progress past them.

Common Signs of Anger

1. You call other people demeaning names.
2. You nitpick yourself and others and nothing is ever good enough.
3. You don't have patience with yourself.
4. There is trauma related to abuse in your past.
5. You are irritated and short-tempered.
6. You have a difficult time accepting responsibility when you have made a mistake. You blame everyone else.

7. You are physically aggressive toward objects, pets, and people.

8. Your family, friends, and coworkers avoid you or "walk on eggshells" in your presence.

9. People try to avoid bringing up complex issues to you, because you can't control your reactions.

10. People appear to be close-off and scared in your presence.

Common Signs of Envy or Jealousy

Below are some of the signs that someone is jealous (69):

1. False commitments

People who are jealous are also generally in denial. They will appear to be pleasant when you are speaking to them, but you will hear their criticisms through other people. These people can be difficult to read, and you may never find out their true nature.

It is advised to limit the flow of sensitive information with individuals that you aren't sure of. Watch how those around you respond to your successes. Envious people will make passive-aggressive comments and send backhanded compliments in your direction.

2. Not appreciating your success

Jealous personalities won't be able to value your success; thus, they will belittle your progress. They try to convince other people that you are not good enough. You should use caution with the friends you tell about your achievements; they may use the information later to belittle your accomplishments to others.

3. Friends boasting about their accomplishments

---

(69) Ekman, Paul (2009) – *Emotions Revealed: Recognizing Faces and Feelings to Improve Communication and Emotional*. Life Malor Books

Someone jealous will talk about their success so that everyone can recognize their progress. These individuals will also be voracious one-uppers and will try to outdo any sentiment you make. They will question the intention or goals of everyone around them whom they consider to be a threat.

4. Anxious to compete

When you have a jealous friend, then you will realize that they always want to show how superior they are. Such people will be full of envy and will always appear to be over-competitive. These individuals are not happy until others are aware that they are the best. They will also try to defame anyone who is perceived as more accomplished than they are. Humiliation is a pleasure for such a person.

Common Signs of Disinterest

You should look in your partner some signs in case you feel they are losing their interests:

1. No sexual desire

Couples all go through dry spells and that is normal. A chronic loss of interest in sex could be due to a number of factors that are not in anyone partner's control. Hormones can bring a sex drive from one hundred to zero, and all the way back. If you are in a relationship experiencing this issue, it can be best to look at the larger picture. Have you been through any recent changes? Is this due to insecurity? Are there any other symptoms?

This lack of desire could be a reason to worry, but only if you are noticing other signs that your partner is no longer interested. Look for manifestations of the other entries on this list before forming an opinion. It can be easy to take something trivial and make it a much larger deal.

2. Fantasy

When love is young, you will often find yourselves planning for a future together. This is a good indication that you are occupying a sizable space in the other person's thoughts. If you find yourself questioning your relationship, try asking your partner about their future plans. Do they struggle to answer? Have they stopped seeing you within those goals? These questions may help you to understand the motives of the person you love.

3. Going out often without your partner

Please understand that taking time for yourself is healthy. You should have your own interests and hobbies; your partner should support these passions. Going out alone is not a sign that the other person does not love you. There is a period in every relationship (that usually occurs around the two-year mark) when partners begin to reclaim a little bit of their space. This is completely normal.

Only you will know when the behavior reaches an abnormal level. If your loved one is going out without you constantly, this could be a bad sign. Watch how protective they are of their phone. Does it seem like they are talking to other people in a romantic capacity? Disinterest is never subtle; it is a harsh and unsettling change.

4. Lonely feeling

Has something changed about the amount of time that you spend with your significant other? Have they been diagnosed with depression or anxiety? Has work been exhausting lately? These are all normal situations that can bring about loneliness. These issues are also fixable and should not indicate that the relationship is over.

When you don't have any feelings of love towards your spouse, then there will be a craving for that brand of connection. Without fulfillment of these emotions, loneliness will set in. Don't be surprised when you find yourself being attracted to other people, physically. This is a sign that you are missing something in your relationship.

Common Signs of Interest

There are very many signs of interest:

1. Breaking away from friends

Notice how girls will start their night out by dancing together? This formation can offer them both comradery and protection. Separating a girl from her group may be a difficult task, as they stick together for safety. When she has an interest in someone, she may walk away from her crew to see the new person, alone. Feeling comfortable with another is a sign of intent and can mean that a connection is forming.

2. Falling in

Body language can give someone a lot of information about another person. You will learn from someone's expressions and movements, even without being told. One of the postures to look out for during attraction is a fall-in towards you. Someone will not inch closer to someone that they do not like. Leaning into the conversation is a sign of interest.

3. Seeking answers

When you meet another person, they form a snap judgment of you before you ever speak. Some information will be missing or inaccurate. You can fill in these blanks by asking and answering questions.

People who are interested in one another romantically, are thirsty for knowledge about the other person. Have you ever met someone and suddenly you find yourself wondering what they think about this or that? This is an indication that you are attracted to this individual. Interested parties will interview one another about even the most trivial information.

4. Facial exploration

You can tell so much about a person from watching their features. Someone who is interested in you is going to hold a steady gaze toward your face. This can be explained both by attraction and by our need to know more.

Maintaining eye contact can also be a sign that another party is interested in you, romantically. This is done to show that they are listening to you and can become a conscious effort in nerve-wracking moments. Look for a slow and constant stare from the person you are speaking to.

Common Signs of Boredom

Being chronically bored can be a sign that you need to seek out hobbies or alternative forms of entertainment. Apathy has the potential to strangle passion, which can lead to a host of other issues. The following are signs you need to add some spice back into your life:

1. Most of your time is spent on the phone

Being on your phone is not all bad because we have a need to connect with the people around us, including family and friends. Nevertheless, when you spend most of your time on a device, then this could a sign that you are missing stimulation. Many people use their electronics to avoid being bored. Wasting large quantities of time searching through apps can be a signal that you need a new hobby.

2. Sleeping a lot

When people are depressed or apathetic, it only makes sense to sleep the days away. Excessive slumber means that you need to find a new place to devote your attention. Find something that you enjoy doing and put effort into this skill, talent or pastime.

3. Loss of personal interest

A common symptom of depression is loss of interest in activities you used to love. When your passion no longer lights up your life, this can be a cue that you need to reinvent yourself or find something else. Joy does not have to be a fleeting emotion. Find the motivation to turn yourself into the person you want to be.

4. You daydream

This can be an imaginative escape from nagging reality. If you find yourself daydreaming most of the time, you should find a way to make the real world exciting again. Forming an interest can have such a positive effect on your emotional state.

Common Signs that You are Searching for Relief

There are cognitive symptoms such as; memory issues, lack of concentration, poor judgment, only being able to recognize the adversity, anxiety, and constant worrying. Physical symptoms such as: being dizzy, chest pains, and heart rates increasing, loss of sex urges, increased illness, constipation, and aches.

Behavioral symptoms such as: eating more or loss of appetite, too much sleep or lack of sleep, neglecting duty, engaging in drugs and alcohol.

Emotional signs include: being unhappy, agitation, angry, isolation, and mental distress.

Common Signs of Stress

Some of the following signs might indicate you are suffering from stress:

1. You are overemotional

Being emotionally fragile and sensitive can indicate that you are having issues with stress. Crying all the time shows that your mental state is unbalanced. Dealing with these issues through therapy can change your life for the better.

2. Overworking

Overworking may result in you being stressed. Becoming anxious can happen for various reasons. Working too much can be a sign that you are avoiding other areas of your life.

3. Moody

When you find yourself always moody, then this is a red flag that something is wrong. There may be some hidden cause making you feel overwhelmed. Feeling this way can bring about a loss of perspective that you won't be able to cope with.

Common Signs of Disgust

1. Anger

Rage is a feeling that connects naturally to feeling that you have been treated unjustly. You can be displeased with any number of things, but when it begins affecting your mood, you need to seek help. These symptoms tend to build to the point of explosion.

2. Fear

This may involve worry over a consequence you will face or just an unpleasant situation. Fear has the ability to consume us, which is why these feelings should be taken care of before they spiral out of control.

3. Sadness

Being disgusted will make you feel frustrated with so many things around you. You will find yourself becoming sad or overwhelmed by these circumstances. These feelings can be addressed properly and overcome.

Common Signs of Shame

Shame does not listen to logic and has the ability to crawl beneath our skin. The symptoms of this emotion include:

1. You want to disappear

You will want to bury your head in the sand or to run away from all people. You won't be in a position to even answer calls just because you are ashamed. This feeling can spawn from an incident or may just come from nowhere if you have issues with insecurity.

2. Anger

Some people react to shame with anger. You will find it easy to blame other people and not take responsibility for your actions. Learning to control your own emotions can help you overcome this hurdle.

3. Addiction

When you have feelings of guilt, then you may find yourself trying to use drugs to give temporary relief. Addiction can result from the abuse of recreational narcotics for the purpose of escape. It can be imperative to address your trauma before you lose your impulse control.

Common Signs of Pity

1. Struggling with everything

When you are in a state of self-pity you will find yourself struggling with a lot of things like relationships, health, and finances. You will find yourself stuck in a negativity tar pit.

2. Distorted reality

You will see things in a warped lens. Everything in your life to you will be horrible and you will always complain. You will have a perception that your life is worse than it is. This negativity may cost you relationships with friends and family.

3. Depression

Pity can be a symptom of depression, which can be difficult for other people to understand. Sadness consumes some people and they need time and space to pull themselves back out. Do the things that relax you. Focus on your own healing and do not place pressure on yourself when you fall short of your goals.

Common Signs of Calmness

1. Handle issues as arise

You won't anticipate problems. You will handle the issues when it occurs. You do not hand your responsibilities off to others and you do not panic. You are a problem-solver and you can stay cool under pressure.

2. Treating yourself kindly

You don't blame yourself for past mistakes or the weaknesses that you have. It is unfair to dwell on bad things that you can't change. Your disposition toward yourself inspires those around you.

3. Always happy even when things are not okay

You will be able to give yourself some emotional space and try to recover from sadness and disappointments. You recognize that problems are fleeting. You aren't bogged down in the details of every little thing that doesn't go your way.

Emotions and Appearance

1. Throw away conventional ideals of beauty

You have to realize that you won't change other people's definition of beauty, but you can alter your own. Stop focusing on the examples you see in advertisements. Try concentrating on the vision you have created for yourself.

2. Take the focus off of your appearance

Looks will always fade away with the sands of time. Nothing lasts forever and even the most youthful skin will eventually wrinkle. By focusing on what you have to offer, as a person, you can ensure that you always admire yourself. You can be exactly the person that you have always wanted to be. Dropping these shallow standards will allow you to adopt new and impressive interests. You can enrich your personality.

3. Don't be afraid to feel bad

Negative emotions are natural. We learn and grow from our pain. You can use the traumatic experiences of your past to shape the person you become. Kindness and patience are necessary along the path to self-discovery, but the results can be impressive.

4. Smile

Smiling is infectious. People want to be around others who are pleasant. We want to surround ourselves with others who exemplify our values, and fun is important to everyone. This can also serve to make you more approachable.

Trustworthiness

Trustworthy people are always surrounded by loyal friends. You will be hurt from time to time, but the experiences that you gain will make your pain worth it. Honest individuals are in short supply.

The Chin

Chins are bony attachments to the face. Connection to the jaw allows for movement when chewing and talking. This is an important element of our face but does not (itself) contain the ability to emote.

The Mouth

This is an entrance to both the digestive and respiratory systems. The mouth has been lined by mucous membranes pink in color when you are healthy. The gums will be paler color and fit very well around the teeth.

The Nose

This is an important structure amid the eyes and serves as the entrance to the respiratory tract. The nose contains an olfactory organ. It gives you air for breathing and also serves to enable the sense of smell.

The Eyes

The eyes are slightly asymmetrical globes, an inch in diameter. It consists of the iris which is the colored part, cornea which is a clear dome over the iris, pupil which lets light inside your eyes, sclera which is white in your eyes, and the conjunctiva which is a thick layer that covers the front part of your eye expect the cornea. This is one of the most expressive parts of the human face (70).

(70) Ekman, Paul (2009) – *Emotions Revealed: Recognizing Faces and Feelings to Improve Communication and Emotional.* Life Malor Books

Chapter 22

Personality Types

The personality of an individual is associated with their behaviors. We spend a lot of time talking about personality and describing people's traits. Many people don't really understand what it is. Even though, we know it is what characterizes a person, psychologists have different definitions to explain the term.

What is Personality?

Personality, according to Randy Larsen and David Buss, remains static throughout the life of an individual. It is a collection of patterns, thoughts, behaviors, and feelings that influences a person's interactions with the environment. We form our traits based upon our genes and our environment.

Feist and Feist, 2009 define personality as involving a unique characteristic and a pattern of permanent traits that gives a person's behavior some consistency and individuality. Funder defines it as all the patterns of thoughts, emotions, and behavior, and every hidden psychological mechanism influencing those patterns.

Even though there are different definitions of personality, we can find some common factors in each description. They all mention patterns of behavior and characteristics that predict a person's behavior. We will compare the categories below.

Categories of Personality

There are four categories of personality:

Introvert vs. Extrovert

In 1960, Carl Jung, a psychologist, described the two personality types: introverts and extroverts. Each has different ways of regaining their energy. Introverts seek a quiet environment while extroverts like being around people.

Many people associate introversion with shyness and having low self-esteem, while others think introverts don't like people. This is not true; introverts may appear sheepish because they keep to themselves and don't like attention. Being timid has a connotation.

Most introverts are comfortable in their skin. Cain mentioned in her book *The Power of Introverts,* that they are warm and interested in other people while also being influential in their own right. When given a chance and space to think, they can come up with great ideas. They are capable of profound insights.

Even though introverts don't always like sharing their problems with others, they will choose outlets such as writing. Many artists share this personality type. They learn to express their thoughts and feelings through other means.

Extroverts, on the other hand, enjoy the company of others. They are outgoing and like talking. While introverts seek time alone to get inspiration, extroverts find motivation from interacting with others and exploring the outside world.

Extroverts are also associated with being the center of attention. They tend to get energy from talking and engaging in social activities. When faced with problems, they will choose to talk it out, unlike introverts who decide to keep to themselves.

They also do not shy away from taking chances. In a recent study, theorists found out that when extroverts engage in risky behavior and succeed in it, they get a boost of dopamine. This is the chemical neurotransmitter responsible for feelings of pleasure, which is precisely what extroverts crave.

Case Study

Mike and Sarah are both seniors in Millbrook High School. The pair attended the same institutions from the time they were in first grade. They didn't find themselves interacting too often. They both have different personalities. Mike is the quiet and reserved guy who prefers to keep to himself. Sarah, on the other hand, is the talkative type; she attends every party and interacts with almost everyone.

On weekends, you will mostly find mike at home, either reading or working on a project. Mike will choose not to go to the party because it's loud and he doesn't want to be in a room filled with new people. Sarah, being an extrovert, will gladly accept any invitation instead of sitting at home on a weekend night.

Sensing vs. Intuition

People use sense and intuition in their daily lives. It's how they have survived in this world. Even though everyone has these traits, one of them is mostly predominant. A person will be more comfortable using one, unlike the other.

Carl Jung believed there were different personality types that dictated how people perceived information. These also had an impact on the thought process and in how people make decisions. Sensing and intuition are all about how a person processes information. It is reported that sensing people make up the most significant percentage on earth. These individuals were also likely to be female.

Sensing people pay more attention to their immediate environment and what is happening in the moment. They are better with processing sensory information that they can see or hear and even touch. Besides being practical and active in their responses, they will often refer back to their past experiences before making any decisions.

There are different sensing personality types, according to Jung. They include:

ISTJ - Introversion, sensing, thinking, judging. Also called The Assessor, they are known to be responsible and reliable. They are quiet and serious in everything they do. For this reason, you will find most of them are successful in business and personal affairs.

When faced with a matter, they take their time to assess the situation and also incorporate logic before concluding.

ISFJ - Introversion, sensing, feeling, judging. Also referred to as The Guardian, they are cordial, quiet, and responsible. They can be trusted with assignments because besides meeting deadlines, they are able to produce quality work. People around them can trust them because they are loyal, and they remember important details about people close to them. They also like to be in a neat place where they can relax and be in harmony with those around them. People with an ISTJ trait value loyalty above everything else. They also respect traditions.

ISTP - Introversion, sensing, thinking, perceiving. Also known as The Expert. ISTPs are known to be flexible and tolerant. They are logical in their thinking. They don't involve emotions in their thought process. They focus on critical details of a matter, considering facts before concluding.

ISFP - Introversion, sensing, feeling, perceiving. Also referred to as The Artist. They are known to live in the moment. To enjoy life with enthusiasm, ISFP is known to go with the flow. Those around them may find it hard to understand or even know them. However, for those who have gotten the chance to really interact with them will tell you that they are friendly and kindhearted. People with ISFP traits are known to be creative, which is why most of them are in the arts industry.

ESTJ - Extroverted, sensing, thinking, judging. This personality type is also known as The Overseer. These individuals are considered hardworking and diligent. When they take up a challenge, they will see it to completion because they are strong-willed.

ESTP - Extroverted, sensing, thinking, perceiving. Also known as The Persuader. They are able to get people on board and make things happen. They are lively and jovial when conducting an assignment. They are well suited in harsh and situations that are considered critical. They don't take things to heart even when given criticism.

ESFJ - Extroverted, sensing, feeling, judging. Also called The Supporter. People with these traits are known to be friendly. They are also good at following rules and caring for others. ESFJs loved to be liked and they have a strong desire to help and make others happy. They are generally popular, and they soak up the attention.

ESFP - Extroverted, sensing, feeling, perceiving. Also known as The Entertainer, they are the outgoing type. They love fun and prefer sharing their adventures with the people around them. ESFPs are likable, and they attract people with their charm and warmth.

Intuition

People with intuition personalities like to go beyond their limits. They seek to explore uncharted territory. They want to challenge and question everything that does not make sense to them. Even when they have found an answer to something, they will pose the question, "what if." Intuitive people are best for situations that require deeper thinking and innovation or a diverse perspective because they are able to see the bigger picture.

ENTJ - Extroverted, intuitive, thinking, judging. Also known as The Chief. They are naturally decisive and hardworking. They like debating and analyzing situations. They focus hard on achieving their goals.

ENTP - Extroverted, intuitive, thinking, and judging. They are known as The Originator. These individuals are innovative and can see all the possibilities in almost everything. They are also considered inventive.

ENFJ - Extroverted, intuitive, feeling, judging. The Mentor. They care about others and desire to assist them with reaching their potential. They like helping others so they focus on multiple possibilities, even during challenging situations. When it comes to relationships, ENFJ strives to establish a meaningful connection with the people they love.

ENFP - Extroverted, intuitive, feeling, perceiving. Also called The Advocate. A person with this characteristic makes a leader who is enthusiastic and charismatic. They go the distance, for what they truly believe in. They are also known to be resourceful.

INTJ - Introverted, intuitive, thinking, judging, also called The Strategist. They enjoy planning and they strive for perfection. These individuals can also adapt to different situations because they are flexible.

Case Study

You are walking on an unfamiliar road with different turns, heading to town "B" from town "A." Just before you get there, a man going the opposite direction approaches you and asks for directions to get to a shop, on the way to town "A." As a person with sensing personality traits, you will direct the stranger to this shop, clearly mentioning which route he should take to avoid getting lost.

An intuitive person using the same route is asked for directions for getting to the shop. Even if he has used the road a couple of times before, the chances are that he will struggle to remember the directions. These individuals are daydreamers and hardly pay attention to reality.

Thinking vs. Feeling

According to Jung, thought and feelings in a person are modes of judging. Thinking involves the mind, while emotions generally come from the heart. Thinkers rely on logic before making established decisions. This means they won't go back on what they have decided.

In a work setting, thinkers are always professional. They focus on their work and have no time for unnecessary interruption. People around them often assume that they are coldhearted and unfriendly. This doesn't mean they have no emotions.

On the other hand, people who rely on feelings for their decision making don't use logic. They consider things like how their choices would affect those around them, social settings, and their hearts. Empathy could be a motto for these individuals.

In a professional setting, feelers are more social, unlike thinkers. They take a few minutes of their time to interact with others. People find them more likable. They are more open to people, which means they quickly get hurt.

Case Study

In a Chicago law office, two coworkers Dan and Steve, are heading out of their elevator.

On the way to their offices, Miriam, their litigator, comes to them and she shares her weekend experience. She will be in-laws soon. Dan congratulates her on her new engagement and quickly dismisses himself and heads over to his office. Steve stays behind to listen to Miriam's story because he would like to know more, and it would be rude if he left without listening to her.

Dan is obviously the thinker here.

Judging vs. Perceiving

No man is an island. We all interact with each other on a day-to-day basis. When we connect with others, we tend to use judging and perceiving. These traits are present in every person, but one is always more predominant. This can be observed through the way one interacts with the other person.

Judging involves organization, order, and structure. People who judge plan to complete their tasks and observe deadlines. Perceiving involves keeping options available. They are flexible in how they act. When they take on a new assignment, perceivers find joy at the start of the task instead of its completion. They are curious about their environment and find pleasure in exploring the boundaries.

Case Study

Susan and Angie are both friends from college. They have both recently secured employment at a firm in their hometown, even though they planned on living in the city. Nonetheless, they are excited because the job offers them unique benefits and room to grow.

Susan is especially happy because her job is flexible; it allows her to work from home. On one particular day, they were offered an assignment that was to be completed in three days with a presentation. So, Angie immediately received the project and wrote down a plan on how to work on it. She then focused on the job and completed it two days before the deadline.

Susan, on the other hand, took her time, and for the first three days, she spent the hours visiting friends and engaging in other work.

Until two days before the deadline when she began working on the assignment. She made sure she was highly energized before taking up the action. Angie is the judging type, and Susan is obviously the perceiver.

Personality or Environment?

Does DNA influence personality? Numerous studies have been conducted to ascertain whether the character is nurtured or is a result of nature. For quite a while, it was believed that personality changes very little throughout a person's life. However, a few psychologists have disproven this theory. It is now understood that there are a few changes that take place over time. However, it is difficult for these shifts to occur.

We have previously mentioned that each person has two different traits. For instance, introverts have a bit of extroversion in them. When it comes to the dominant trait, which in our case is introversion, a change occurs, but it will be very minimal. The introvert becomes more outgoing. Nonetheless, this doesn't mean that the person's personality will transform into extroversion.

The extrovert will also become more like an introvert in some ways. He/she may choose to have their moment away from all the hullabaloo of the world. When the personality changes, it has just been modified to include a few traits of introversion. The shifts that occur are as a result of the different experiences that each person encounters throughout their lives.

The other question is whether the environment has any effect on a person's personality. The environment shapes us. There are different factors present in the background that influence our character. The place we live in, the people around us, and our daily interactions affect us.

Researchers have been conducting studies on foster families, twins, and even adopted children to understand more about the environmental effects on our personalities. One of the studies carried out in Minnesota on 350 twins who grew apart, from 1979 and 1999, showed similar traits within the siblings. This information has expanded our understanding of the subject.

The twins that were included involved both identical and fraternal twins. They shared the same characteristics even though they grew up apart. Identical twins, who were separated, showed similar traits. Fraternal twins also showed some identical characteristics, while they grew up without one another. Even though this indicates that genetics influence a person's personality, researchers found out that the identical twins in the study shared about 50% of the traits while the fraternal twins included only 20%.

The study suggests that both genetics and the environment affect a person's personality.

The Four Temperaments of Personality

The temperaments are one of the oldest personality traits. It has its origin from the medical field of Greece, where it was used by healers to treat illnesses. Even though the tradition is from ancient times, it is still used by many people practicing traditional healing.

Temperament is formed from birth and remains the same throughout the life of a person. The brain stem processes determine a person's temperament. When you find a person with a different temperament, it means their brain stem works differently from everyone else.

The concept behind this typology is humorism, which comes from the word "humors." They are the fluids within a person's body. This fluid is responsible for the temperaments in people. There are four different types of temperaments:

Melancholic

Melancholic people seek to contribute to the environment in whatever way. Besides being social, they are thorough and accurate in their dealings, which is why they make great managers. They also respect traditions; that's why you will still find some women cooking for men and men being respectful (like pulling out a seat for a woman). Melancholic individuals excel in careers that involve administration, management, and even social work.

Choleric

Someone with choleric temperament is focused and goal-oriented. They always use logic in their decision making. People close to them find them to be unfriendly and not fun to be around. They are also considered to be impatient and are quick to anger. Men are mostly considered to have this trait because testosterone is dominant. Choleric people are aggressive and self-centered. They don't take their time to nurture or work on any relationship.

Phlegmatic Temperament

Most people with this trait are introverts. The majority of them are also females. They follow the given rules and despise it when people go against the establishment. They also like making people happy. They put other people's needs first, even when it costs them.

Phlegmatic people also have a high level of emotional intelligence. They empathize with others even if it's someone they don't know. These individuals are prone to being taken advantage of.

Sanguine Personality

People with sanguine personalities are known to be adventurous, lively, and cheerful. They find joy in being around people. You will always see them talking and discussing ideas because of their creativity. They have no problem with making friends.

A sanguine person has difficulties with tasks. When given an assignment, they may delay in completing it or forget that they had a responsibility to begin with. They also don't pay attention to what they are told; they talk more than they listen. If they find you annoying and not up to their fun activities, they will immediately dump you for someone else.

Chapter 23

Deception

Generally speaking, deception involves some type of cheating or trickery. While deception may not necessarily involve fooling someone into believing something that is not true, it may involve manipulating someone's perception of the situation around them.

A simple example of this could be tricking your boss into believing that you are sicker than you really are, so you can get an extra day off. While you are not lying insofar as being sick, you are exaggerating the extent to which you are actually ill. In this case, there is a great deal of trickery, even though you are being relatively forthcoming.

Deception is widely used by manipulators to get their way, especially when the circumstances surrounding their plans don't favor them too well. Think about people who include false information on their resume in order to get a job or manipulators who pretend to be someone else when seducing a potential romantic partner.

The ways in which deception can take place are numerous. Likewise, the motivations that a person may have can be quite abundant. It is important to keep in mind that an individual may feel compelled to resort to deception when they feel that they are unable to get things on their own. This means that when a manipulator estimates that they won't be able to achieve something by traditional means, they will resort to deception to get it.

Depending on the type of ruse, this can be a one-time affair, meaning that they will get their way, but the end result will alienate them from the people they affect with their machinations. On the other hand, deception may be well-timed, meaning that the manipulator may be able to keep the ruse going for an extended period of time. There have been cases in which manipulators can keep a deception going on for years without raising the slightest bit of suspicion.

Types of Deception

When dealing with deception, it should be noted that not all deceptions are created equal. This implies that there are various forms in which a manipulator may go about deceiving their victims. So, here is a list of the various types of deception which can be implemented (71).

1. *Lies*. This is, by far, the most common type of deception. The degree of effectiveness of the lie will depend on how clever and credible it is. If the lie is outrageous and exaggerated, then there may be little chances the lie will work. However, the truth may be more outrageous than a lie. So, when you build up your trust capital, people will be far more likely to believe you. Nevertheless, you need to be careful not to get openly caught. Otherwise, you may destroy your entire trust capital.

2. *Equivocations*. This type of deception consists in making inaccurate or ambiguous statements. This is used to avoid giving a straight answer to a question or providing enough information, which may be damaging in some way. Equivocations are also common when a manipulator does not know the answer to a question.

---

(71) Carson, Thomas L. (2012) – *Lying and deception: theory and practice*. Oxford University Press.

3. *Concealment*. This tactic is about hiding information. The reasons for withholding information may vary greatly. For instance, the manipulator may be looking to cheat someone into agreeing to something. Also, concealment can be used in an attempt to justify actions that we have done or not in any given situation.

4. *Exaggeration.* This tactic is quite common. Exaggeration can be seen in the embellishment of accomplishments, or perhaps in the effects of a given situation. So, just like exaggerating the symptoms of an illness, a typical manipulator will exaggerate their injuries in an accident. Moreover, exaggeration may be used to avoid doing a task by indicating that it will take far longer than anticipated.

5. *Understatement.* This maneuver looks to minimize a fact or situation. Perhaps a manipulator is looking to downplay someone else's achievements out of jealousy. Also, a manipulator may look to minimize someone else's symptoms when ill. All of this is done to create a feeling of inferiority in the victim.

6. *Misrepresentation.* This technique looks to provide an alternative perception of the truth or reality. When this occurs, the manipulator may attempt to convince the victim that things did not happen as they think, or things happened in a manner that isn't entirely accurate. Misrepresentation may appear to be similar to gaslighting, though gaslighting generally involves a denial of abuse. As such, misrepresentation doesn't seek to deny events happening; it simply looks to provide an alternative interpretation of what really happened at the convenience of the manipulator.

Main Components of Deception

Deception is predicated on the gullibility or ignorance of the victim. Manipulators will do their best to scope out people who don't know any better. That way, they can lie, misrepresent, exaggerate, and so on, without their victim actually being able to tell the difference.

Therefore, deception preys on people's lack of knowledge in a given area. But beyond that, deception is also about the logic and common sense that goes with it. For instance, it is far more believable to say that you are a neurosurgeon than an astronaut. While you may, in fact, be an astronaut, the fact of the matter is that doctors are far more common.

In addition, the execution of the deception is critical. Skilled manipulators will deliver lies so naturally because they actually believe, for a fact, that the lie they are telling is real. This plays on the old adage that a lie is "not a lie if you really believe it." The most skilled manipulators are able to embrace their lies to such a degree that they are able to convince others it is really based solely on the sincerity with which they were able to deliver it.

However, it should be noted that the devil is in the details. So, the more detailed a deception can be, the more credible it will be. For instance, if a manipulator is looking to understate someone's accomplishments, the manipulator had better produce another accomplishment that can top the one they are looking to understate. If they lack an accomplishment (whether real or not) that can top the accomplishment that they are looking to downplay, the manipulator may simply look foolish.

Lastly, deception is a pattern of behavior. Manipulators don't generally use all types of deception. They tend to use one or two types more than the rest. As such, it is possible to detect patterns in their behavior based on the type of deception they commonly use. For example, a person who tends to exaggerate their accomplishments will do so every time they have an audience who will listen to them. By the same token, they may attempt to downplay others' achievements when they feel bested by someone else.

Simulation

Highly skilled manipulators will go as far as creating the circumstances they need in order to carry out their plans. While this may require a good deal of planning and organization, they may very well have the means to do it.

Consider this situation:

A fraudster is looking to deceive a bank into giving them a loan. One simple approach may be to present the corresponding paperwork and lie about their income. Ultimately, the bank may, or may not, approve the loan. Simulation occurs when the fraudster falsifies documents that prove employment, income and so on. Under these circumstances, the level of sophistication with which fraudsters can produce the necessary documentation may prove to be very complex.

A good example of this is identity theft. When thieves are able to get enough real information on a person, they can create an entirely fake persona using real information. Therefore, the victims may very well fall for the ruse as the cover seems perfectly legit. In the end, the fraudster may, or may not, get away with their crime. But the important thing to keep in mind is that they are able to pull off clever and sophisticated "simulations" by creating situations and circumstances which very closely resemble the real thing.

In the end, your powers of perception will allow you to detect whenever anyone is looking to deceive you. However, there are times when a ruse is so cleverly put together, that it might be virtually impossible to tell the difference. In the meantime, it is always important to trust your instincts. It could be that you may not be able to tell the difference straight up, but something inside you can tell you whether you're dealing with a ruse or the real deal.

Using Deception

First of all, it should be noted that deception is not to be used lightly. When a person habitually engages in deception, they may end up exhausting their victims. As a result, they may need to move on and find a new set of victims.

Think about a romantic relationship that was formed under false pretenses. There may come a point in which the victim eventually realizes the manipulator is not being entirely forthcoming. This may lead to a series of questions and issues in which the end result may be the termination of the relationship. At this point, the manipulator has no choice but to move on and find another victim.

When using deception, it is important to keep in mind your behavior. Any deviation from your usual behavior may tip off victims that something is up. Some manipulators like to keep an aura of unpredictability, thereby keeping their victims off balance. However, if you abuse this approach, you may end up being dismissed as a whacko. As such, no one will believe you when you are trying to push your agenda long.

Being consistent is highly important. When you're consistent, people will believe you because you are not deviating from your usual self. Therefore, no one will have any reason to doubt your actions. In addition, whatever deception you're looking to carry out, it must be congruent with your persona. Thus, if you're looking to pretend to be rich, then you need to create this persona from the beginning. Otherwise, it may be hard for others to believe that you have suddenly come into money.

Lastly, when using deception, gaslighting and misrepresentation need to go hand in hand. You need to convince your victims that what they perceive to be real is not. Also, you may have to adamantly deny certain events in order to keep the deception going. If you fail to acknowledge this, you may end up being betrayed by the circumstances around you.

A good example of this is when others around you make comments or tell stories that contradict what you're trying to push across. In this case, you need to have solid counterarguments and be insistent on why these people are wrong. You may even have to justify their actions by framing their motivations in such a way that others side with you (72).

In the end, your deception skills will grow in the measure that you are able to practice them. If you are serious about implementing deception into your way of life, then it's a good idea to progressively build up the level of sophistication with which you carry out these tactics.

How to Detect Deception

The easiest way to detect deception is when you know, for a fact, that someone is not being truthful. For example, you can immediately pick up on exaggeration because you know that the events that occurred did not happen in that manner. Also, you can pick up on a lie because you are aware of the truth.

While this may seem like a very simple way of detecting deception, it is often the most effective. Generally speaking, most manipulators

---

(72) Carson, Thomas L. (2012) – *Lying and deception: theory and practice*. Oxford University Press.

won't stop to think that others around them may have a keen understanding of the events they are looking to misrepresent or embellish.

Things get tough when you are dealing with a skilled and able manipulator or you don't have any idea regarding the veracity of the lies being put forth. In such cases, your only recourse may be to ask questions. The truth is that when you see something that may not be too believable, you can dig deeper by asking questions.

Consider this situation:

A manipulator is looking to boast about how much they paid for their car. If you happen to know how much the car costs, you can determine if they are lying or not. However, if you don't have any idea how much the car really costs, you can begin by asking questions about the car itself. Perhaps you can keep them talking long enough so that they contradict themselves. When this occurs, you can catch them in their deception.

Often, detecting deception is just a matter of keeping your eyes and ears open. When a manipulator is looking to pull the wool over your eyes, your better judgment will keep away from falling into their trap. Moreover, using common sense generally aids in detecting when someone is looking to deceive.

Chapter 24

How to Identify a Lie: Key Behaviors that Indicate Deception

Deception is something that we have all dealt with, in one form or another. Everyone has told a lie, no matter how hard they have tried to walk the "straight and narrow." We avoid the truth to keep from hurting the feelings of those around us. We do it to keep ourselves out of trouble or to dodge responsibility.

You can learn to detect dishonesty in others. This can be a useful skill when your job mandates that you do such. Interpersonal matters can also be improved with the ability to seek out the truth. Below, you will find a list of features to watch in order to know when you are being lied to (73).

---

(73) Vrij, Aldert; Hartwig, Maria; Granhag, Pär Anders (2019) – *"Reading Lies: Nonverbal Communication and Deception"*. Annual Review of Psychology.

The Eyes: Clues to Revealing the True Intention

The eyes are one of the most principal expressive areas of the face. They may act as deception detectors. Reading dishonesty is dependent on the non-verbal cues, and thus through the eyes, it becomes easy to reveal the exact intention that an individual has. The eyes also communicate the next action that someone is likely to take, whether bad or good.

A break in eye contact is one determinant of deception. This occurs when an individual refrains from directly looking at the other party. This action is associated with no emotion other than shame.

In most cases, it is essential to understand that those who tell the truth are able to directly look at the other individual. They don't feel ashamed of their actions. Whenever someone breaks the eye-contact sometime after the conversation starts, then this is a clear indicator that they have changed their intention. This shift is evidence that such individuals are lying.

Consequently, detecting deception through the use of eyes is complex since it requires the interviewer or the investigator to continuously ask various questions. It is applicable whenever an investigator applies a series of questions to a particular subject, which requires the person to conform to the process.

To determine if these individuals are lying, they are allowed to diverge from the main subject, which is an indicator of deception. In the session which involves questions and answers, it is the principal role of both parties to maintain eye contact. Keeping this gaze could allow the liar to avoid detection, but they are likely to be unable to manage their movements. It is essential to note that as a principal organ, the emotion of an individual is directly tied to the movement of their eyes (74).

---

(74) Carson, Thomas L. (2012) – *Lying and deception: theory and practice*. Oxford University Press.

Body Language

Body language is a vital aspect of detecting deception. We all gesture unconsciously while we speak. Watching someone's movements may allow you to discern if they are being honest on the subject matter. These motions are composed of various components: including head movements as well as breathing.

Body language is essential because it portrays exactly what an individual feels. Whenever someone's movements (such as that of the head) do not complement the various affirmations and verbal denials, then it is a clear indication of deception. Consistency is imperative during this process.

A good example is a consistency in the head movement. Whenever an individual's head steadily moves, it indicates that they are telling the truth. Whenever they nod their head erratically, they are lying. Most of the investigators fail in the determination of dishonesty because they don't correlate the inconsistencies which are observed between the nonverbal behavior and also the spoken words. It is vital to note that whenever someone is comfortable about what they are saying, the body movements (specifically the head) conform to their words.

One essential element of body language which can be applied in the detection of deception is the aspect of breathing. Individuals who lie are often burdened with fast breathing due to the increased speed of their heartbeat. Interestingly, other than rapid breaths, whenever an individual starts lying, they are plagued by fear. This eventually results in a change in the breathing pattern. Deception is detectable through watching these features.

The Hands

Hands also act as a determinant of deception since truthful individuals are not nearly as worried. They can easily spread their fingers. Those who are insecure, due to their lying nature, need to fold their palms and also tend to try to occupy a minimum amount of space.

Interestingly, liars are also known to fold their legs since they strongly believe whenever they occupy too much space, they could be easily detected. Furthermore, deception can be determined whenever an individual's fingers or hands tremble without any climate change noticed. They may also attempt to cover their appendages with a sleeve.

Most of the individuals that are experts in the art of dishonesty will barely move their hands or bodies. They speak in a measured tone and are very careful not to give away any extra information with their motions. Someone who is tasked with interviewing a known conman would be wise to watch for this lack of change. No one sits completely still.

Slouching may also serve as an indicator that a person is lying; it directly helps in boosting confidence. While yawning, those who are being deceptive also stretch their hands to ensure they can confuse the parties that they are addressing. Watch for motions that could be used to misdirect attention. Liars are either going to have a decent poker face, an issue with fidgeting or weird and disjointed gestures.

The Face

Facial expressions also play a significant role in the determination of lies. There are several types of facial movements that clearly indicate an individual is dishonest. This is the most expressive region of the human body and should be watched intently.

Facial expressions may be caused by various emotions (like nervousness) and other physical reactions. They can be identified to act as a scale for detecting dishonesty. One of the common ways to identify that a person is lying is when someone blinks their eyes between four or five times, within less than a minute.

The closing of eyes can also be used as a way to show that someone is lying. Under normal circumstances, an individual should not close their eyes when they answer a certain question. Whenever an individual shuts their lids for more than two seconds, it is a clear indication that they have not told the truth.

Based on the facial expression, deception can also be detected whenever an individual who is right-handed is asked a question regarding what they had seen in the past, and they look to the left side and upwards. They are directly lying to you and they are trying to diverge your attention. However, whenever they look right side but upwards, they are sincere. These are some of the facial expressions which clearly show an individual is lying.

The Voice

Variation in the voice is also one of the ways to determine whether a person is lying or not. In most cases, the trembling sounds are associated with fear. Under normal circumstances, it is essential to note that an individual's tone should not vary in every answer that they give.

Whenever an individual's voice trembles as they answer complex questions, it is essential evidence that they are lying. The shakiness is an indicator that people are applying various kinds of defense mechanisms. This is mostly observed among those who cannot justify their claims. It is essential to conclude that someone's voice gives a direct glimpse of whether they are lying or not.

Big Lie vs. White Lie

You may have encountered people telling lies in their everyday life. Some of these are categorized as "big lies and white lies". In the two forms of lies, a person intentionally deceives the other person or groups of persons by communicating misleading information.

There is a big difference between big lies and white lies. In big lies, the deceptive person tries to gain something from the deceived person. This means that the dishonest individual seeks to exploit the other party, out of self-interest.

Telling a lie to gain personal benefit is condemned across all cultures of the world. For example, a used electronics dealer may mislead his/her customers about the condition of the TV he/she is selling. The salesperson will pass the device off as being in a good working condition, even when they know too well that the TV is faulty. He/she will then sell the TV at a high price in order to maximize the profits.

On the other hand, white lies involve manipulating information in order to motivate or please the deceived. Sometimes situations may compel you to mislead others. You may be forced to say what the other person is expecting to hear, even when the situation is different. For example, you may have told your friend how great their new hairstyle was, even when you secretly loathe it. You do this to make your friend happy.

White lies usually don't harm the other person's feelings. In fact, when you tell a lie in order to please the other person, you are just exercising an innocent part of your daily interactions. These are sometimes necessary to keep the peace.

The difference in the two types of deceptions lies in the motives of the deceiver. While the big lies are often condemned, the white lies are sometimes encouraged depending on the context. In some scenarios, white lies cause harm, especially when you use it to foster relationships and connections. When you desperately want to bond with others, you tend to agree with all of their opinions in order to please them or to gain favor from them. This may greatly hamper your decision-making skills.

Case Studies of a Big Lie and a White Lie

Case study 1

Big Lie: Black Men are Inherently Violent towards White People

White supremacists have long held a destructive belief that black people present a threat of violence and rape to white people. This narrative has been prevalent in the United States for so many years. The idea is used by the nationalists to justify calls to oppress black people. These sentiments are echoed under the pretense of protecting the country. Our case is that of a 21-year-old white man called Dylann Storm Roof. In June 2015, Roof walked into a Charleston church and fired 70 rounds of ammunition on a Bible study group, killing many and injuring others. While he was shooting, he kept shouting, "you have been raping our white women, you have been taking over the world."

He saw himself as a victim standing up for the "oppressed whites" rather than the aggressor he was. Some white supremacists' websites spread big lies like that the black people are waging a war against the whites. A good example of such a website is that of the council of conservative citizens.

258

Case study 2

White Lie: Telling White Lies to People with Dementia can Actually Help Them

There is new research that shows if you tell a white lie to people suffering from dementia, it can actually help improve their condition. These are beneficial to such persons because it serves to ease their stress and to reassure them. Imagine slowly forgetting everything that you knew. Being comforted is important.

The research which was conducted by NUI Galway, Ireland, focused on people with memory problems. Such persons usually keep asking for their loved ones, especially the deceased ones. The study found out that lying or giving incorrect answers to such people actually prevents them from being distressed. However, the study considered blatant lying that deceives and harms, as unacceptable.

The study also established that it might be acceptable for caregivers and other health professionals to tell white lies in certain situations. However, before you do this to the patient it was important to consider the wishes of the family. Every patient is a complex person with unique needs (75).

Other Things to Note: When it is and When it isn't okay to tell a White Lie

When it is Okay to Tell a White Lie

1. When Someone Asks How You Are

When you pass greetings to your friends or acquaintances ask how you are, the standard response to such a question is usually "I am fine, thank you, what about you?" This answer applies even when you are experiencing problems. The person asking you that question is probably being polite; they don't actually have the time or interest to listen to your challenges.

2. When Complimenting Someone

---

(75) Vrij, Aldert; Hartwig, Maria; Granhag, Pär Anders (2019) – "*Reading Lies: Nonverbal Communication and Deception*". Annual Review of Psychology.

It is fine to tell a friend a white lie when you are complimenting them. If they are sporting a new haircut that you dislike and they ask for your comment, it is okay to tell them you like it because after all, there is nothing they can really do to change it now.

3. When You are Late for Work

If you know telling the truth about why you are late for work will get you in trouble, it is okay to craft a good lie to save your situation.

When it is Not Okay to Tell a White Lie

1. When You Want to Delay the Inevitable

If you are hiding something from someone that you wish to reveal later, then avoid telling small lies. These may lead to other bigger lies that will get you found out. It is always best to be honest from the onset in such scenarios. For example: imagine you are out shopping when you spot the significant other of a close friend, out with a different person. You should immediately tell your friend, so the situation doesn't spiral out of control.

2. When You Are Ending a Relationship

Once you feel uncomfortable dating someone you have been with for a while, it is a good idea to communicate your feelings as soon as possible. Make it clear to them that you are no longer interested in the romantic relationship. Don't give them false hope with your white lies.

3. When Someone Needs a Wakeup Call

When you feel there is some information that someone needs to know in order to improve their decision making, then it is wise to tell them the truth, even if being honest will make them uncomfortable. A good example is an artist whose performance is horrible. Such a person needs to be told honest truths rather than white lies in order to improve their performances in the future.

Chapter 25

How to Analyze Yourself

Through self-awareness, you gain an understanding of yourself and your personality. You can also get to know about your behaviors and tendencies. Part of this process is coming to accept the unsightly corners of your own mind you would rather keep locked away. It is through embracing our whole being (even the darkness) how we are able to achieve true contentment. Some strategies listed below will allow you to take a closer look at the person that you have become.

Be Aware of Your Feelings

Notice Your Thoughts

Your thoughts are essential in defining who you are. They will assist in guiding how you feel and your attitude and perceptions of situations. You should keep in touch with your mind. You need to be able to tell whether they are harmful, if you are pinning yourself down, or within which areas you are hard on yourself. This reflection is good to encompass all of your perceptions, even the ones that need to change.

Keep a Journal

Keeping a journal can be a wonderful way to stay in tune with your patterns. Emotions and reactions will be documented. You can review the pages to gain an objective perspective on your values and consistency.

Be Conscious of Your Perceptions

Your perceptions can lead you astray, thus making you have the wrong conclusions about what occurred or what you saw. For instance, you can blame yourself that your friend was mad at you during lunch break; thus, you will think you did something wrong. When you are conscious of your interpretation of her mood, this can assist you in knowing why you came to the conclusion that she is mad at you.

With such situations, you are supposed to take your time to study your moves and beliefs about what happened. Write down what you saw, heard, or had feelings about that made you understand the situation the way you did. You must be able to get answers about what made your friend moody, and if there are any outside reasons, you should be aware of it.

Identify Your Feelings

The feelings you have will readily tell you the person you are from the way you react to situations you have at hand and the people around you. You are supposed to try and analyze your feelings and how you respond to different topics, interactions, tonal variations, facial appearances, and body language.

You should be able to tell why you have certain feelings and why you experienced such emotional responses. You must understand how you are responding, and what directed you to make such choices. You are allowed to use physical cues to assist you in understanding how you feel.

Scrutinizing Your Values

Know Your Values

When you are aware of what you value, this can give you an overview of who you are at your core. Many of your beliefs are based on your individual experiences. They will change, the more you get to know about yourself. You may find it very difficult to identify your values at times. The concept can be intangible and unclear.

Identify Your Values

Values are the beliefs that you remain loyal to. They are usually based on morality. There are some things that you believe that others may not agree with. One of your core values may be to never steal. This is an idea you have thrown meaning behind, and you hold to this sentiment even when theft would benefit you in a significant way.

Your values describe the type of person you are. The caliber of friend or partner you are (to someone else) may be based upon these ideals; the things that you consider important. Defining unmoving moral mission statements can take some work! Imagine knowing off-hand, every aspect of yourself that you consider to be worthwhile. Most people aren't able to do this.

Start identifying your values by inscribing answers to questions like:

1. Think two people you admire, what qualities do they have that make you admire them? What particular thing do they believe to make you admire them?

2. Think of the person you hope to be in the future and write down all the positive aspects of their character.

3. What are you passionate about?

4. What good thing have you done, even when it would have been easier to walk away or take advantage?

Plan Your Core Values

When you have answered the above questions, you should have an idea of the qualities you consider important. Writing these values down will allow you to create a map. Pick one or two of these at a time, and form a plan for being the sort of person who better embodies these beliefs. You have always been completely in control of the person you are. It can be so easy to forget that we are steering this vessel. Our daily grind can fog up the lens of our abilities. **YOU** decide all you wish to embody.

Do you look up to people who are brave? Right this moment, plan an activity that places you outside of your comfort zone. Do you want to be charitable? Call that homeless shelter, right this instant, and offer your services. You are being the steering wheel. You can be as cool, well-red, honest, or kind as you want to be.

Discover Yourself

Write Your Story

Writing down your story can be both fun and rewarding. This is your chance to document the events that changed you and the beliefs that you hold dear. Not only is this a brilliant way to pass the time, but it can also allow you to look back on your life, like a spectator. Can you imagine the feeling of accomplishment that will come from completing a project of this nature?

Evaluate Your Story

After writing down your story, you should be able to evaluate yourself by asking yourself questions like:

1. What are some of the themes that recur in your narrative? Are you always saving people or you are the one who is always saved? Is your story based on a topic? Is it a love story, drama, comedy, or some other genre?

2. What is the title of your story?

3. What are the chapters your story is divided into?

4. Have you labeled yourself and others in the story?

5. What kind of words are you using to talk about yourself and the others? Are you using positive language?

6.

Resolve What Your Analysis Means

You have to decide what your story means after writing it down. What is interesting about authoring your own account, for review, will be referred to as narrative therapy. It will highlight your moments in life when you felt essential or worthy. It will also show you the way you see yourself and the path of your life up to where you are.

For instance, you can tell your story as if it were a drama, due to a feeling that your life is dramatic and very intense. If it was written as a comedy, then you will think that your experience has been full of fun up to where you are. Or maybe it feels like a cosmic joke? A love story could indicate that you are a romantic.

Put it in Your Mind That it Takes Time

You can follow all the steps, but still, you have to remember that it will need to take time. You should be aware that its vital to analyze yourself and put your ideas into action. The person you are will change in the days to come.

Track Your Sleeping

When you lack sleep, exhaustion will have some negative impacts on your body. This can encourage stress. You should be able to look at the hours you spend sleeping every night. Amount of sleep needed for an individual varies. This can result in your anxiety levels getting higher than they should be. When you don't sleep:

1. You will think and learn slowly.

2. There will be an increase in accidents.

3. A lot of health challenges will be experienced.

4. Increase in depression and forgetfulness.

5. Lower libido.

6. You will age faster.

7. Weight will fluctuate.

8. You will have impaired judgment.

You should have a list of things to help you to enhance your overall life experience. This will aid you in a thoughtful self-analysis. Brainstorm ways to promote growth. You should always see yourself evolving and changing based on your ambitions and life experiences.

It's extraordinarily vital to take your time and engage in self-analysis. This will assist you in changing into the person that you are meant to be. You can live by your own values. You can make the rules and steer yourself toward realizing your goals.

Chapter 26

Interpersonal Communication

The process by which people exchange feelings, emotions, and information using verbal and non-verbal cues is known as interpersonal communication. This type of interaction mainly takes place between two or more people and defines the relationship. For example, the bond between you and your boss will be different from that between you and your siblings. You will speak to these individuals in different ways.

Interpersonal communication involves a sender, who put out the message and a receiver who returns feedback to the initial party. For this to take place between two or more people, there has to be a set and setting (meaning, context). This influences the direction of the conversation.

In every communication process, noise is a constant factor referring to interference with the conveyance of the message. This may be psychological, external, or semantics. While developing your interpersonal communication skill set, it is essential to think about who the parties are, the message, noise, feedback, and context in every part of the interaction.

How to Improve Interpersonal Relationships

Interpersonal relationships can be improved in a few ways:

Self-Awareness

Write down a list highlighting your non-verbal cues, your emotions, and your thoughts. Becoming aware of what you are feeling will help you become better at interpersonal communication.

Maintain Empathy towards Other People

Make a conscious effort to listen to other's body language and non-verbal cues. This will help you hear more of what they actually have to say. Try to put yourself in their shoes; what are they feeling or thinking? Remember that communication is a two-way street; it is more effective if you understand what the other person is saying.

Listen Attentively

More people are concerned with their response to the other person rather than listening. Unfortunately, many people do not consider listening to be a useful skill that can be acquired and sharpened, but it is. The person that you are interacting with, will come away with a much better impression of you if they feel as though they were heard.

Practice a Calm Tone or Approach

Avoid talking over people and shooting them down. They are entitled to their opinion just as you are to yours. Allow the other party to finish their message; avoid speaking for them. An open, calm tone will show your dedication in trying to build a relationship and also shows that you are an open-minded person.

Collaborate More

Say "yes" and build upon it. It is a simple trick to take into consideration when you are improving your interpersonal skills. In case your expected outcome did not produce the intended results, developing a positive attitude will pull you through to the other end. For example, improving classes are an excellent example of collaboration exercises.

To develop interpersonal communication skills, one must become a trained listener. This helps you understand the other person on a more profound level. You can get more than their words; you also gain insight into their situation with all their body's cues.

Steps to Becoming a Better Listener

1. Be attentive

Good listeners maintain eye contact and pay close attention to what you are saying. Remaining interested in the message being conveyed is a curious, open-minded, thoughtful, and selfless act.

2. Avoid distractions

Remove distractions like phones or external noises; don't tune into the person talking behind you.

3. Use positive body language

A good listener uses body language to suggest interest by leaning forward, nodding, and uttering an agreeable murmur like, 'mm-hmm.' By expressing yourself in this manner, the speaker will see that you are relaxed and enthusiastic.

4. Watch for subtle cues like voice inflection and tonal variation

For example, you can tell from someone's tone if they are angry, distressed, or experiencing other emotions. Note if they talk too loud, fast, take long pauses, or emphasize specific words, etc. These will help you relate to the speaker.

5. Be a mirror

Reflect the tone of voice and body language of the speaker without appearing to mimic them. This action allows you to develop a rapport. For example, "I do not like it when you take a day to respond to company emails." You may reflect as, "What I understand is that when I take a day to respond to company emails, it upsets you."

6. Empathize

A good listener acknowledges and empathizes with the speaker. Instead of offering platitudes as feedback, you can reflect the message of the speaker. Focus on being responsive, not reactive.

7. Remember

A good listener remembers conversations not only to repeat them to the speaker but also to use them for ongoing dialogue.

8. Ask follow-up questions

Asking questions shows the other person that you are interested in what they have to say. When doing this, it may be helpful to use an open-ended approach. For instance, "Tell me more," is an appropriate response when someone tells you, "I had a terrible day at work." Do not limit your answers to "yes" or "no." Keep in mind, however, that your queries should not be intrusive in any way. It is a friendly conversation, not an interrogation.

Building listening skills takes patience and practice. A good listener develops trust between herself and her companions. A good speaker is not always a perfect listener, but an excellent speaker who grows their listening skills may develop a conversational aptitude.

Why You Need to Become a Better Listener

Being a good listener builds a meaningful relationship with others and can encourage our personal growth. They are better at solving problems; they make better colleagues and establish healthier interpersonal relationships. This skill requires one to denounce all distractions, self-centered attitudes, and know-it-all mentalities. Listening, like all abilities, becomes better with practice. Even if you think that you are already decent, you can always improve your performance.

The benefits of active listening include but are not limited to:

1. Avoid misunderstandings.

The most common communication failure is a misunderstanding. This happens when there is a breakdown in meaning. To avoid these, ensure that the message is received as the speaker intended it. Try using mirror language to aid with this task. Avoiding this pitfall leads to briefer and more accurate conversations.

2. Foster trust and improve relationships.

When you listen keenly to other people's words, you will be in a better position to respond to their needs. The speaker is likely to trust you more and be vulnerable with you.

3. Increase critical-thinking skills.

A problem shared is half-solved. A good listener is more collaborative; therefore, they create an element of positivity when finding solutions. By taking in the information, understanding the nature of the problem, and asking questions, you will be more skillful and productive.

4. Promote cohesiveness.

A good listener aims to engage with the speaker to drive the message home. When feelings become charged discussing sensitive topics, the listener should use her knowledge to reassure the speaker that they are being heard. This can keep both sides of the conversation calm and avoid "emotional flooding."

Empathy: The Cornerstone of Authentic Human Interaction

Empathy is valuable in building successful social relationships. In business, the owner's priority should be to understand and cater to the needs of the clients. Compassion involves putting yourself in someone else's shoes. It helps us communicate our thoughts in a way that others will understand.

Some people are naturally empathic, while others may require training. Below are the types that you should familiarize yourself with:

Cognitive Empathy: Psychologists refer to it as the theory of mind. Cognitive empathy helps you increase mindfulness of what others are thinking and their mental state. This helps us communicate transparently. When building this level of understanding, you need to make educated guesses based on what you know about the person. Do not rush into hasty assumptions; instead, take time to consider the feedback you receive through particular gestures and remain impartial.

Emotional Empathy: This involves the ability to share the emotions of others. This may cause personal distress or concern for someone else's well-being. Emotional understanding helps you create connections with others.

Ask yourself, "Have I felt similar to what they feel?" To answer this question, you would be inclined to understand the other person's emotions and then reflect upon them. Find a way to relate it to yourself. Then you can find the courage to take action.

Somatic Empathy: Also known as affectionate or compassionate empathy, this involves physically reacting to someone's emotions. It consists in taking action to ease someone else's suffering. Begin by asking what you can do to help the other person.

Sometimes, the other person is unable to respond, and therefore, in this situation, you may suggest doing something that worked for you in the past. If that does not help, do something else because what worked for you may not necessarily work for everybody else. It can be a comfort for others to have someone willing to listen and help.

Choosing an Effective Communication Strategy

Different forms of communication exist to cater effectively to different situations. Several factors are taken into consideration while selecting the most effective mode of communication, such as:

What is the Purpose of the Message?

Different motivations will compose different messages for different groups of people. Your motivation might be to make an announcement, create a relationship, educate, etc. Finding the purpose will drive you to form a compelling statement. Let's take the purpose of teaching teens and preteens on the dangers of drug abuse as an example.

What is the Message?

Knowing what message to use helps you also find out how to do it and what audience to target. When constructing the statement, consider mood, design, content, and language. In our example, our information would focus on the consequences of drug abuse.

The language used in the message would be simple and informal. The channels used may include social media platforms, comic books, animations, and community outreach programs, among others. Other elements to consider would be the urgency and confidentiality of the message.

Who is the Audience?

Determining your target audience for a piece of information plays a crucial role in selecting the most effective communication strategy. Your listeners may vary according to demographics such as age, gender, etc., geographical location, health, and ability, etc. Our audience would be teenagers and preteens across the country.

What Resources Will You Need?

Find out what it will cost you to convey your message in terms of money, labor, equipment, and materials, etc. If you seek to gather feedback, then tools are required to collect this data. Organizations that share a similar agenda are effectively useful as resources. When determining these options, you should also consider contingency plans. Prepare for crisis management, in the process.

Communication Styles

There are three main styles of communication, out of which others emerge. These styles are:

Assertive

Assertive communication is about expressing yourself while remaining mindful of another person's thoughts and feelings. It involves "I" statements such as "I feel unheard because..." or, "I think it is best to..." and so on. These statements express ownership of emotions without blaming the other person. It is the most effective way to interact with others.

Aggressive

Aggressive communication expresses dominance and involves winning over the other person, at whatever cost. For example, "It's my way or the highway!" These individuals are often loud and rude. This style of communication is not practical because the listeners are either distracted by the delivery or too frightened, hurt, or defensive to understand the message.

Passive-Aggressive

In this style of communication, the person seems to be calm on the surface while indirectly acting out their anger. They are usually quietly aggressive and sometimes sarcastic. This kind of individual lacks proper interpersonal skills and may use body language to convey their genuine feelings. For example, "Sure, Einstein, let's do it your way."

Other types of communication include:

Passive or Submissive

Passive communicators ignore their feelings acting indifferently and often giving in to the other party. They avoid confrontation and are unsure of how to express their thoughts. When they fail to assert their thoughts effectively, they may harbor resentment toward themselves or the situation. For example, "I am good with whatever." These individuals use a meek voice and make themselves as small as possible. Their body posture and gestures do most of the talking.

Manipulative

These communicators are gifted at steering conversations with others, to their advantage. They use cunning and deceptive devices unbeknownst to the other person. They may pout, cry crocodile tears, or even lie to force the other person's hand in helping them.

How to Improve Your Body Language

On top of these communication styles, body language plays a role in ensuring effective interpersonal communication. You can use gestures in your favor.

Start with the **power pose**. Also called the Superman, practice by putting your hands on your hips, head, and shoulders upright. You should try this posture before an anticipated, emotionally stressful situation such as a meeting where you will be presenting.

Increase your **energy level**. Being energetic shows enthusiasm and interest in the subject of discussion. This, however, does not mean you fidget. Do not seem desperate, or you will annoy others. This is all about keeping a good attitude. How you feel is ultimately echoed by your body.

Smile more. Smiling keeps us stay relaxed in harsh circumstances. It also shows people that you are confident and positive. Others are more likely to engage with you if you look friendly. However, do not put on a fake smirk because this, too, is visible to the other person.

Talk more with **controlled hand gestures**. Use your palms to add emphasis to what you are saying. Do not unnecessarily wave them around or lay them limply on your side. When giving a presentation, avoid gesturing above the shoulders; this provides a radius of motion that is comfortable and impactful.

Relax your posture. Sit upright and relax your shoulders, but do not slouch. Tension indicates discomfort, while slouching indicates disinterest. When sitting, do not cross your legs or your arms. That posture suggests that one is guarded.

Maintain **personal space**. Keep a respectable distance between you and the other individual. Human beings behave in the same way that animals do when their area feels invaded. Without permission to approach, getting too close may be viewed as aggressive or intrusive. Wildlife also takes it as an invitation to fight.

As you aim to improve your body language, it is easy to exaggerate the new postures at first, but with practice, these behaviors will become second nature.

Chapter 27

How to Influence and Lead

Are you a manager, or do you have any leadership position within your workplace? As an authority figure, your primary role should be seeking the best for your subordinates while completing the tasks assigned. For you to have your associate's trust, you have to win their respect and admiration.

How will you make sure that everything works out? How can you be able to lead and inspire your people at the same time? How can you be someone that your workers or peers look up to? For you to get answers to these questions, you have to be a mentor and guide your employees down the right path. Different guidelines assist you, as shown below (76).

1. Always Expect the Best From People

When you are a good leader, you will understand that people always try and live up to the expectations that have been set for them.

---

(76) Jonah Berger, (2016) – *Invisible Influence: The Hidden Forces that Shape Behavior*. Simon & Schuster.

When you set low expectations, then you will make subordinates lazy, and the result will be underperformance. As a great leader, you will have to set high and realistic expectations; thus, your team can strive to achieve them.

This will allow you to expect the best from the people you manage. You should be able to give your associates challenges that they can live up to. You should also have encouraging words that will have a positive impact on your audience. This will give them some encouragement to rise to any task.

2. Always Encourage Them

As a great leader, you must empower your team at any given time. You should be able to praise them even for the slightest achievement or progress. You should do this due to your understanding that goals aren't reached in a day. Projects take a lot of time.

By encouraging the small improvements, you will assist in guiding them in the right direction and higher goals and visions. This can keep your associates more focused motivated, going ahead. This will build a good momentum and encourage a positive change.

3. Encourage Positive Change

As a great leader, you will be able to understand that no one is perfect. Everyone has a personal defect that can impact their work. Don't make big deals out of people's limitations but instead, go in the opposite direction and put up clear standards that will enforce good morale.

You won't be concerned with how a particular person is at that moment. Your main agenda will be to lead them down a path where insecurities can't hinder them from working to their best. When you correct your subordinates, do so in a kind and gentle manner.

How to Be a Great Leader

A strong leader should have certain qualities like intelligence, adaptability, and empathy. An authority figure should embrace certain values to be healthy and capable. The following tips can help you to become great:

1. Learn to Understand Your Leadership Style

You should be able to understand your leadership style as this is very vital. You should know your strengths and the areas that you can improve upon. Assess your people skills. You should be able to tell if the qualities will help or hinder your team.

2. Value Creativity

Intellectual motivation is considered to be a quality that defines transformational leadership. Your team should be encouraged to voice and act upon their creativity. You should be able to give new challenges and support them to accomplish your goals.

3. Give Rewards and Recognition

This is an important ability that you, as a good leader, should have. Be able to recognize and award your people, this will ensure that they feel appreciated. Happy workers will always give their best. As an authority figure, you can ensure that your team is satisfied with your direction.

Body Language of a Leader / Confident Body Language

Body language is a fundamental skill when communicating with others. It is a talent that is given very minimal attention. As a leader, you have more incentive to work on this ability. The following are concepts that will help with comprehension.

1. Tell Us that You are Attentive or Listening

As a leader, you should be able to tell your workers from your body language that you are observant. There are simple things that can show your intent; sitting upright, maintaining eye contact, using open movements while gesturing, and putting your fingertips together when you are resting your hands.

2. Maintain Eye Contact to Build Trust

Maintaining eye contact is very important. Always look at your associates directly in their eyes and listen to them. This will create trust between you and your team. When you are not looking at them or are busy staring around, then this can distract them. It can eat away the faith you'd earned and what you say won't matter as much.

278

3. The Balance Between Open and Closed Body Language

You can't reach too far on either side of the spectrum. Being free with your body language can make your team uncomfortable. For example, power poses can make you feel like a confident presenter, but they may be perceived as arrogance. At the same time, you can be too closed off, thus making your members think you don't care. When you keep your head down, you will be assumed to be doubtful. Your decisions or leadership may come into question. The best action you can take is to relax and control the message being portrayed with your body language.

How to Influence and Persuade

You can improve your powers of persuasion in many ways. It is imperative that your team trusts your guidance and listens to your advice. By allowing yourself to learn more about influencing those around you, you can also improve your leadership skills (77).

1. Reasoning

This is a vital tactic that can help to persuade others. Most of you will isolate it rather than including it as part of the influencing strategy. You will be required to explain the facts and demonstrate them with confidence. This is a method that people of any profession can put into use. This can be characterized by the word "because." Anytime you are using "reason" go for quality and not quantity or else your challengers may look down on your weaknesses. Use logic to breakdown information and decisions. Account for even the most trivial of details and illustrate your line of thought to your team.

2. Inspire

This is a tactic that will work according to your emotions. Be enthusiastic and try to picture a future where your goals have been accomplished. Use active language that will involve the listener. You

---

(77) Tali Sharot (2018) – *The Influential Mind: What the Brain Reveals About Our Power to Change Others*. Picador USA.

must also sound confident about your ideals. Show every single person how they are able to contribute.

Anytime you are using "inspire", make sure whatever you say is something that will attract and appeal your audience. You don't need to be someone famous to encourage others. You can use powerful images and words that can encourage your boss, coworkers, and your team.

3. Ask

This can be effective for individuals of high power. Avoid giving solutions and ask the other individual how to resolve the problem. Journalists or lawyers use this technique. Consider questions that have a satisfactory response.

Those who are selling vehicles will also put in use this technique. Using "leading questions" most of the time can backfire. You should always try to evaluate if the honesty of the queries. In such a case the other people can persuade themselves to work with you if you are interested in working with them.

How to Lead Different Personality Types

Being a leader, it's extraordinarily vital to understand the people you are working with. A strong relationship with your team will only improve the organization. This can encourage productivity and enforce success in your company. There are different ways to help you enhance great teams.

1. Recognize Yourself

Some industries will require you to have a Myers-Briggs personality test. This will allow you to be accustomed to the different types and it can also be a friendly conversation starter. You will be able to read your results and talk about how worryingly precise their portrayal was. This description will allow you to know yourself much better. This is honestly the first step toward being able to work with others and to lead teams.

2. Recognize Your Team

Personalities may clash at times. This is not possible to generate a team that has one personality type, and in case it is, then you are advised not to do it. For you to have a high energy team, then you will note that it's key for you to be knowledgeable about the traits of everyone in the room. You have to note that many members of your team are like a puzzle, and when to put the pieces where they fit, the results can be wonderful.

3. Accept Feedback

Everyone makes mistakes and unfortunately, you are not infallible. You should not be afraid to take feedback when you misstep. Being a leader, you will be giving suggestions daily. Be open and accepting when your teams provide you with notes. You may feel it hard to accept, but their words will allow you to improve.

Handling a team isn't an easy task. There are different personalities, wants, and motivations from every member of your organization. Seeing different people come together to defeat a common challenge can be so rewarding. You must trust them, in the same way that they trust you.

Case Study: Teacher

Case study learning can assist leaders in the classroom. As a teacher, you give your students a video about a specific case to watch. Then they will either work in groups or individually to come up with a solution. You provide a guideline to assist the students in what they are expected to do.

Case study learning should asses every student's learning capability. There are examples of projects that can be given in a classroom, such as journaling, interviews, and student discussion. Some of these tips help in setting up a case study.

1. Provide Outlines to Assist in Giving Solutions

The amount of support that you give your students will be contingent on their level of skills and development. An answer to the case study can be from different pieces of information you have given to your students. This can be from the specific headings you give then from the parts of an essay.

2. Have a Clear Introduction

Give your students guidelines to follow. Allow them to express their different learning styles within the body of the project. By giving them clear instructions, you can ensure they are able to create a quality result.

3. Give Context

This step should be thought of as a movie preview or a book summary. Try to make the students understand that the problem requires them to learn more and challenge themselves.

4. Get a Challenge to Examine

This should be a topic the students can relate to and has some relevance to their lives. The problem should be complex to bring out different solutions with a variety of layers.

Case Study: Coach

1. Stunning Characters

A lot of coaching engagements will put focus on enhancing an administrator's weaker leadership skills, which can expose character flaws or blind spots. Others must be open to learning about changing their style, and coaching can be a positive platform to promote this evolution.

2. Growing Business

Coaching can be very vital to CEOs and entrepreneurs who want to grow their companies despite the challenges they may come across. You will meet with small business owners who wish to expand their trade.

Case Study: Promotion

1. Have a Devoted Case Studies Page

You should be able to have a webpage that will accommodate your case studies. This should be easy for guests to visit. The page can be called "case studies" or "success studies." The structure of the site will be important, and the previous challenges should be clear on your goals, processes, and outcomes.

2. Have Case Studies On Your Home Page

Give your website visitors a chance to see evidence of happy clients. Your homepage is the best place to do this. You can include case studies to your website in such ways; client testimonials, call to action to see certain case studies among others.

What Makes A Bad Leader?

1. Poor Integrity

Integrity is an essential quality of leadership. Learn to keep your word. You won't be successful as long as you lack moral integrity. Employees will look at your unacceptable character, and this will as well make them act poorly.

2. Lack of Flexibility

You should be able to employ a variety of leadership styles according to the situation you have at hand. You must be aware that not all the employees will be motivated by the same factors. As a good leader, you should recognize this, but a weak leader won't be able to see this and will stick to their ways.

You must be able to change and adapt to suit the needs of the clients and your team. Learning new skills is a valuable way to strengthen your organization. You should also work alongside your team to earn their trust.

Cult Leaders

Combine the traits of fringe beliefs, propensity for violence, and charismatic personality and you will be able to understand the character of a cult leader. There are two common traits of cult leaders:

Narcissistic

This will be obvious when it comes to people who deal with abusive traits in those around them. These individuals grow up thinking they are superior to others. They make a lot of demands due to being driven by their ego. They are the hero in their own story, and no one else matters. They use other individuals like pawns in a shady chess game.

Charismatic

Pop culture has taught us this about cult leaders. This is a very complicated term as it can describe a leader's style of talking, dressing, or how they treat their followers. These individuals are charming. They are able to convince anyone of anything. People with this trait are able to command attention.

Chapter 28

Mastering Persuasion

What is Persuasion?

Persuasion refers to the act of convincing someone to do something or act in a certain way. When thinking about persuasion, it should be noted that we are talking about voluntary action. This means that you are not openly coercing an individual to go along with your ideas. In fact, your ability to convince someone largely depends on the various factors that comprise effective persuasion.

On the whole, persuasion is about making a compelling argument that can resonate with others. If you have a weak argument, it may be nearly impossible to get others to go along with your ideas. By the same token, manipulators may rely on things like charm and physical attraction to be persuasive.

Practitioners of dark psychology use persuasion effectively by playing on people's emotions. In some cases, they play on people's fears. Other times, they play on their greed. In general, persuasion can be quite effective when you play on negative emotions rather than positive ones. If you seek to motivate someone by telling them the benefits they will gain, you might be successful. However, you might be even more successful if you highlight what they stand to lose if they don't go along with you. That's why punishment is usually more effective than reward.

Elements of Persuasion

A number of elements may factor into persuasion. Persuasion can be very hard to achieve, especially when you are facing highly defensive individuals. Also, there is a great deal of resistance any time you are looking to change behaviors deeply rooted in the psyche of individuals. Moreover, appealing to individuals is harder than appealing to a collective group. Yet, your ability to be convincing can be magnified by reaching a broad audience rather than appealing to individuals (78).

Here are five crucial elements to effective persuasion:

The Message

The message is not always the most important aspect when looking to persuade others. Even when you have a convincing argument, you may not be effective, especially if someone else is a better showman. There are times when a good song and dance is better than having a reasonable argument. Still, your message needs to be congruent with your aims. Otherwise, you leave yourself open to attacks. If you rely on looks and charm to get by, don't be surprised if someone who dislikes you looks to make your arguments look like Swiss cheese. Substance is always best.

The Delivery

How you say things is just as important as what you say. Your delivery and your confidence will tell people that you mean what you say. If you show insecurity, it opens the door to criticism. Moreover, the best manipulators are able to make blatant lies seem real by the confidence they exhibit. While you may not necessarily

---

(78) Jonah Berger, (2016) – *Invisible Influence: The Hidden Forces that Shape Behavior.* Simon & Schuster.

be lying, it always helps to seem convinced of what you have to say even if it's just a pile of rubbish.

The Platform

In today's modern world, the platform you use to communicate is vital. This largely depends on your audience. For instance, social media is the go-to place for anyone who is looking to make serious headway. By the same token, print media may be your best bet if you're looking to reach an older, more traditional crowd. Perhaps television and radio may work for you depending on the type of segment you're looking to reach. Then, there's always that face-to-face factor that may be needed. While you might want to focus on one platform in particular, it's always best to focus on various types. That way, you can ensure greater coverage.

The Messenger

The messenger is critical. This could be the person who speaks, a social media profile, or an organization. The messenger needs to be presentable while also credible. If the messenger does not live up to the expectations of the audience, then the message might as well be delivered in Esperanto.

This is why attractive, well-groomed people garner a lot more attention. In addition, large organizations which large visibility also tend to be more effective as compared to those with less visibility.

The Credibility

Credibility is the most valuable currency in the persuasion business. If you are not credible, then you are wasting your time. Building credibility can take a long time to achieve and seconds to smash. This is one of the particular reasons why social media is a double-edged sword. Building traction on a social media site can take a great deal of effort, but one bad post and that credibility can come crashing down.

If you are marketing yourself, individually, then always take care with what you say and do. Even things of the past may come to haunt you at some point. So, it's always best to make sure that your message is wrapped within a bubble of credibility.

Methods of Persuasion

Traditionally, three main methods of persuasion are used to compel targets to go along with the wishes and desires of the manipulator. It should be noted that these methods aren't necessarily intended to manipulate others. However, they can be powerful tools used to convince others to go along with you. As a result, the effective application of these strategies can lead you to win just about every time. Also, these tricks can be relied upon any time you need to engage in a situation in which you are communicating with others.

The Ethos Method

By "ethos" we mean "ethic." In short, this method refers to the ethics that come with persuading others through your character. In other words, you are leading by example. The most effective leaders are those who can build up a track record and then stand by it. With these individuals, there comes a point in which they don't need to say much. Their mere presence leads them to become unquestionable sources in their respective fields.

When this concept is applied within a darker context, you may find that these leaders are the so-called, "gurus," "experts" or "whisperers." There are times when they are the result of media hype. Other times, they completely fabricate their personas. In some of the most extreme cases, these gurus make up credentials, fabricate experiences and testimonials while even simulating techniques that supposedly work.

Examples of these manipulators can be seen all over: dietary experts, religious cult leaders, political candidates and self-help gurus to name a few. When you dig a little bit deeper into the lives of these individuals, you may be able to detect just how forthcoming they really are.

The Pathos Method

In this case, "pathos" refers to emotion. As such, skilled individual can evoke passion and emotion to get people to comply with their wishes and desires. Earlier, we mentioned the use of fear. And while fear is very effective, plenty of other emotions out there can be used.

In general, triggering negative emotions seems to be much more effective than triggering positive ones. For instance, appealing to people's greed, lust, gluttony (the seven deadly sins, basically) seems to resonate at a primal level much more than sublime emotions such as love, kindness and compassion.

Manipulators who understand that greed is more powerful than compassion, may use these primal instincts to carry out their own agenda by offering people wealth in exchange for their support. By the same token, marketing of most products seems to appeal to this aspect of people's character.

Nevertheless, fear is the most effective tool. Fear-based persuasion generally entails describing a problem, saying who's to blame, outlining the consequences and then presenting the solution. This happens across all various aspects of life. It is seldom you hear, "improve your life and get the love of your life." Rather, it's common to hear, "stop being rejected by the love of your life." In the latter statement, you can see a negative emotion being triggered. The manipulator would then present their plan designed to overcome the problem.

On the whole, the Pathos method is highly effective if the individual in general (not just a manipulator) is able to convey seemingly genuine passion. If this is the case, then there is a much higher probability of being successful as opposed to simply laying out a plan or solution to a situation (79).

(79) Tali Sharot (2018) – *The Influential Mind: What the Brain Reveals About Our Power to Change Others*. Picador USA.

The Logos Method

In this regard, "logos" refers to using logic to achieve persuasion. This ought to be the most effective method, but it often takes a backseat to pathos, that is, emotion. When the Logos method is used effectively, you present a situation that makes sense to people. The most skilled users of this method are able to take highly complex and abstract concepts and bring them down to a more manageable level. When this happens, you are able to get through to people in a way that they feel smart even when you are dumbing down things for them.

Also, the Logos method appeals to the rational side of the brain. This is important, particularly when fear and panic set in. When you lay out a rational solution, people will comply as it makes sense. When you trigger fear, presenting a rational solution gives people something to hold on to. However, if you appeal to logic as a means of controlling emotion, then you may be facing an uphill battle.

Think about it.

How often do people who believe they are in love listen to others?

Even if you present a compelling argument as to why the object of their affection is not suitable for them, their emotions get in the way. As such, these individuals don't listen and follow their emotions. However, once the individual is heartbroken, you can then appeal to their rational side by offering a logical explanation for the events that occurred.

With these three methods, your efforts to be persuasive will be highly effective. In the end, you will be able to make the most of your efforts and multiply the effects that you achieve through the art of persuasion.

Chapter 29

Empathy and Persuasion

What is Empathy?

The ability to identify and understand others' feelings and situations; that is, to communicate with others at a meaningful level, is empathy. Sometimes it is spontaneous and can be unintentional most of the time, especially for a natural empathic individual. Empathy is a sensitive person who is extremely compassionate, caring, and understanding of others. Deep compassion produces a function where the empathic actually appears to "see" people's emotions around them.

Most people do not know how it works. Still, some have long since accepted that they are open to others. Most people are learning how to conceal their genuine feelings and expose the world beyond out of fear of being hurt or affected in some manner. Empathy can often be linked to the true emotions of an individual and how these can be used to connect at a personal level with others. Empathic have a big heart and will help others compassionately. Empathy with the parents, children, colleagues, close associates, visitors, animals, plants, and even inanimate objects is quite common in true empathic.

Although there are many aspects that we still don't understand about how empathy functions, we know that everything has an emotional pulse or pitch, which can be sensed by empathic. Empathic can even perceive the subtlest shifts, which the naked eye or the five senses cannot identify. Words have an energetic pattern from the speaker which can be picked up by empathic.

That is why true empathic my find it hard fitting in society as they are constantly receiving input from all around them. This can make it hard to cope with the circumstances around them, especially if others are hurting or suffering. Natural empathic people need to find the best way to handle these emotions (80).

How to Tell If You Are Empathic

Empathic are often said to be poets in constant motion. They are the born poets, musicians, and performers, so the creative world is packed within them; they are born with a high degree of creativity. They are well-known for their varied, wide, and eclectic interests. Empathic often have a broad perspective of the experiences in their lives. They explore many areas of life which may include experiences from many cultures around the world. They have a broad view of the world.

There is no clear-cut definition as to the characteristics that make up an empathic. There is no way to determine an empathic by their place of birth, age, physical or personality traits. What we do know is that empathic come from all walks of life. In some cases, children can be highly empathic while older individuals may exhibit great signs of wisdom and compassion.

Empathy also solves problems. It is a means of helping others cope with the world around them and the circumstances they may be facing. This is why empathic make great therapists and counselors.

---

(80) Jonah Berger, (2016) – *Invisible Influence: The Hidden Forces that Shape Behavior*. Simon & Schuster.

It should be noted that empathy is not the same as sympathy. When you experience sympathy, you are able to understand a situation. But you are not able to fully appreciate what people are going through. In a manner of speaking, sympathy is a precursor to empathy.

Empathic often have the ability to feel others at various levels. They can also become extremely knowledgeable in interpreting another person's body language. They can observe their eye movements and facial expressions to determine what others are thinking and feeling.

Also, empathic have their tool kit. This kit includes being a good listener. Empathic are able to help people calm down in their presence. This is especially true when people find themselves in difficult emotional situations. The true empathic is able to have a soothing effect on people by simply being in their presence. For this reason, in careers connected with compassion, we find so many natural empathic, such as healers, clergy, counselors, and caregivers.

Empathic will always try to influence others around them in a positive manner. However, it is important to distinguish the true empathic from those pretending to be empathic. When a manipulator pretends to be an empathic, they fake all sorts of reactions. Yet, they really couldn't care less about what happens to others. In such cases, manipulators almost always slip up. It is during these slip ups that they reveal who they truly are and what they truly feel. All telltale sign of this behavior lies in individuals who seek to go good deeds so they can be acknowledged for them.

How to Use Empathy to Attract and Influence Your Target

Firstly, it's important to define the difference between seeking to influence someone and looking to push your own agenda. True empathic generally act out of their own goodwill. They don't seek attention. All they want is to help and that's it. End of story.

However, there are those who seek to come off as great humanitarians. It is this kind of individual that seeks to show how compassionate they are. They will support charities and organizations with the sole purpose of being known for their efforts.

These individuals use their humanitarian efforts to influence others by leading them to think they are genuinely kind people.

In fact, it's common to see great humanitarians use charitable organizations as a front for their own purposes. This may include exerting control, acquiring wealth or calling attention to themselves (this is very common in narcissistic people).

If you wish to show yourself off as a great humanitarian, you need to be prepared to put in the time that is required for charity and other types of altruistic endeavors. This may also mean donating money to charity at some point. In the end, being a great humanitarian is more a question of well-placed and well-timed efforts as opposed to a long track record of contributions.

Manipulators will use all sorts of fronts to show off their kindness and compassion. Their agenda may be as simple as seeking attention to a more complex agenda, such as building their personal brand. Ultimately, you can tell the difference since these individuals are always pushing something. The true altruistic empathic does not seek adulation. They just act out of the sheer desire to help others and make a difference in the world.

Chapter 30

Persuasion in Business

Persuasion in Sales

An understanding of various effective persuasion techniques will allow salespeople not only to sell and achieve their goals, but will boost them to have a lead over the market's competitors. Some of the most effective techniques of persuasion you can use are discussed here (81).

1. **Find common ground**. Many people purchase products from people they like, so a salesperson should have a connection with potential customers. You should identify the areas you have in common, and you should ask questions about their criteria and be genuinely aware of the prospective customer if you do not know what you have in common. By being optimistic, enthusiastic, quick, and polite, you should always smile and strive to be lovable. A salesperson should never argue with their customers.

---

(81) Morin, C. (2019) – *The Persuasion Code: How Neuromarketing Can Help You Persuade Anyone, Anywhere, Anytime.* Wiley.

2. **Display the advantages**. You can show the major advantages of using the product or service. You should try to show how nice it is, for instance, to buy the product in accordance with their specific priorities and expectations. You can highlight how it is better for them to purchase from you and not the competition. You must not strive to offer discounts because it makes you look desperate.

3. **Transform objections into strengths**. It so happens that most of the time, a customer will object. Thus, a good understanding of the goods can benefit against any complaints or criticism. This is common in selling. You must consider the criticism from a customer and explain that your product or service will easily overcome these criticisms. Also explain how the brand's benefits will eliminate pain points and lead to the satisfaction of their needs.

4. **Commitment and consistency principle**. Try to make the customer believe in something small or allow them to take a small action first. After the customer has committed, a bigger step could possibly be approved at a later date. This tactic uses the idea that when people are consistent in their actions, you can rely on them to follow through.

5. **Use the principle of reciprocity**. The rule suggests that we feel obliged to return the favor when someone does something good for us. When a salesperson goes the extra mile for their customers, they might make orders in the future. The reasoning behind this is that there is a feeling of mutual support when both sellers and customers strive to help out one another.

6. **Providing ample information and support**. People tend to follow other people more when they don't have enough information about something to make their own decisions. This strategy works by telling your customers that other people use your goods. For example, you can show them the logos of current clients and their testimonials. Celebrity endorsements are a good example of this kind of tactic.

7. **The scarcity principle**. This means that people are told that they have a chance to get to lose a special product or that they have to wait longer for access to the product. You can use this technique to achieve quick sales, but you should be sincere on time limits and quantity limitations.

These persuasion techniques should be used as well as learning about human behavior and how people decide to buy. This awareness lets you easily achieve sales success more comfortably.

Persuasion in Marketing

1. **Reciprocity**: Let your customers feel happy about something. Often, marketing strives to create good feelings among customers rather than pointing out negative issues. Try your best to associate your product and brand to positive feelings.
2. **Authority**: When you buy something, that means you are trusting a brand. Most people tend to follow credible leaders. If a person named Peter tries to sell you a flat, you are less inclined to buy it from him as compared to a real estate professional who has over 20 years' experience with a reputable brand backing him up.
3. **Social proof principle**: people tend to do what others do. It's easier to get someone to alter their behavior by showing them what other people have done in circumstances of the same kind, instead of telling them what to do in a particular situation.
4. **Commitment**: When customers can have their say in what the brand, product, or service offers, they can buy more from you. Start small, and you will find that you can snowball your advertising activities when your customers are committed. The foundation of a good relationship is commitment.
5. **Liking**: People buy more from those they like. We are narcissistic creatures that easily purchase from people who complement and value us. Naturally, the main issue is genuineness; how can you genuinely thank and appreciate your consumer, naturally and believably? For example, try to invite them to a closed online community and ask their thoughts and suggestions on what you are doing.
6. **Scarcity**: People love to buy products that others can't purchase. We tend to rush for rarely available items. The problem is: how can I make my brand look and feel extremely rare and scarce?

Persuasion in Customer Service

Customers who have shared experiences, needs, and/or frustrations or are striving to view things in their perspective are more likely to agree with and be open to customer service representatives. It is also much easier to persuade a customer you have related to and built a rapport with than one whom you have made no connection with at all. This is why connecting with customers through great service is an unbelievably effective and rather simple technique to implement. The main attitude to keep in mind is being genuine about the needs of the customer.

You will more easily convince a person to act by using action words and speaking in the present tense than using in the past tense. Some examples are: "Purchasing this item saves you money in the long run" or "Putting your order in now will ensure that it's installed promptly." How about, "it's not hard to make room for the product in your home." Speaking in the now and actively will allow you to help the consumer resolve past difficulty and disappointment and move towards solutions here and now.

Consumers will be convinced more often by plans, ideas, and approaches that are comprehensible, and your ability to quickly bring about understanding will boost your ability to convince customers of the merits of your suggestions.

Sometimes a customer service representative can use repetition to persuade a customer as one of the most effective tools. The skills of this approach are successful when you learn to be repetitive without being annoying. That is to say, when you repeat the same ideas or suggestions consistently without the client being annoyed by your insistence. You can do this by modifying the phrases used. If you are trying to convince the client, for instance, that you they save precious time in the morning by buying your coffee maker, you can include the following statements in your dialogue: "You'll have more time to get ready for work in the morning because the coffee maker automatically brews your coffee." This restates the same idea, but without actually using the same words.

Chapter 31

Persuasion in Negotiation

The Relationship between Persuasion and Negotiation

People think negotiation and persuasion are the same thing. While persuasion can be an effective technique in negotiation, persuasion and negotiation are separate tasks. Negotiations can be described as two or more people communicating with each other to reach an agreement on one or more issues. This includes reaching a compromise with another party whenever possible. Therefore, the end result of a negotiation is to find an outcome that satisfies as many of the stakeholders involved.

On the whole, negotiating is about using persuasion to get your goals. Ruthless negotiators don't care about what others gain. All they care about are their own outcomes. Yet, skilled negotiators will at least give the other party that they have gained something from the negotiation. Whether that's actually true is a moot point or not. As a result, the art of negotiating is bridging a gap that will lead you to getting your own wishes and desires (82).

---

(82) Tali Sharot (2018) – *The Influential Mind: What the Brain Reveals About Our Power to Change Others*. Picador USA.

Persuasion in Business Negotiation

Negotiation is where two parties arrive to an agreement regarding a matter. The critical skill is the ability to persuade the other party to agree with you. Knowledge of persuasion skills is a key factor in a successful negotiation. You have to be able to convince your counterpart to understand your position and to accept this position. Of course, the other party has their own agenda. But when you are an able negotiator, you can take their position and use it to your own advantage.

Why is persuasion critical in negotiations?

Persuasion is what ultimately gets the other party to follow along with your ideas and your proposals. If you are unconvincing, the other party will be reluctant to agree with you. Even if you present a compelling argument, it's important to employ persuasion techniques so that they can become an effective part of your repertoire. That way, you can ensure that others will follow you even if they don't necessarily agree.

Persuasion in Personal Negotiation

You must first believe in yourself if you wish to convince others to support your beliefs. By practicing this skill, you can build confidence in yourself. Such skills can be built either through trial and error or through negotiation training courses. You will better be able to persuade the other party when you are self-confident and motivated. You should think about things correctly and critically determine what decision is in the best interest. You should understand your position and be able to convince the adversary to support your views through the compilation and analyzing of facts.

The greatest mistake in negotiations is believing that everything will go smoothly and without any challenge from the other side. Yet seldom does this happen. You should expect your counterparty to raise criticisms. In a negotiation, that's natural. You cannot be caught off guard by not anticipating criticism from the opposing party. Preparation helps you to grasp any questions from the other party easily and answer them. In this way, objections will become strengths that pave the way for effective negotiations.

You must also highlight the advantages of the proposal in order to convince others. You must answer the simple question, "What is in it for me?" in the mind of the counterpart. Responding to this issue will help to bring the proposal into line with the other party's interests. Finally, you must master the straightforward but incredibly important and effective ability to persuade while knowing critical steps to improve your negotiating capacities. Having such skills and experience will help you persuade the other party to consent to the validity of your views.

Chapter 32

Persuasion in Relationships and Sex

Persuasion in Dating

In dating, persuasion can be used to either spark attraction or establish a relationship with a person. This is an important distinction as being able to use persuasion effectively in dating can make or break an individual's attempts at gaining the favor of the object of their affection. As such, it's important to keep in mind that this isn't some kind of voodoo trickery that is going to be used. The idea is to use persuasion effectively in order to create attraction and lead the relationship through its natural course (83).

It should be noted that dating almost always relies on emotion. So, if you are able to persuade using emotions, you should succeed more often than not. In fact, using well-timed tactics can help you achieve far more than you could have ever imagined. For instance, if you are approaching someone who has been through a difficult breakup, you may find it useful to approach them with empathy. By the same token, if you find that someone is defensive, you may want to approach them with a laid-back attitude.

---

(83) Chadderton, C., & Croft, R. (2006) – *"Who is kidding whom? A study of complicity, seduction and deception in the marketplace"*. Social Responsibility Journal.

Generally speaking, logic and reasoning don't always mesh well with dating. In fact, if you seek to approach potential romantic interests by giving them reasons as to why you would be good together, you may not necessarily be able to spark the attraction you seek.

Yet, you may be able to connect at a more personal level, that is, connect by showing leadership. This could come in the form of security and confidence. If the person you are approaching sees how confident you are, they may very well follow your lead.

Persuasion for Commitment

When you are looking to establish a long-term commitment with someone, it's almost always important to demonstrate confidence in what you are doing. The reasoning behind this is that a commitment is not something to be taken lightly. So, if you are seeking a serious commitment with someone, say in the realm of marriage, it's important to display security in what you are doing. Any signs of flaking out will almost always work against you.

When you are looking to get others to commit to your cause, you will have to persuade them through your ethos. When you are able to demonstrate your ethos fully and clearly, others will feed off that lead. This is why the best leaders you can find always have some sort of value structure that they transmit to others. Often, they may not articulate it in a verbal sense, but they will do it through their actions and attitudes.

One of the most important aspects of commitment is sharing passion. Often, great leaders share their passion and their vision. So, they are able to communicate their feelings effectively in such a way that they inspire others to follow their lead. When this occurs, such leaders can develop a wide audience and following.

Persuasion in Family Life

In family life, persuasion can play a very important role. When you are dealing with your spouse, children, parents, or siblings, persuasion can be an effective tool in order to help the entire family circle get along as best they can. Often, this means evoking both passion and example. If you don't walk the walk, then you might end up losing respect from your family. While they may still love you, they won't respect you. Needless to say, this is not a good place to be.

When considering your family, it's always good to be on the same page in terms of values and goals. When you are unable to communicate along those terms with your family members, it can be tough to have a shared agenda. As a result, family goals aren't always met.

Persuasion in Sexual Encounters

It should be noted that persuasion isn't meant to be used in order to engage in non-consensual sexual encounters. The truth is that persuasion can be used to spark feelings and emotions in such a way that your potential mates will feel an affinity for you. In this manner, you can ensure pleasant encounters.

It's important to note that persuasion, when effectively used, can lead to consensual sexual encounters. For instance, if you manifest your passion and feelings toward the other person, they can feed off your lead and follow suit. While this isn't foolproof, meaning that everyone you seek will follow, at least you can be sure that when you do get someone to follow your lead, you will both have a pleasant experience (84).

---

(84) Buss, D. M., & Schmitt, D. P. (1993) – "Sexual strategies theory: an evolutionary perspective on human mating". Psychological Review

Chapter 33

Case Studies on Dark Psychology

Throughout this book, we have touched on a number of concepts and ideas which have enabled us to gain a clear perspective on what dark psychology is and how it can be used to the advantage of a manipulator. We have also provided practical examples of each situation. Nevertheless, it is important to consider presenting relevant case studies that can provide very good insights into the way that dark psychology can function in real-world applications.

As such, this chapter is dedicated to presenting three very relevant case studies which will surely help you get a keen understanding of how dark psychology can be used, by manipulators, to make the most of their position. In addition, we will analyze the principles and techniques which were implemented and how each of these tactics could have been counteracted had victims been aware earlier of the manipulation they were being subjected to.

Ultimately, it is up to you do distill the most relevant aspects to your personal situation. On the whole, we're sure that you will find a great deal of information which can help you come full circle with this topic. Best of all, you will have a much deeper understanding of the way dark psychology can be used to achieve your agenda while being able to guard against other types of manipulation that exist in the world today. While the aim is not to be paranoid, it is important to have a good understanding so that you can guard against unwanted attempts.

Case Study #1: Bernie Madoff

Bernie Madoff is notorious for having run one of the largest Ponzi schemes in history, defrauding investors of millions of dollars. In 2009, Madoff pled guilty to a total of 11 charges as a result of the investigation conducted by the Securities and Exchange Commission (SEC). In total, Madoff was sentenced to 150 years in prison.

But how did it come to this? How was Madoff able to get away with $65 billion of his investors' money?

Bernie Madoff was known to be a charming man who could sweet talk anybody into investing in his fund. He had built up a seemingly prosperous empire that had invested millions upon millions of dollars in startup companies and in the stock market. Investors felt they were safe with Madoff in charge as he always had answers to any questions that investors had.

The Investor's Next Door

Madoff was approachable and very sympathetic to his investors' concerns. He projected a calm demeanor which really helped put investors at ease. It seems like he was in full control of his empire. There wasn't anything that he wouldn't do to quell investors' apprehensions. People with inside knowledge to case describe Madoff as a harmless man who didn't seem to have any malicious intent; he never showed any signs that he was up to something.

The only reason Madoff ever got caught was because he started running into financial trouble. Since he was running a Ponzi scheme, he used the money from new investors to pay off old investors. In order for a scheme such as this to work properly, there needs to be a consistent influx of new investors. When new investors don't get into the scheme, the money dries up and the whole ruse crumbles.

What's even more telling is that Madoff never broke character, even when lawsuits from investors piled up. Madoff seemed like a guy who was down on his luck rather than the most prolific fraudster in history. Ultimately, Madoff pled guilty to the charges he was facing, not because he had something on this conscience, but rather, he acted on the advice of his lawyers.

To this day, the money has not been recovered. So, investors are essentially out of their money.

Analysis

Madoff is a narcissist with psychopathic tendencies. He was completely aware of what he was doing and never really stopped to think how it would affect others. His narcissistic tendencies are clear as he relished in the idea of being a billionaire hedge fund manager.

This is an important distinction to make as the average criminal simply takes the money and runs. <u>Madoff had a high degree of intelligence and put it to good use.</u> He was able to build an empire that lasted for decades. He had built up an alternate reality that was so convincing, that no one was able to tell the difference.

<u>Skilled manipulators are quite able to blur the lines between reality and fantasy.</u> Madoff did so in a remarkable fashion. To this day, there are people who can't believe they were duped by such a nice man. However, his front, his alternate persona, was so well crafted that the average investor was unable to even come close to figuring out what he was really up to.

Moreover, it could be speculated that Madoff could have kept up his scheme for even longer had he not run into financial constraints. After all, his cover was intact: he was able to lie and deceive the people around him, including his closest collaborators, into believing that he was acting in a forthcoming and transparent manner.

While many observers point out that greed was at the root of this entire plot (it certainly played a key role), the fact of the matter is that Madoff is a narcissist with psychopathic tendencies. Sure, he did rip off some very wealthy folks, but in the end, he also took money from average families leaving them in financial ruin.

Madoff, to this day, has shown little remorse and has done nothing to show any type of contrition whatsoever.

He was completely aware of his actions and did so for decades. Perhaps it could be argued that he was delusional, especially toward the end of his scheme. But Madoff could not have pulled off such a scheme if he had lost touch with reality. He was perfectly aware of his actions. As such, there is a clear element of premeditation in his demeanor.

The underlying moral of this story is that if investors had done their due diligence, they may have never fallen into the trap. But that's debatable, especially when you consider that Madoff had spent years building up his trust capital.

That's the type of persona that criminals love to fabricate.

Case Study #2: Charles Manson

Charles Manson gained a great deal of notoriety in the late 1960s after his cult followers committed a series of grisly murders in San Francisco. In particular, the murder of Sharon Tate, wife of film director Roman Polanski brought worldwide attention on Manson and his cult.

Manson styled himself as a messianic type in which he proclaimed to be the "savior" to his group of followers. His cult grew in size and diversity as any number of orphans, runways and homeless people joined. Manson proclaimed his version of the Gospel in which a racial war was to precede final Armageddon.

While Manson was found to be clinically insane during his trial, his actions showed a great deal of deliberation and premeditation. His followers were seduced by his charm and appeal and essentially did his bidding without question.

Urban Legend

Research into Manson's cult has dispelled urban myths that he had some sort of demonic possession which granted him powers over the minds of people. The fact of the matter is that Manson surrounded himself with people, particularly young women, who had very little to their name and much less to choose.

The Manson cult notoriously experimented with hallucinogenic drugs such as LSD. It is believed that it was under the influence of these drugs that the Manson cult followers perpetrated the gruesome acts of violence they carried out.

Mason, himself, was not believed to have committed any of the murders. However, the prosecution was able to determine that Manson's ideology and manipulation of his followers, who did commit the murders, was reason enough to convict him of first-degree murder and conspiracy to commit murder. He was sentenced to life in prison in 1971.

His death in 2017 shed new light on this case. Manson had been a drifter who was convicted of petty crimes before embarking upon the building of his cult. He often told followers that he was a "God" while convincing his followers that they were the chosen ones. Some accounts detail how Manson's cult was part of the 144,000 people that would survive the "end of the world."

Manson was known to be a violent drug addict and alcoholic who came from a broken home. Research into his life revealed an abusive upbringing and troubled adolescence. Manson left his home at an early age and settled into the underworld of drugs and prostitution in California's major cities, particularly in San Francisco.

Analysis

While the clinical evidence is clear on Manson's insanity, the fact remains that he possessed an extraordinary ability to manipulate his followers to the degree that they would blindly do his bidding. Manson exploited a fundamental human need; the need for affection and belonging. That's why it's no surprise that the bulk of Manson's followers we comprised of runaways, orphans and teens who had escaped foster care.

Manson was especially surrounded by young women as he was able to afford them a sense of community and protection that no one else had been able to provide before. Some of the girls in his cult had been forced into prostitution and subsequently "saved" by Manson. Therefore, he played a dominant male role which many of these girls had lacked during their upbringing.

Moreover, Manson frequently used lies and half-truths to confuse his followers. Since he was quite adept at quoting Scripture, his followers believed that he had some magical knowledge and understanding of the world. The fact is that his confidence (most likely derived from his delusions) was enough to convince scared runaways that he was the real deal.

In the end, the Manson cult proved to be a fascinating case study into the ways a madman is capable of preying on the primal needs and fears of people to the degree that they are able to commit murder on his behalf. While it has also been claimed that Manson used brainwashing tactics on his followers, there is no clear evidence of that being the case. If anything, Manson was very skilled in recognizing that he could create a high degree of dependency on his followers by getting them addicted to drugs. As such, his followers would not stray too far as they would be in constant need of drugs to fuel their addiction.

Charles Manson has gone down in history as a textbook manipulator. This case proves that by mastering even rudimentary techniques, a manipulator can cause quite a bit of chaos in the world around them.

Case Study #3: Adolf Hitler

Adolf Hitler is a classic case study for psychologists, students of behavioral science, not to mention political science and military. Hitler was the supreme leader of Nazi Germany in the 1930s and 40s. He was the face of the Nazi occupation of Europe and one of the main combatants during World War II. Hitler is often described as a madman though it's also a fair assumption to say that he was perfectly aware of his deeds.

Among his most heinous acts, the Holocaust stands out as the most gruesome and vicious of attacks perpetrated on a single ethnic group. While estimates vary on the number of Jews that were killed during the Holocaust, a likely figure of about 6 million deaths seems reasonable.

But, how did Hitler come to power? Most importantly, how did he stay in power? After all, he was able to seduce millions of Germans so that they would buy into his outlandish world domination schemes. Furthermore, he was able to persuade millions of men to join the ranks of the Nazi army and go fight in the war.

Hitler as a Seducer

It's important to note that Hitler's rise to power coincided with the collapse of the Weimar Republic in Germany. The Weimar Republic was a system of government that emerged following World War I.

Germany had been one of the main combatants in World War I and was defeated by the Allied Forces of France, England and the United States.

The Weimar Republic was characterized by an economic collapse that saw millions of Germans fall into destitution. So, the rise of Hitler was spurred by this collapse. Hitler did two things that resonated with the German people at the time. First, he was able to clearly articulate the problem that people were going through. He was able to sympathize with people's plight. He seemed to genuinely care about what they were going through. The second, he told people who was to blame for their misfortunes. In this manner, Hitler was able to create a persona, that is, the persona that was responsible for the suffering of the German people.

In the end, Hitler pinned the cause of all ills on an ethnic group (the Jews) while embarking on his conquest of the world. He fought against both the Allies and the Soviet Union until he was ultimately defeated. However, Hitler's legacy is predicated on both evil and his ability to seduce an entire country to go along with his madness. The end result was the death of millions upon millions of people and the destruction of Europe.

Analysis

Multiple theories call Hitler everything, from a paranoid schizophrenic to a classic narcissist. While he definitely exhibits signs of traditional narcissism, the fact of the matter is that he was able to play off one of the primal concerns of people: fear. Hitler recognized that the German people were going through a very rough time and found someone to blame for it. Of course, the Jews had nothing to do with the situation Germany was going through. Still, Hitler sold a convincing lie by mixing lies with the truth. Since Hitler was a brilliant speaker, people bought into his ideas.

Adolf Hitler was an astute man because he recognized the German people's desire to take control of their own destiny. He knew that if he gave them someone to blame for their ills, and if he could give them a way to solve it, that the people would follow him, and they did.

Beyond that, Hitler created an alternative reality in which Germany would emerge as a powerful nation that would essentially control the entire world. And while they were close to getting away with it, the fact of the matter is that Hitler's ambitions fell short of the mark simply because he did not account for the fact that the truth would shine through. When it did, the German army lost its morale while the German people simply backed away.

Hitler is remembered as both a madman and a skilled manipulator. He was able to use his exceptional speaking skills to convince people that he was being forthcoming in his intention. Had people been able to see through his ruse, they may have been able to stop him before the Holocaust and World War II took place. While that is nothing more than mere speculation, the truth is that the entire world was fooled.

One specific event puts this into perspective. Germany was the host of the 1936 Olympic Games. The Nazi government put on one of the most incredible events for its time. The entire world was convinced that Nazi Germany meant no harm to the world. After all, why would they go to the trouble of organizing such a wonderful event if they had devious intentions in mind?

Of course, the 1936 Olympics were meant to be a distraction. Hitler and his cronies wanted to lure the world into a false sense of security. And did they ever! Many world leaders were confused by Germany's overt plans to conquer Europe especially in light of the way they had been so inviting in earlier years.

Looking back at this episode, it's clear that Hitler and the Nazis had attempted to hide their agenda long enough in order to catch their victims unawares. This is a typical manipulation technique used to get victims to lower their guard before pouncing on them when the time was right.

It worked for Hitler until someone finally put a stop to him.

Chapter 34

Ten Strategies of Mass Manipulation by Media

The renowned critic and linguist Noam Chomsky, one of the classic voices of intellectual dissent in the last decade, has compiled a list of the ten most common and effective strategies for mind control used by governments to establish a manipulation of the population through the media (85).

1. The Strategy of Distraction

One of the most powerful weapons used by rulers to manipulate people is "distraction." Continuously, shifting the attention to the less important trivial news, allows diverting the interest from much more vital issues as they are decided by political and economic lobbies, to pass into the background.

---

(85) Noam, Chomsky (2011) – *Media Control: The Spectacular Achievements of Propaganda*. Seven Stories Press

2. The Gradual Strategy

Get an unacceptable measure accepted is enough to introduce it gradually, little by little for consecutive years, in such a way that it is virtually imperceptible.

This is what has happened, for example, with the reduction in workers' rights. In several companies, measures or ways of working have implemented, which have ended up making it accepted as normal that a worker has no guarantee of social protection. These changes would have caused a revolution if they had been implemented at one time.

The gradual strategy is based on the "Boiled Frog Principle" which is a metaphorical principle told by the American philosopher Noam Chomsky, to describe the bad ability of human beings to adapt to unpleasant and harmful situations without reacting.

In truth, the boiled frog phenomenon dates back to research conducted by "John Hopkins University" in 1882. During an experiment, some American researchers noticed that by throwing a frog into a pot of boiling water, it inevitably jumped out to save itself. On the contrary, by putting the frog into a pot of cold water and heating the pot slowly but steadily, the frog would inevitably end up boiled.

This principle is applied daily in modern society through devious techniques of mass manipulation and conscience. These disguised techniques as "well-being," apparently are for the benefit of humanity, having such as better living, health, prolonging life, more and more products, more services, progress, technology, but where is all this taking us?

In fact, the principle of the boiled frog shows us that when a change is made slow enough to become invisible, it escapes to the consciousness and does not arouse, for most of humanity, no reaction, no opposition, no revolt.

3. Create Problems and Offer Solutions

This method is also called "Problem - Reaction - Solution." It consists of degenerating a given public situation or artificially creating a "problem," to cause a certain "reaction" from the public, with the aim of the instigator of the measures that desired to accept as a "solution" to the problem. For example: to let urban violence escalate or to organize terrorist attacks, with the objective that the citizens themselves who require the government to enact new security laws at the expense of freedom.

4. The Strategy of Deferring

Another way to get an unpopular decision accepted is to present it to the citizens as "painful but necessary," and obtain immediate public acceptance for its future application. It is easier to get a future sacrifice accepted than an immediate one. This gives the public more time to get used to the idea of change and to accept it resigned when the time comes.

5. Treat People Like Children

Many of the television messages, especially advertisers, tend to speak to the public treating them as if they were children. They use words, arguments, gestures, and intonation as if the viewer were a child.

The goal is to overcome people's resistance. This is one of the strategies of mass manipulation that tries to neutralize people's critical sense by leveraging their suggestibility. Politicians also employ these tactics, sometimes showing themselves as father figures.

6. Taking Advantage of the Emotional Aspect

Often, the messages proposed by power aim at generating emotions and reaching the unconscious of individuals. Using the emotions, is a classic technique to cause a kind of "short circuit" on the rational part of the individual. In this way, the critical capacity is neutralized.

Also, the use of the emotional register allows you to open the door to the unconscious grafting ideas, desires, fears, or induce behavior in individuals.

315

7. Keep the Public Ignorant

Keeping people ignorant is one of the methods used by the power to exercise control over citizens. Ignorance means preventing people from having the tools of analysis on their own. Therefore, means drowning out curiosity for knowledge, not increasing the quality of education, and promoting a strong discrepancy between the quality of private and public education.

8. Making the Public Complacent

Most fashions and trends brands are not created spontaneously. Almost always, they are induced and promoted from a center of power that exerts its influence to create waves of mass tastes, interests, and opinions.

The media usually promote fashions and trends brands, most of them around ephemeral, unnecessary, and even ridiculous lifestyles. They persuade people "in fashion."

9. Reinforcing Self-Blame

Another of the strategies of mass manipulation is making the individual believe that only he is guilty of his misfortune, because of his insufficient intelligence or useless efforts. Thus, instead of rebelling against the system, the individual self-assesses and holds himself responsible. This, in turn, creates a depressive state, one of the effects of which is the inhibition of his action. And without action, there is no revolution!

10. Knowing People Better Than They Know Themselves

Over the past 60 years, rapid advances in science have generated a growing gap between the knowledge of individuals and that possessed and used by dominant lobbies. Thanks to neuroscience and applied psychology, the "system" has managed to know the individual better than he knows himself. This means that the system exercises are more in control over people than the individual himself.

Chapter Bonus

10 Psychology Tricks to Influence Anyone

Here are 10 powerful psychological tricks you can apply right now. I recommend you to practice gradually and practice one psychological tricks for day and you will see that after 10 days you will have become a master of mental manipulation.

Trick # 1: Use the Word "Because..." to Get What You Want

If you have to ask a favor, always try to explain the "because..." you ask, because giving a reason makes a favorable answer more likely.

In 1978 Ellen Langer, professor of psychology at Harvard, took a test to prove the true power of this word. In her fascinating research, participants had to try to skip the line that was created in front of the copier (86).

The first group had to use a banal sentence like, "Excuse me, I only have five pages, can I make copies right away?";

The second group was instructed to say, "I'd like to use the copier right away because I'm in a hurry, can I?";

The third and last group of volunteers had to say, "I'd like to use the copier right away because I have to make copies."

Curiously enough, even an excuse as unconvincing as that of the third group was successful, as 93% of the people in line gave priority to the test subjects. So it was the word "because" that triggered the automatic response in people's brains. In short, it doesn't matter how crazy an argument is, because if you use the word "because" to give a reason, you will significantly increase your chances of success in a debate.

If, for example, you use a phrase like *"Come to the cinema with me tonight because they're showing a film that's going well"* it'll be much more effective than *"Come to the cinema with me tonight"* no matter what motivation you give, any kind of motivation will still be more effective than a sentence without the "because."

Therefore, always motivate your request, because that's just the way it is!

Trick # 2: Use Exactly the Same Words as Your Interlocutor (Hot Words)

Pay attention to the words your interlocutor uses in his or her communication, in particular the words he or she uses most frequently.

If you also use exactly those words, you will create a feeling of total affinity and closeness in your interlocutor, which will lead him/her to perceive you as a nice person.

---

(86) Langer, E., Blank, A., & Chanowitz, B. (1978) – *The mindlessness of Ostensibly Thoughtful Action: The Role of "Placebic" Information* in Interpersonal Interaction. Journal of Personality and Social Psychology, 36(6), 635-642.

If a person, when describing something beautiful, often uses the word "fantastic," for example, says *"this holiday was fantastic,"* *"this movie is fantastic,"* you would like to convince him to take a holiday with you, you don't have to say, "would you like to come like in a "wonderful" place, because for the "wonderful" interlocutor it's not his "warm word," but to influence him you have to say *"would you like to take a holiday with me in a "fantastic" place"*?

If you use exactly these words, unconsciously the person you are talking to, will feel that they trust you and are more likely to accept your proposal.

Just try to believe it!

Trick # 3: Nod Slightly and They Will Agree With You

Sometimes the only thing you want to achieve in a debate is to hear the other side say YES and agree with you. No problem! To get a positive response, use this simple subliminal message: *nod slightly while asking a question*. In your counterpart's brain, your nodding will activate her mirror neurons and will be unconsciously perceived as a signal of agreement and this will trigger an instinctive response in her; that is, they will nod in turn and end up giving you the answer you wanted. Remember, however, to always maintain eye contact.

In a negotiation, if you want to conclude the contract and get the signature while saying "you need to sign the contract," <u>nod slightly with your head in the affirmative</u> to subliminally pass the message "Ok sign" I just advise you not to exaggerate, because nodding too openly will not help.

Trick # 4: Use Similarity to Surprise Your Opponent

A similitude is a rhetorical figure that consists of comparing two identities, in one of which we find certain qualities (or defects) similar and comparable to those of the other, thanks to the use of adverbs including how, like, etc.

Example: a gang of boys is like a pack of wolves.

Thanks to the similarities we can also create comparisons that go beyond the reality of the facts that will have a certain influence in the mind of our interlocutor.

In the sale, thanks to it, is possible to make important a choice that initially did not seem.

For example, a salesman friend of mine asked a customer: *"What changes between the Home version and the Professional version of Windows?,"* he replied: *"Having the Windows Home version is a bit small"!*

The similarity must have hit the nail on the head because my friend was able to sell the Professional version.

Trick # 5: The Sensory Overload

The conscious mind of the human being is very limited in its capabilities, as it can handle about 7 pieces of information simultaneously.

Overloading the mind of our interlocutor, for example, by providing a lot of information, speaking quickly and simultaneously administering different stimuli, (tactile, visual, and auditory) will create a momentary mental confusion in our target, generating a receptive state in his mind.

Any suggestions are given exactly during this "altered state of consciousness" will go deeper and will increase the probability of being accepted by the recipient.

This loss of critical capacity lasts very little, about one second.

Sensory overload and mental confusion are strategies underlying instantaneous hypnosis induction techniques.

Tricks # 6: The Exaggeration Model

The exaggeration model leads to exasperate the meaning of the interlocutor's words by transforming each of his sentences into an emotional accusation that will bring him under your control and leave him speechless.

Let's analyze these examples:

"Madam, have you experienced the potential of this cream yet?"

"No, I don't care."

"Are you saying you don't care what your skin looks like?"

Or else:

- *"Our offer will get you a year's subscription for only $67."*

- *"I'm sorry, but I'm not interested."*

- *"So, you're saying you don't want to save money?*

As you can see, the operation is simple: you take the client's answer and use the ambiguity to exaggerate its meaning to the point of implying something the client didn't think about.

Trick # 7: The Black/White Model

This model consists of proposing two alternatives, painting them as the only ways out and opposite to each other (one good and the other bad).

"Either you buy our pills to lose weight, or you're going to keep this belly forever."

"There are loser runners in life and winning runners... the latter wearing X shoes."

"I don't want to talk you into buying this slimming cream, it's your choice, but if you leave here without it, don't come back to me complaining in a year..."

In this scene, the trick is to propose the other choice so painful or disgusting that they will have to follow your advice: the less explicit you are and the less you will be able to "catch" this trick.

This model is often used in the sales pages of digital products giving an illusion of choice: *"Now the choice is yours: red pill or the blue pill? You can order this product now, start creating your business and receive your first earnings in the next few days OR you can decide to leave this page to continue to lead a miserable life forever thanks to your poor employee job."*

Trick # 8: Learn to Use Reinforced Truisms

Truism consists of making a series of 5 or more statements that are strictly true and immediately afterward in inserting a suggestion. You need to know that if you can educate a person's mind to say "Yes" many times the mind will then be ready to respond "Yes" to a later stimulation.

We can use these phrases, in our speech, by repeating them and linking them to another phrase that "hides" the behavior we want to induce.

For example, assuming you want to motivate a person to face change and encourage them to learn new things, I can tell you: *"Remember when you started taking your first steps as a child, so you learned to walk, then without knowing the grammar you learned to speak, and then you learned to read and write the first words, today you can do all these things well and many more, <u>and now you can learn many new things!"</u>*

You can see that I've highlighted the behavior I want to induce.

We can summarize the meaning of truisms in the formula: if this is true, and this one is true, then this one is true too.

A fine example of truism can also be found in Obama's speech when he says to the nation, *"Today I stand before you to say that what we have already achieved gives us hope for what we can and must achieve tomorrow.*

This sentence, after a series of truisms, "installs" the conviction in the citizens that they can obtain in the near future and other fields, the same success obtained with the elections... Interesting, isn't it?

If we want to strengthen a truism, we can add a "strengthening."

For example, suppose that we want to motivate a person to join a gym, I could say:

"We all want to stay in shape, isn't it? And we also know that exercise is important for weight maintenance, do you agree? Then joining a gym is an appropriate solution, right?"

So, I'm using after every trick I've done, "isn't it?" "Right?" "Do you agree?" If you use a reinforcement at the end of the sentence, you'll increase your chances of getting a yes by 17%!

Not only that, if you nod slightly with your head at the same time as you use the strengthener, but you also increase your chances of getting a yes by another 23%.

17 + 23 = 40% more likely to get a yes!

This is one of the easiest communication techniques in the world, right?

And I bet you didn't think this technique could be that powerful, did you?

So, I guess as of tonight, you're going to enjoy putting it into practice, aren't you?

Trick # 9: The Simple Bind

Milton H. Erickson, a famous therapeutic hypnotist, used to say, "I like to give my patients as many choices as possible to do what I want."

The "Bind" (or Linguistic-Presupposition) is one of the most powerful and easy to use tools to give someone "apparently" a choice and at the same time "trap" them inside your idea, almost without any way out.

Bind is a hypnotic technique used to force a choice with words. It is also called the "illusion of alternative."

Let's see some examples:

- *"Do you want to tell me now what's bothering you or would you rather wait a while?"*

- *"After you go to buy bread, could you come by the newsstand and buy me the paper?"*

- *"When are you going to take me to the movies?"*

- *"Have you decided which foreign country to take me to for our anniversary?"*

Each of these questions already provides a choice, and the trick is to take for granted a fact that is slightly hidden.

This technique is often used in online sales to assume that the potential buyer will do what we want, for example:

- *"When you get to the order form, be careful to enter the coupon code before buying, so that the discount is activated";*

- *"After the purchase, you will be taken to the member's area and have immediate access to the course videos."*

You can use these two factors to create your simple Bind:

1. Choice: What will be the next product you buy?"

2. Time: How fast do you think you'll get here?

Remember: Don't give a choice; increase the conversions!

Trick # 10: The Power of the Double Bind

If you know the simple Bind, double Bind will be very easy for you to understand. It is propose two specific alternatives.

This bind even more powerful because all the client has to do is choose one without thinking too much.

-*"Do you want to order white or red wine with pasta?"*

-*"Do you want to move into your new house tomorrow or next month?"*

-*"Would you prefer to sit in the front row or the middle for the VIP seat?"*

The formula to create it is the same as the simple Bind; simply as far as quality is concerned, take two specific options and propose them instead of asking an open-ended question.

"Now you have two options to proceed. By purchasing the product with a one-time payment, you will pay $997 and save 20%. If you prefer a deferred payment, there are 3 installments of $333 available. You will pay slightly more, but not all at once."

Conclusion

We have come to the end of this fascinating discussion into the world of dark psychology and the various components which comprise the vast array of facets involved in this study. As such, thank you for making it all the way through to this point. We certainly hope that you have found information that is not only useful, but also interesting to read.

The next step is to put the techniques you have learned into practice out in the real world. Find a target that you want to manipulate and try some of your favorite techniques out, whether that means trying to control the narrative, attempting to manage your target's expectations, or making an effort to manipulate your target's beliefs. Do not expect to get everything right the first time, and do not be afraid of failure; if something goes wrong, simply learn what you can from the experience and move on to the next target. Learning a new skill is always a process, and that includes learning how to manipulate people in the world around you. If you feel that you have to, take a break from manipulation and come back to it at a later time. Frustration is never good for the learning process, and will only serve to make you want to give up altogether. As long as you keep trying, you will get there eventually. I know that I have repeated myself over and over, but remember that practice makes perfect. Once you practice long enough, you will find that you have mastered the techniques of manipulation and influence, and you will have very little difficulty in making targets bend to your will.

You should also take the time to come back to this book every so often and review the topics covered within, from the most basic concepts to the more advanced material. Even if you are practicing what you have learned on a regular basis, it is always a good idea to review in order to make sure that you are using the techniques correctly. The practice is a great thing, but only when you are not enforcing bad habits instead of developing good ones. The best way to tell good from bad is to go back and read about whatever concept you might be struggling with, instead of letting bad habits take hold for the foreseeable future. If you have any further questions about dark psychology, the art of manipulation, or any of the concepts or techniques discussed in this book, do not be afraid to research topics yourself.

Throughout this book, we explored the various motivations that manipulators have for engaging in the activities they do. Moreover, we explored the reasons why manipulators act out in the manner they do. In addition, we also discussed how you could guard against any unwanted attempts on yourself.

Here are the main takeaways from this discussion.

1. *Generally speaking, manipulators have nothing personal against you.* This means that a manipulator, when looking to take advantage of you, or any other victim, don't do it because they hate you, or have something against you. They do it because they have an agenda and will essentially look for anyone they can take advantage of. If that happens to be you, then you need to address that issue before serious damage comes to you.

2. *Manipulators are usually scared and often insecure individuals who look to prey on someone who is weaker than they are.* This is something that you need to keep in mind especially when dealing with toxic people. For instance, bullies tend to be individuals who feel inadequate and will do everything they can to make others feel worse than they do.

3. *Most manipulators seek validation and affection.* In the particular case of narcissists, what they really seek is to be loved. They seek the attention and validation of those around them. However, their toxic attitude alienates them from actually getting what they way. In the end, they end up destroying any semblance of a meaningful relationship which could lead them to get what they desire most.

4. ***Guarding against manipulators is a lot easier than you think.*** However, it requires you to keep your eyes and ears open regularly. Also, keep an eye out for the red flags we have pointed out throughout this book. In doing so, you will provide yourself with a fighting chance. In the end, you will be better off while making it know to manipulators that you are no easy prey.

If you find yourself exhibiting any of the behaviors we have described in this book that are consistent with manipulators, then it would be a great idea to make an assessment of what's really driving you to act in this manner. Perhaps there is something out there that isn't quite making you feel entirely comfortable about yourself or your surroundings. If that is the case, then perhaps seeking professional help may allow you to dig deeper into the root causes fueling your attitude. In the end, you may have the chance to develop a much more balanced outlook on life.

As you gain more experience and knowledge in the topic of dark psychology, you will be able to further expand on them thereby achieving a deeper knowledge and understanding of this fascinating topic.

So, thank you very much for reading this book. If you have found it to be useful and informative, please tell your friends, family, and colleagues about it. They too will surely find it to be useful and informative as you have.

Finally, if you found this book useful in any way, a review on Amazon is always appreciated!

Bibliography

Jonah Berger (2016) – *Invisible Influence: The Hidden Forces that Shape Behavior.* Simon & Schuster.

Morin, C. (2019) – *The Persuasion Code: How Neuromarketing Can Help You Persuade Anyone, Anywhere, Anytime.* Wiley.

Tali Sharot (2018) – *The Influential Mind: What the Brain Reveals About Our Power to Change Others.* Picador USA.

Vance Packard (2007) – *The Hidden Persuaders.* Ig Publishing.

Burg, B. (2011) – *The Art of Persuasion: Winning Without Intimidation.* Tremendous Life Books.

Richard M. Perloff (1993) – *The Dynamics of Persuasion: Communication and Attitudes in the 21st Century,* Hillsdale, New Jersey: Lawrence Erlbaum

Dale Carnegie (2010) – *How to Win Friends and Influence People,* Simon & Schuster

Cacioppo, John T., Petty, Richard E. (1984) – *The Elaboration Likelihood Model of Persuasion,* in *Advances in Consumer Research, Association for Consumer Research*

Robert B. Cialdini, (1993) – *Influence: The Psychology of Persuasion* (3rd ed.). HarperCollins.

Cialdini, R. B. (2001) – *Influence: Science and practice* (4th ed.). Boston: Allyn & Bacon.

Cialdini, R. B., (2017) – *Pre-Suasion: A Revolutionary Way to Influence and Persuade.* HarperCollins.

Cialdini, R. B. (2001) – *The science of persuasion.* Scientific American, 290, 32-55.

Asch, S. E. (1956) – *Studies of independence and conformity: A minority of one against a unanimous majority. Psychological Monographs,* 70 (Whole no. 416).

Asch, S. E. (1951) – *Effects of group pressure upon the modification and distortion of judgment.* In H. Guetzkow (ed.)

Kenrick, D. T., Neuberg, S. L., & Cialdini, R. B. (2002) – *Social Psychology: Unraveling the Mystery* (2nd Ed.). Boston: Allyn & Bacon.

Guadagno, R. E., & Cialdini, R. B. (2002) – *On-line persuasion: An examination of differences in computer-mediated interpersonal influence.* Group Dynamics: Theory, Research and Practice, 6, 38-51.

Sagarin, B. J., Cialdini, R. B., Rice, W. E., & Serna, S. B. (2002) – *Dispelling the illusion of invulnerability: The motivations and mechanisms of resistance to persuasion.* Journal of Personality and Social Psychology, 83, 326-354.

Cialdini, R.B., Wosinska, W., Barrett, D.W., Butner, J. & Gornik-Durose, M. (1999) – *Compliance with a request in two cultures: The differential influence of social proof and commitment/consistency on collectivists and individualists.* Personality and Social Psychology Bulletin, 25, 1242-1253.

Cialdini, R. B., Sagarin, B. J., & Rice, W. E. (2001) – *Training in ethical influence.* In J. Darley, D. Messick, and T. Tyler (Eds.).

Social influences on ethical behavior in organizations (pp. 137-153). Mahwah, NJ: Erlbaum.

Kahneman, D. (2011) – *Thinking, fast and slow*. New York: Farrar, Straus and Giroux.

A. Tversky, D. Kahneman (1974) - *Judgment under Uncertainty: Heuristics and Biases*. Cambridge University Press.

24 Cognitive Biases That Are Warping Your Perception of Reality https://www.visualcapitalist.com/24-cognitive-biases-warping-reality/

Galperin, A., & Haselton, M. G. (2013) - Error management and the evolution of cognitive bias. In J. P. Forgas, K. Fiedler, & C. Sedikides (Eds.), Sydney symposium of social psychology. Social thinking and interpersonal behavior (p. 45–63). Psychology Press.

Martie G. Haselton, Andrew Galperin (2011) – Error Management and the Evolution of Cognitive Bias

Do you want to see more on cognitive biases? In this link 188 of them in one infographic. https://www.visualcapitalist.com/every-single-cognitive-bias/

Tversky, D. Kahneman (1983) – *Extensional Versus Intuitive Reasoning: The Conjunction Fallacy in Probability Judgment*

Kahneman D., Jack Knetsch J., Richard Thaler R. (2008) – *The Endowment Effect: Evidence of Losses Valued More Than Gains*, in Handbook of Experimental Economics Results, vol. 1, pp 939-948

Jack B. Soll, Katherine L. Milkman, John W. Payne (2015) – A User's Guide to Debiasing

Samuel McNerney (2015) – Living in a Post-Kahneman World

Buss DM, Gomes M, Higgins DS, Lauterback K. *"Tactics of Manipulation"*, Journal of Personality and Social Psychology, Vol 52 No 6 1219–1279 (1987)

Adelyn Birch, (2014) – *30 Covert Emotional Manipulation Tactics: How Manipulators Take Control* in Personal Relationships

Hofer, Paul. *"The Role of Manipulation in the Antisocial Personality"*, International Journal of Offender Therapy and Comparative Criminology, Vol. 33 No 2, 91–101 (1989)

Crawford, Craig (2007) . *The Politics of Life: 25 Rules for Survival in a Brutal and Manipulative World*

Carson, Thomas L. (2012). *Lying and deception: theory and practice.* Oxford University Press.

Dantalion, J. (2008) – *Mind Control Language Patterns.* Mind Control Publishing.

John Marks (1979) – *The Search for the Manchurian Candidate: The CIA and Mind Control*, Times Books, p. 77

Brehm, S. S., & Brehm, J. W. (2013) – *Psychological reactance: A theory of freedom and control.* Academic Press. Christie, R., & Geis, F. L. (2013).

James, O. (2018). *Love bombing: Reset your child's emotional thermostat.* Routledge.

Dilts, R., (2017). *Sleight of Mouth: The Magic of Conversational Belief Change.* Dilts Strategy Group.

Bandler, R. (1992). *Magic in Action.* Meta Publications.

Brown, D. (2007) – *Tricks of the Mind.* Channel 4 Books.

Jonason, P. K., Li, N. P., Webster, G. D., & Schmitt, D. P. (2009). *"The dark triad: Facilitating a short-term mating strategy in men"*. European Journal of Personality.

Bursten, Ben. *"The Manipulative Personality"*, Archives of General Psychiatry, Vol 26 No 4, 318–321 (1972)

Christie, R., & Geis, F. L. (2013) – *Studies in Machiavellianism.* Academic Press.

Behary, W. (2013) – *Disarming the Narcissist: Surviving & Thriving with the Self-Absorbed.* New Harbinger Publications.

Aglietta, M.; Reberioux, A.; Babiak, P. *"Psychopathic manipulation at work"*, in Gacono, C.B. (Ed), The Clinical and Forensic Assessment of Psychopathy: A Practitioner's Guide, Erlbaum, Mahwah, NJ, pp. 287–311. (2000)

Taylor, K. (2006) – *Brainwashing: The Science of Thought Control.* Oxford University Press.

Dennis M. Kowal (2000) – *Brainwashing*, Oxford University Press, pp. 358–457

Schein, Edgar H. (1971) – *Coercive Persuasion: A Socio-Psychological Analysis of the "Brainwashing" of American Civilian Prisoners by the Chinese Communists.*, New York, W.W. Norton

L.J. West (1989) – *Persuasive Techniques in Contemporary Cults: A Public Health Approach*, Washington, CULTS and New Religious Movements American Psychiatric Association

Bromley, D., & Melton, J. (2002) – *Cults, religion, and violence.* Cambridge University Press

Anthony Dick (1999) – *"Pseudoscience and Minority Religions: An Evaluation of the Brainwashing Theories of Jean-Marie"*. Social Justice Research. *12 (4)*, pp. 250–364

Simon, George K (1996) – *In Sheep's Clothing: Understanding and Dealing with Manipulative People.*

Alessandra, Tony (1992) – *Non-Manipulative Selling*

Forward, Susan. Emotional Blackmail (1997)

Klatte, Bill & Thompson, Kate. (2007) *It's So Hard to Love You: Staying Sane When Your Loved One Is Manipulative, Needy, Dishonest, or Addicted*

Chadderton, C., & Croft, R. (2006). *"Who is kidding whom? A study of complicity, seduction and deception in the marketplace"*. Social Responsibility Journal.

Buss, D. M., & Schmitt, D. P. (1993). *"Sexual strategies theory: an evolutionary perspective on human mating"*. Psychological Review.

McMillan, Dina L. (2008) – *But He Says He Loves Me: How to Avoid Being Trapped in a Manipulative Relationship*

Murphy, Christopher M.; O'Leary, K. Daniel (1989). "Psychological aggression predicts physical aggression in early marriage"

McCoy, Dorothy (2006) – *The Manipulative Man: Identify His Behavior, Counter the Abuse,* Regain Control

Nathan Blaszak (2004). *How to Hypnotize Anyone Without Getting Caught.* Life Tricks Inc.

Kevin Hogan (2006). *Covert Hypnosis: An Operator's Manual.* Network 3000 Publishing.

Kevin Hogan and James Speakman (2006). *Covert Persuasion: Psychological Tactics and Tricks to Win the Game.* Wiley.

Glenn Twiddle (2010). *Advanced Hypnotic Selling.* Glenn Twiddle Publishing.

Steven Peliari (2009). *The Art of Covert Hypnosis.* Life Tricks Inc.

Richard Bandler, John Grinder (1996) – *Patterns of the Hypnotic Techniques of Milton H. Erickson,* Grinder & Associates

Abramson, Kate (2014) – *Turning up the Lights on Gaslighting.* Philosophical Perspectives. p.28

Stern, Robin (2008) – *The Gaslight Effect: How to Spot and Survive the Hidden Manipulation Others Use to Control Your Life*

Pease, Allan & Barbara (2004) – *The Definitive Book of Body Language.* Orion Books

Albert Mehrabian, *Silent Messages: Implicit Communication of Emotions and Attitudes*, Wadsworth, Belmont CA 1981

Albert Mehrabian, *Nonverbal Communication,* Aldine-Atherton, Chicago 1972.

Bradbury, Andrew (2006) – "Talking Body Language" in Develop Your NLP Skills Kogan Page

Fast, Julius (2014). *Body Language.* Open Road Media

Candler, Wendy; & Lille-Martin, Diane. (2006) – *Sign Language and Linguistic Universals.* Cambridge University Press.

Vrij, Aldert; Hartwig, Maria; Granhag, Pär Anders (2019*). "Reading Lies: Nonverbal Communication and Deception"*. Annual Review of Psychology.

Alan J. Fridlund *(1994) – Human facial expression.* Academic Press.

J.A. Russell; J.M. Fernandez Dols (1997). *The psychology of facial expression.* Cambridge University Press.

Ekman, Paul (2009) – *Emotions Revealed: Recognizing Faces and Feelings to Improve Communication and Emotional.* Life Malor Books

Ekman, Paul (1993) – *"Facial Expression and Emotion".* American Psychologist

Noam, Chomsky (2011) – *Media Control: The Spectacular Achievements of Propaganda.* Seven Stories Press